Women, Feminism and Biology

Women, Feminism and Biology

The Feminist Challenge

Lynda Birke

Research Fellow in Biology
The Open University

DISTRIBUTED BY HARVESTER PRESS

First published in Great Britain in 1986 by
WHEATSHEAF BOOKS LTD
A DIVISION OF THE HARVESTER PRESS PUBLISHING GROUP
Publisher: John Spiers
Director of Publications: Edward Elgar
16 Ship Street, Brighton, Sussex

© Lynda Birke, 1986

British Library Cataloguing in Publication Data
Birke, Lynda
  Women, feminism and biology: the feminist challenge.
  1. Feminism. 2. Biology
  I. Title
  305.4'2   HQ1206

   ISBN 0-7108-0765-1
   ISBN 0-7108-0706-0 Pbk

Typeset in 11/12 point Times by Ormskirk Typesetting Services
Printed and bound in Great Britain by
Biddles Ltd, Guildford and King's Lynn

All rights reserved

THE HARVESTER PRESS PUBLISHING GROUP

The Harvester Press Publishing Group comprises Harvester Press Limited (chiefly publishing literature, fiction, philosophy, psychology, and science and trade books), Harvester Press Microform Publications Limited (publishing in microform unpublished archives, scarce printed sources, and indexes to these collections) and Wheatsheaf Books Limited (a wholly independent company chiefly publishing in economics, international politics, sociology and related social sciences), whose books are distributed by The Harvester Press Limited and its agencies throughout the world.

Contents

Introduction		vii
Chapter 1:	Feminism and its Concern with Biology	1
Chapter 2:	Determined Women: Feminism and Biological Determinism	13
Chapter 3:	The Political Effects of Biological Determinism	36
Chapter 4:	Reducing Women: Feminism and Reductionism	56
Chapter 5:	Developing Gender	83
Chapter 6:	On Female Nature	107
Chapter 7:	Feminism as a Herald of Change?	126
Chapter 8:	Towards a Feminist Science	143
Notes		172
Name Index		204
Subject Index		206

Introduction

The theme of this book is the relationship between women, feminism and biology. The starting point of my interest in the relationship between these topics was my own experience, both through working as a biologist, but more importantly, through my involvement in the Women's Liberation Movement. At various times, and in various ways, the ideas contained in this book have emerged in discussion with other people; often in workshops at feminist conferences; sometimes in radical science conferences. One of the greatest sources of that development, however, was my involvement with the Brighton Women and Science Group, with whom I worked for about five years,[1] and with whom I developed much of the interest and understanding that, a few years later, led to this book.

In this book my concern is to explore some of the ways in which biology is relevant to feminism. It is relevant in that, at present, biological arguments are all too frequently adduced to provide justification for women's continued oppression, and in that sense feminism has had to confront biology. The first few chapters of the book are principally concerned with the ways in which such arguments have been used, and the political context of their use. It is inevitably impossible to cover all fields of biology in this way—even if it were desirable—and I have focussed on two areas in which a detailed consideration of how we think about biology is relevant to feminist theory. The first of these is human development, since theories of development incorporate ideas of how we acquire our sense of gender. The second is the way that we view our relationship to nature, a topic which is becoming of increasing concern within feminism. The final part of the book attempts to pull together some of the ideas that have been expressed about creating a "feminist science". Feminism is not only about fighting our oppression within contemporary society: it is also about the possibility of change. And, if biology can be said to contribute to that oppression, then we have to consider how—or if—it might be changed if we are to move towards a more "feminist" society.

That consideration, however, begs the question of what we mean by "feminism". In the sense that throughout history there have been women who have recognised their subordination as women and have tried to resist, then feminism has always existed. Its forms, on the other hand, have been many and varied, depending upon historical circumstances, and it is only relatively recently that it has become identifiable as a collective social movement.[2] The present wave of feminism grew up in the context of the radical politics of the 1960s and 1970s, which emphasised liberation and active struggle against oppression. The term "feminism" has, since the beginning of the 1970s been used increasingly widely. Media images of feminism, for example, range from what the press terms the "bra-burning women's libber"[3] who is portrayed as some kind of "militant extremist", to the more acceptable woman asking politely for equal opportunities at work. While the Women's Liberation Movement does consider that equal opportunities are important, equal opportunities are not enough. The Women's Liberation Movement (WLM) is, generally, more concerned with active struggle against women's oppression in its various forms (and in particular with those areas of struggle defined in Britain by the WLM's seven demands).[4] In this sense, it is indeed more militant than those who are concerned principally with legal reforms for putative equal rights.

When I refer to feminism, or to feminists, in this book, the sense of 'feminist' that I use is one grounded in WLM feminism, and generalisations about "feminists" are ones that I feel would approximately represent the beliefs and interests of a large proportion of women involved in women's liberation. However, generalisations are not often possible, if only because there are large differences of perspective within the WLM on the nature and sources of women's oppression, as well as on the strategies and tactics that might be used to fight that oppression. Moreover, in recent years, there has been much discussion (and some acrimony) about divisions between women in the WLM, divisions such as those based on class or ethnic differences, or between women with and without physical disabilities. Despite these, I have written this book about "women" as a generalisation. I have done this not because I think that those differences are unimportant but because I believe that, if feminism has anything unifying it, it is that feminism is opposed to *women's* subordination. Subordination is something which women have in common, even if it varies markedly across other social divisions.

Different feminists take different views about the significance of biology in our understanding of women's oppression. Some emphasise that our understanding of gender—the roles ascribed to women and men—is a social product, and that biology is largely irrelevant.[5] Some have argued that the subordination of women and the concomitant power accruing to men are rooted in biological differences between the sexes.[6] Of all the differing political perspectives, it is radical feminism to which the latter view has often been attributed;[7] that is, it is frequently claimed (although not commonly by self-defined radical feminists themselves) that radical feminism is biologically determinist, that it believes that existing gender differences are firmly rooted in, and determined by, underlying biological differences. In Britain, the claim that radical feminism is biologically determinist in its beliefs was made particularly during the 1970s, at the time when radical feminism began to emerge as a clearly separate current within the WLM. The prevailing attitude towards biology at that time within the WLM was that it was not relevant to the ways in which we become women or men.

In Britain at least some of the feeling that radical feminism is biologically determinist arises from attempts made at that time to define what radical or revolutionary[8] feminism *was* and how it differed from socialist feminism. In opposition to the claim that gender was wholly socially constructed, some radical feminists emphasised that biology was not irrelevant to our understanding of gender. It may not determine gender, it was argued, but we cannot ignore the fact that biological differences do form part of the way in which we understand concepts of gender. Moreover, biological experiences do contribute to the way we experience our lives as women. But that belief was heresy to the WLM in the mid-1970s, and those who stated it were accused, among other things, of fascism. The problem was then, and remains, that the belief that gender is socially constructed was the only alternative to a belief in biological determinism. If you did not agree with one, then by implication, you must believe in the other.

This opposition has had dire consequences, both for feminism and for the Left in general. Pure social constructionism of the kind advanced by the Left in the 1960s and 1970s did not appeal to popular "common sense", a failure which contributed to its demise. Into the breach stepped the appeals to commonsense notions of human nature made by the New Right, appeals which have found a willing audience, since they contribute both to the popularity of right-wing ideas in the 1980s and to the dismal failure of the Left to provide an electorally viable alternative. Within feminism itself that opposition has not only opened the way for the anti-feminism of the New Right, but it has also given birth to what Judith Stacey has called the new "conservative feminism", in which biological determinism is used to underwrite feminist claims.[9] One theme of this book is that this opposition, whatever its political consequences have been, is a false one.

This book is founded upon my belief in the relevance of biology to feminist thought: that relevance is not, however, biologically determinist, as I hope the following pages will indicate. The book begins with a brief outline of the ways in which current feminism has concerned itself with biology and what biology has had to say about women. One central concern has been to draw attention to the prevalence of biologically determinist arguments "explaining" women's oppression and to emphasise the effects of these on women's lives. It is to this theme that I turn in the second chapter, where I draw on examples from three particular areas of contemporary concern to feminism, namely, sexuality, paid work, and violence towards women. Chapter Three considers more explicitly the political consequences of biological determinism for feminism, and some responses to it. One response is simply to accept it as based on fact, a view that cannot be found only in arguments against feminism, but is also held by some feminists. Another is simply to say that biological arguments are irrelevant to feminist politics; and the third is to reject biological determinism altogether.

Chapters Four and Five explore in more detail some of the philosophical and political objections to the determinism and reductionism of biological theories relating to gender, and the implications of such theories for feminism. My concern here is not only to explore the objections, but also to consider some of the alternatives—feminist or otherwise—that have been proposed in opposition to biological determinism. Chapters Six and Seven turn to our relationship to nature in general. Contemporary feminism has become increasingly concerned with environmental issues, particularly the struggle against the arms race. One problem with the "ecofeminism" that has emerged in Europe and the United States is that it is often based on a belief in the innate superiority of females and femininity, a view that implies biological determinism. On the other hand, some writers have seen in the convergence of the women's liberation and ecology movements hope for the future, both for the earth and for humanity in general. Some of the ideas put forward in this context are significant in relation to how we might construct a "feminist science", a theme to which I turn in the final chapter, where I bring together a number of ideas about what feminist science might look like, and what it might hope to achieve.

There are, inevitably, a great many people whose ideas and inspiration have contributed to the development of my own thought, and it is impossible to thank them all. Many of the ideas developed in this book have emerged from discussion with women in the Brighton Women and Science Group, in which I was involved between 1976 and 1980, and from discussions with the people involved in the Dialectics of Biology Group which met at Bressanone, Italy, in 1980. My interest in trying to think about a more radical or progressive approach to biology owes much to members of that group, particularly to Bruno D'Udine, Pat Bateson, Brian Goodwin and Hilary Rose and Steven Rose. I have been involved in the Women's Liberation Movement and many of its campaigns for several years, and it is thus impossible to acknowledge the contributions of all the women I have met who have helped me to think about feminism. The feminist implications of some of the ideas in this book have, however, been usefully discussed with some of the women with whom I worked on the "Changing Experience of Women" course at the Open University, particularly Veronica Beechey and Sue Himmelweit, to whom I am very grateful.

I am particularly grateful to the people who have taken the time and trouble to read earlier drafts of all or part of this book, notably Deirdre Janson-Smith, Brian Goodwin, Hilary Rose and Steven Rose—even if they have not always agreed with everything I wrote—and to Beverley Simon for deciphering the manuscript and transforming it into typescript. I also wish to thank Sandy Best for her help with the Figures and Gail Vines for her help with proof-reading and compiling the index. Finally, there are always people whose forbearance makes writing a book possible, and mine is no exception: this book would not have been written without the help of Dawn Sadler, who kept an eye on the research when I had a date with the typewriter, and the help of those with whom I live—Sue, Sandy and Jan, not to mention the various four-legged friends who have sometimes got in the way, but sometimes provided a helpful nudge. Perhaps it is because of their intervention that the book got written at all.

1 Feminism and its Concern with Biology

This book explores the relationship between feminism and biology. More precisely, the book explores what biology has had to say about women, and about what feminism has had to say in reply. In the first part of the book I shall outline some of contemporary feminism's changing concerns with biology, outlining ways in which biological arguments about women and their place in society can be interpreted from a feminist perspective. Feminists, among others, have been quick to criticise the ways in which biological arguments have helped to perpetuate gender inequalities, and they have been quick to criticise the patriarchal[1] nature of science as it is currently practised. But in biology, as elsewhere, we need to do more than criticise, and in the second part of the book, I want to consider ways in which feminism might move beyond the level of merely criticising. An important question that constantly faces feminism and other political movements is to ask: what kind of society are we aiming for? And with respect to science, might it be possible—or desirable—to try to change that biology that we so often criticise? It has been suggested that we might create a "feminist science",[2] which might better serve women's (or, indeed, human) needs. Is this possible; and if so, how can it be achieved?

This chapter begins with a brief sketch of the ways in which feminism has confronted biology. This outline is intended to be sketchy, to set the scene for the rest of the book. It will raise many themes that I will explore further, but will also raise some topics to which I will not return. Any book makes a somewhat arbitrary choice of available material, and this one is no exception. On the other hand, the initial scene-setting is important, particularly if, towards the end of the book, we are to consider the possibility of rethinking biology.

An important question with which to begin is: why *should* feminism have become concerned at all with biology and the natural sciences? The primary reason for this concern is that gender differences have tended to be seen principally in biological terms within our society; moreover, women have been depicted as passive victims of their biology in ways that men, in general, have not. That is, women as a group are often portrayed as having an underlying biological nature, an essence of femininity, which provides constraints on what is individually possible for them. The social position of women thus becomes seen as determined—and limited—by their biology. This preponderant view thus acts as an ideological constraint; that is, it acts to justify women's relative lack of power in society.

There are many instances of this kind of argument, and some will be dealt with at greater length in Chapter Two. In general, they are based on the notion that existing gender divisions are *natural*, that they are rooted in an eternal, unchanging, biology in one way or another. Arguments such as these are frequently employed by those opposed to feminism; the idea, for example, that women are naturally less capable of intellectual endeavour than men—because of the biological demands of their childbearing—was employed in the nineteenth century as an argument against extending opportunities for higher education to women.[3] In this century accusations are frequent that, because of their biology, women are less suited for particular kinds of work than men. The chief value of these arguments that ground women's social position in biology—to the antifeminist—is that they suggest that social change is impossible, or at best, very limited. If existing social inequalities are firmly rooted in biological differences between women and men, then there is little that any reasonable person can do to effect change. Feminism would thus be misguided.

Not surprisingly, feminists have reacted against such arguments. During the early years of the current wave of feminism (from the late 1960s onwards)[4] the response was usually simply to reject biology altogether, along with the biological arguments. To some extent this was understandable, partly because of the vigour with which such arguments had previously been used to oppose feminism, and partly because contemporary feminism grew up in a time when there was considerable anti-science feeling arising largely from the horrors of the Vietnam war. At this time, feminism concentrated on drawing attention to the social and historical context of women's oppression as a condition for gender divisions, a context in which biology had no obvious place. However, this initial rejection has changed, and "biology" has been the focus of a number of analytical critiques in recent years. In part, this shift of focus has occurred because of the realisation that if biological arguments have been used to oppose feminism, then feminists must grapple with biology in order to deal effectively with the arguments at all levels. In part, too, a greater concern with women's biology emerged from the success of the women's health movement,[5] whose emphasis on self-help meant that the women involved needed to deal with some aspects of biology as part of their concern with medicine.

Thus the initial rejection of biology began to give way to increasing interest in it. From analyses of the ways in which biologically determinist arguments have been used against women's interests, feminism has also become concerned with such issues as the ways in which human biology is actually involved in the development of gender differences, with the broader relationships between science and society, with future possibilities for technological control of reproduction, and with the ways in which we conceptualise nature as female in Western thought. Within each of these broad areas, of course, there are different feminist approaches. I am not going to go into these here in detail, since the purpose of this sketch is only to indicate why these issues have become of interest to feminism. The major strands of feminist enquiry concerning biology are shown in Figure One. This shows "feminism" as the central concern, with the various kinds of question it has raised about biology radiating outwards from that.

The first part of the diagram concerns the critiques that have focussed upon ideas of biological determinism and women's role. These ideas have largely been opposed by feminists because they serve to justify the status quo, in which women in general have less power than do men, which in turn is sometimes attributed to underlying biological differences. These ideas are dealt with in detail in Chapters Two and Three;

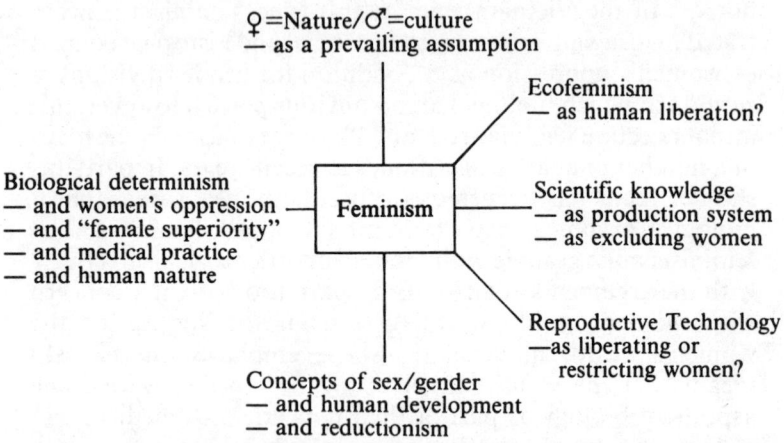

Figure 1: The principal areas of concern of contemporary feminism, outlining the key questions addressed in this book

here, it should be noted that they are to be found in a variety of guises, ranging from the rhetoric of right-wing ideology (emphasising, for example, that a woman's "natural" biological place is in the home), to many of the professions (the argument, for example, that women should not be employed because they are biologically less suitable for the job). Biological determinism can also be found in some feminist writing which implies that women are intrinsically (i.e. biologically) superior, and this view seems to be gaining popularity. It is not, however, a view that I would defend, and its implied biological determinism is also criticised in later chapters.[6]

One significant area in which biologically determinist arguments abound is medicine and its practice, as shown in the diagram. Such arguments have, for example, been propounded in the pages of medical journals, giving ostensibly medical reasons why women should be denied access to higher education, or certain kinds of work. By their citation in the medical literature they are given medical authority, and hence greater credibility, given the prevailing belief in the absolute truth of medicine and science in general. As will become evident, a number of examples on which I draw in later chapters are drawn from medical writing.

Biologically determinist arguments have become particularly important in the 1980s, as they are increasingly used by the Right to defend the status quo. Traditional conservatism has always relied heavily on appeals to "human nature", which is assumed to have a fixed, biological basis. Thus the Tory minister Ian Gilmour could write that "Tories are involved in a ceaseless struggle to improve the world, while not embarking on the impossible and dangerous project of trying to change human nature".[7] This human nature was fixed, rooted in the "natural family", and conformist with traditional values. But the concept of human nature espoused by the Right has changed somewhat, with the rise of the neo-liberal New Right in both Western Europe and the U.S.A. This strand of right-wing thought emphasises authoritarianism and an aggressive individuality, a human nature that is fully in accord with the precepts of monetarism.[8] Individuals are, according to this new biological determinism, inherently selfish and competitive, conveniently enough for capitalism. It is, of course, an innate "human" nature, although what is described is quintessentially male. When the New Right considers women's nature, it is to describe "human" nature's antithesis—cooperative, nurturant, and inherently suited to domesticity.[9] At a time when the gains of the last decade for women are increasingly being eroded, the policy implications for such claims of innate human natures are obvious.

A second area of concern is how biology might be relevant to the development of gender. The biologically determinist view suggests that gender roles—our behaviour and self-identity as women or men—are a product of underlying biology. One response to such proposals is to stress that our sense of gender is socially learnt; that is, children learn from an early age what is appropriate or not appropriate behaviour for girls and boys. But if gender is a socially learnt division, it is also one that is founded upon a biological division—sex. Children are generally taught (and learn) what is gender-appropriate behaviour according to the biological sex by which they were recognised at birth. Biology is then relevant to our understanding of gender insofar as it specifies the primary division by body form, female or male, upon which we erect massive social significance. There are problems with this, as I shall argue, in that the view that socially constructed gender differences are based on underlying biological differences posits a largely unchanging biology somehow underlying the edifice we have socially constructed. I shall discuss the ways in which this is problematic, as well as other ways of considering the role of biology in the development of gender differences, in Chapter Five.

A third area of increasing concern to feminism has been the increased use of reproductive technology. By this is meant a variety of technological interventions at any point in the process of reproduction, from conception (including its prevention) to the possibility of developing an artificial womb. Since it is women who bear children it might be tempting to suggest that such technologies should be welcomed by women. Shulamith Firestone put forward the suggestion that women's subordination has historically resulted from the necessity for them to bear and nurse children, which in turn restricted their mobility and created different spheres for women and men.[10] For Firestone, liberation for women could follow when this necessity was removed. Further technology, she supposed, might offer the solution by providing the means for children to be conceived and carried to term entirely outside the bodies of women.

Some forms of technological intervention in the processes of reproduction have been hailed as in some sense "liberating" for women. When the contraceptive pill was first launched, for example, it was widely advertised (and just as widely condemned) as offering sexual freedom for women, with greater choice. More recent developments similarly seem to offer freedom of choice; the technology involved in producing what the media have called "test-tube babies" seems to offer reproductive choices to women who might otherwise not be able to have a child. Other technologies may offer the choice of the sex of the child.

The potential of such changes for women's liberation has been questioned, however. In the first place, many feminists have been critical of what they see as Firestone's "technological fix" for social problems.[11] In a society that devalues women, they argue, such technological changes will not be in the hands of women, and are thus more likely to increase male power over women's lives and bodies. Secondly, feminists have pointed out that when new technological interventions become available, they are not made available to all women; middle-class women may be free to choose the new technology if they wish. Black, working-class or lesbian women may not.

Consider, as an example, the development of some intervention by which one could infallibly choose the sex of one's child. In the West it would no doubt be praised by the media as offering more choice for couples in planning their families. But consider what would happen in countries such as India, in which the birth of a son is always accorded greater prestige than the birth of a daughter. Some writers have speculated on the consequences of such a scenario for women: the number of females born would decline, and there would be greater pressure on those surviving to adulthood to reproduce, thus further eroding what little freedom of choice women now have. And this is not simply feminist paranoia: the Indian feminist magazine *Manushi* has reported increasing numbers of abortions of female foetuses by those who can afford the cost of the tests required to determine foetal sex.[12]

In general, feminists have tended to be cautious, and often critical, of new forms of technology aimed at intervention in biological reproduction. The caution arises from the recognition that women in our present inegalitarian society are unlikely to have full freedom of choice; it also arises in part from a recognition that new "advances" may often prove hazardous. Feminists might, however take a different view of reproductive technology if the society were one in which genuine freedom of choice for women were available. I shall return to this theme in the final chapter, when discussing the potential of "feminist science".

The fourth area of feminist involvement shown in Figure One concerns the practice and process of science itself, including biology—the processes by which scientific knowledge is produced. That scientific knowledge is not always beneficial to the society is now widely recognised; however, the predominant view of the relationship of this knowledge to society is that "science" simply produces knowledge—the facts about nature. What society then does with this knowledge is not the scientists' fault, it is sometimes argued; it can be used, or misused, but the scientists themselves are absolved from blame. This is the kind of argument put forward, for instance, by advocates of the view that intelligence (as measured by I.Q. tests) is inherited: when criticised for the political implications of this view, they have usually argued that all they are producing is facts. It is up to society to evaluate these.[13] This use-abuse model has frequently been criticised, including criticism from feminists.[14] There is, perhaps inevitably, a broad spectrum of views within this critical trend, although most critics would agree that what science is engaged in is not the disinterested pursuit of truth; rather, its processes, progress, and theories are intimately tied into the values of the larger society—which are essentially capitalist and patriarchal. What differentiates different viewpoints is how they see these links.

On the other hand, there is the view that the operation of science can be understood principally in terms of its social relations; at its most extreme, this view is expressed as though science is "nothing but" social relations, reflecting in microcosm the class and gender relations within capitalist society as a whole.[15] For others, such social relationships are indeed important in structuring the activity of science, but there is a danger that, in stressing social relations, the material reality of the natural world is denied. If science is portrayed as "nothing but" the social relationships obtaining between those involved in its practice, then what happens to the nature that it claims to describe?[16] While we may agree that what science produces is undubitably a social product, nature does have a material reality that science purports to study. In this sense science, even within capitalist patriarchy, is surely more than just social relations.

It is not my intention to pursue this debate in detail here, although I will return to similar themes in the final chapter. What is more relevant here is to note one important implication of the broad view that science is intimately part of capitalist patriarchy, and that is that the simple critiques of biological determinism in relation to women are not enough.

We can criticise this or that idea about women's biology as much as we like, but the criticism does nothing to challenge the basic assumptions and organisation of that science as a whole. This will continue to be riddled with particular sets of values derived from the society in which it is embedded. We can challenge one bit of biological determinism, but another will pop up to take its place. In this sense the struggle to understand the workings of science—its institutionalised character, its funding, its modes of operation, as well as its values—is an important part of the struggle to change it.

The final part of Figure One refers to the historical association of science with what are stereotypically "masculine" values, in antithesis to the allegedly "feminine" qualities of Mother Nature. Some feminist writers have argued that a distinction between nature (feminine) and culture (including science: masculine) has been central to Western thought for some time, and inevitably influences the theories produced by science about nature, and about women.[17] This view is rooted in the old idea that there exists a hierarchy of creation, stretching down to the earth from God, an idea which contained within it not only justification for the notion that men were superior to women, but also notions of racial and class superiority.[18] The "inferior" groups in this hierarchy were seen as closer to nature, and thus more readily influenced by her.

If a particular group of people is seen as somehow closer to nature, then it is easier for it to be categorised in terms of biology. If it is claimed that, for example, it is in women's nature to be passive, or to behave maternally, then what is usually meant is that their "nature" is an essential, unchangeable, part of women. The implication is that this unchangeable nature is a product of a uniquely female biology. Thus the popular stereotypes of women as moody and unpredictable can be attributed to woman's nature, and thence to her biology. Karen Paige, in an article discussing the menstrual cycle, cited one male American doctor who felt that it would be disastrous to have a woman as bank manager: after all, you would not want her "making a loan under those raging hormonal influences at that particular period".[19] Her nature is unpredictable: the cause, her biology.

The Western distinction between "masculine" science and

its assumptions of a feminine nature is, then, a fundamental one, underlying the biological determinism of which feminists have often been critical. It is also important that we bear it in mind when we consider the possibility of a feminist science. Whatever views we hold on a feminist society, we will have to take into account our relationship not only with other groups of people, but also with the rest of the earth—with nature. This carries with it implications about the kind of science that we might envisage—a point to which I shall return later in the book.

The starting point of feminist interest in biology was, and is, a critique of biological determinism. This is important because, as I have emphasised, such arguments are frequently used against women's interests. Before going on to examine specific instances of biological determinism in Chapter Two, however, I want to make two caveats. First, in concentrating on *women* and biological determinism, I am not trying to deny that such arguments are at times applied to men: the idea that men are innately aggressive, for instance, is met with frequently, and is referred to in this book. By concentrating on women I am not saying that ideas of men's behaviour being biologically determined either do not exist or are not significant. Biological determinism is fairly pervasive, forming part of the armory of those seeking to defend the status quo.

Biological arguments are particularly relevant to women however, in two ways. First, socially oppressed groups are more likely to have biological arguments levelled against them than are socially dominant groups. This is true whether the division is one based on gender, ethnicity, social class, sexual preference, or whatever. The chief significance of biological arguments is that they reinforce relationships of power: for the group relatively lacking in power, such as women, the biological arguments buttress their powerlessness. When biological arguments *are* used in relation to the more powerful group, they generally serve to reinforce or legitimate that power. Thus it is women's passivity that is said to be a biologically determined, while it is men's aggressiveness; in both cases, what is attributed to biology is behaviour that maintains women's subordination.

Second, I would argue that biological arguments are anti-feminist precisely because they are conservative. Since feminism is a social movement emphasising the injustice of present social organisation and the need for social change, then the biological arguments cannot serve feminist causes. That is not to say that feminists never use biological arguments, as I have already indicated. But claiming that some female qualities, even "good" ones, are biologically inevitable and built-in, is only the other side of the determinist coin that ascribes our less desirable traits to biology. We cannot have it both ways. However it is used, biological determinism is conservative simply because it argues against the possibility of change and denies the social context of our lives.

The second caveat is that biologically determinist arguments frequently involve massive generalisations. As I noted in the Introduction, crudely deterministic arguments might refer to "women" as though they were a homogeneous group. Perhaps at a simple biological level, women do have something in common; nearly all women menstruate, or develop breasts at puberty, for example. There is, too, some common ground of oppression, to which feminism is opposed. But the *experiences* of different women are markedly different, including their experiences of the biological events themselves.[20] When biologically determinist arguments are used to defend and legitimate existing social arrangements, this is usually done without reference to differences between women, as though women's experiences are everywhere and always the same. Irrespective of race, social class or whatever, "women" are conceived of as a single entity. They may for example be eulogised as the centre pin of the nuclear family, whose biologically ordained nature best fits them to domesticity—even when they simply cannot afford to remain at home.

Because of the generalising nature of the arguments with which I am dealing in this book, I will necessarily have to refer to "women" in a similar way. That is, usually, the way in which the arguments themselves are articulated. But it is important to note that the *power* of those arguments to constrain and limit what is actually possible for women will actually differ between women. Thus, for example, the idea that women should be denied access to higher education because of the limitations imposed by their biology was often put forward in the nineteenth century, at a time when women were trying to gain such access.[21] The prevailing biological model put forward was that women were weak by nature, subject to fainting fits, and lacking in stamina. The power of such arguments was that, if they were believed, they would serve to restrict the educational mobility of middle-class women—precisely those who were demanding access to the universities and medical schools. Working-class and black women could hardly be said to be lacking in stamina—except perhaps as a result of too many hours of back-breaking labour. It was not them for whom the biologically determinist arguments were intended since they were unlikely to be breaching the citadels of the ivory tower anyway.

This chapter has been concerned with outlining the broad areas with which feminism has been concerned within biology. Some of these are not pursued further, but have been included here by way of introduction to feminist approaches to the kinds of questions raised by the biological sciences. In the rest of the book I take up some of these concerns in more detail, beginning with a closer look at the biological arguments themselves, and the implications these have for women.

2 Determined Women: Feminism and Biological Determinism

Gender differences, we are sometimes told, are natural. But what is meant by the concept of "naturalness" in such a context? "Natural" and "nature" can have a variety of meanings, so which meaning is intended by such a statement? In the first place, assertions of the naturalness of gender differences are usually intended to mean that the trait is biologically determined, preordained by nature. The idea that women "naturally" want, first and foremost, to be mothers is, for example, part of the wider notion that there resides in every woman an inherent maternal instinct: women naturally want to be mothers because it is in their biological nature to do so.

A second sense of the word natural is that it represents closeness to "nature". This also has connotations of being less refined, less changed, and possibly more wholesome—rather like talking about natural versus processed food. This sense of naturalness implies that closeness to nature involves a degree of immutability: whatever is closer to nature is more likely to be influenced by it, and hence is less subject to cultural modification. As I noted in the previous chapter, several feminist writers have pointed to the association in Western thought between this sense of "nature" and women.

A third sense of "natural" is to imply statistical normality. That is, the speaker is saying that something that is most commonly done is more natural. This sense of natural often forms part of what is meant by the term. Thus, if someone says that they think that it is natural for people to get married, then—in part—they may mean that this is in fact what most people do. However, the statistical meaning of "natural" is quite often confounded with a normative meaning: that is, the statement may partly mean that is what most people do, but it may partly mean that the speaker believes that this is what people should do. So the normative—what people ought to be doing—is a fourth sense in which the term "natural" may be used.

There are other senses in which concepts of natural or nature may be used, or implied, but these four illustrate the multiplicity of meanings that can be given when statements are made about the naturalness of gender, or, indeed, about any other feature of human behaviour. The most important thing to note about statements implying naturalness is that it is often impossible to tell from the context of the statement which (or how many) of these different meanings is implied. To say that it is natural for women to want to be mothers may imply biological determinism, closeness to nature, statistical normality, and may also be a statement implying that this is what women ought to be. And whatever else it is, it is usually a statement intended to discourage any attempts to change things. If it is natural then we would be unwise to try to upset the apple-cart, because if we did, then we would be going against inbuilt human nature.

This, then, is the political significance of biological determinism: its assumption of a universal nature implies that there are strict limits to the social changes that we might seek. In Chapter Three I will turn to the political consequences of these arguments for feminism (including those biological arguments evoked within feminism itself). Here, I want to consider biological determinism in more detail by looking at three areas of feminist concern in which biologically determinist arguments have been rife: sexuality, work, and violence. This selection is somewhat arbitrary, reflecting to some extent my own interests. By making it, I necessarily omit other areas in which biological determinism is equally extensive, such as reproduction and mothering,[1] areas which occupy a large feminist literature. My concern here, however, is to illustrate the nature—if you will forgive the pun—of biologically determinist claims about women, and to show some of the ways in which these can affect women's lives.

1. SEXUALITY

The popular mythology of gender differences in sexuality has it that women are more passive and receptive, men more active and aggressive. It is an idea with a long history in Western thought. Aristotle, for example, maintained that it was the male who was the active sex, both sexually and reproductively: it was his seed (sperm) which gave bodily form to the offspring, while the role of the female was passively to nurture it through pregnancy.[2] This kind of view persisted through subsequent centuries, although the form of its expression was variable. It reached perhaps its most extreme form during Victorian times, when at least some women were supposed not to have any sexual feelings at all.[3] And despite the alleged "sexual liberation" of the 1960s, it is still prevalent today. In an article on female sexuality, Beatrix Campbell observed that we tend now to think of sex as one of the wonders of the world, yet woman is still perceived as relatively passive: " 'it's the most beautiful thing that can happen to you' said one of my teachers. Precisely, it happens to you. You don't do it, it's done to you"[4] Women are no longer denied sexual feelings and pleasure, but their role remains that of the receiver of sexual acts.

The masculine activity/feminine passivity stereotypes of sexuality are fairly pervasive, and are frequently attributed to underlying biological differences between the sexes. In this section I want to focus particularly on two questions that raise feminist issues. These are the questions of whether or not humans have an "innate sex drive", and whether or not heterosexuality is innate and more natural than other forms of sexual expression. Both questions are founded upon assumptions that are frequently made about underlying biology, and both, I shall argue, are related to the active/passive stereotype.

(a) Is there an innate sex drive?
The idea that humans, and particularly men, have an innate sexual urge that propels them towards sexual activity is a familiar one. There are three consequences of this prevalent idea that I want to consider here: In the first place, it is biologically determinist, making assumptions about underlying biology. Second, it implies that that sexual urge might become thwarted or repressed;[5] and third, it implies that people might turn to alternative outlets if the urge is repressed. I shall look at each of these in turn.

The first point is that the idea of innate sex urges assumes that sexuality is an inbuilt trait of the individual. The problem with this is that it is impossible to understand much about sexuality outside the realm of its expression: it is what people *do* sexually that indicates their sexuality. But if it is an inborn trait, then it is one that is remarkably divergent in the forms of its expression. "Sexuality", however it is defined, is expressed in many different ways in different human societies: some accept and condone some sexual practices, while others would find them distasteful.[6] Positing some underlying biological urge cannot usefully explain something as rich and varied as human sexual expression.[7]

The second consequence of viewing sexuality as an innate urge is that it can be seen as something necessarily requiring an outlet. The concept of repression of sexuality and the consequences of such repression have been expounded by several writers, from those writing in the psychoanalytic traditions, such as Freud and Reich, to more recent feminist writing drawing on classical psychoanalysis.[8] Wilhelm Reich, for example, used the concept of repression extensively in his analysis of the "authoritarian personality", arguing that physical sexuality has potentially liberating power. That sexuality may become repressed, leading to undesirable consequences, is, however, an idea that implies that "sexuality" represents some essential quality, an inborn force to be reckoned with. Reich wrote of the consequences: "The compulsory regulation of sex-life works by means of sexual inhibitions which it anchors in the individual in childhood . . . inhibitions produce an insoluble conflict . . . . As a result . . . the capacity for gratification does not and cannot equal the instinctual tension, and sexual illnesses, neuroses, perversions, and antisocial modes of sexual behaviour appear as compensatory reactions".[9] All kinds of social ills might thus be laid at the door of a repressed sexual instinct.

The sexual instinct is also often assumed to be different for women and for men. Women's sex drive, according to this belief, is containable: with a few exceptions (which are then denigrated by labels such as whore, or nymphomaniac) women are assumed to have a low to moderate sex drive. Men, on the other hand, are often assumed to have a much greater, and sometimes insatiable, sex drive. It is this which, according to popular belief, needs alternative outlets, a belief which is sometimes given as a reason, or excuse, for rape and pornography.

This putative difference also rears its head in the concept of promiscuity. The supposed biological bases of male promiscuity have received much attention recently, particularly in sociobiological writing. According to sociobiological theories, males of most species are, other things being equal, likely to be promiscuous and mate with many females; by doing so they may propagate their genes in as many offspring as possible. Females, on the other hand, often have the responsibility of rearing the young: it is in their interests, sociobiology predicts, to remain faithful and find ways to persuade males to remain with them to help rear the young.[10] By this strategy the female propagates *her* genes more effectively, since she ensures the survival of more of her young. Hardly surprising, this biological defence of male philandery was met with joyous glee by publications such as *Playboy*.

What, then, are the feminist implications of the idea that there exists an innate sex drive, having different levels of intensity in the two sexes? First, for women, it reinforces the notion of their relative sexual passivity. The biological basis of women's passive sexuality was the vagina. For Freud, for example, the female would normally transfer her sexuality from the clitoris to the vagina as she grew up;[11] the normal adult woman was thus expected to experience her sexuality as vaginal, receptive to the active male penis. The view that normal female sexuality is passive and receptive in this way has been a particularly tenacious one, and one that contemporary feminists have challenged with, for instance, the publication of Anne Koedt's article, "The Myth of the Vaginal Orgasm."[12] Nonetheless, the myth persists that women's sexuality is centred on the vagina, a myth that has provoked much anxiety among women believing themselves to be "frigid". If prevailing orthodoxy had been that women learnt their sexual responses, then presumably there might be acceptance of the idea that women could learn to reach orgasm during intercourse. Unfortunately for women, the prevailing orthodoxy has been that sexuality is an inborn trait. in which vaginal penetration somehow releases the biological potential. As a result women often feel guilt or a sense of failure if they do not achieve orgasm during vaginal penetration.[13]

The idea that women were passively receptive took different forms in the nineteenth century, with different associated biological explanations. Apart from the double standard which allowed men promiscuity while expecting women's chastity, women themselves were divided by Victorian ideology into two types, the virtuous and the fallen.[14] Virtuous women, particularly of the middle and upper classes, adhered to Victorian values of purity and chastity, values which denied them sexual pleasure. The biological imperative was towards motherhood and the maintenance of the family ideal. But despite this apparent denial of any biologically based sexual urge in women from certain social backgrounds, "fallen" women were assumed to have given in to their inherent urges.[15] Women who thus succumbed became prostitutes; "bad" women coming largely from the poverty-stricken working class. So women were divided into those for whom the biologically preordained sexual passivity was so great that they were denied pleasure altogether, and those for whom the biology imposed an active seeking out of sexual gratification. Either way, the belief in women's receptivity to men was maintained.

Prostitution has long been viewed as something which "bad" women do, rather than as something for which the client is culpable. The law generally acts to support this view, by attempting to control the activities of the women rather than the men who pay for their services. What is particularly significant about the view upheld by Victorian morality was the claim that women turned to prostitution for some *inherent* reason, a "bad" nature, rather than because of some temporary sinfulness. William Acton, a doctor who wrote extensively about the prostitution he studied in the mid-nineteenth century, included among his list of possible causes of prostitution such characteristics as "natural desire" and "natural sinfulness", for example.[16] Alexandra Kollontai similarly made reference to the common belief in the "bad nature" of prostitutes in her speech on prostitution, delivered in 1921:

Bourgeois science and its academics love to prove to the world that prostitution is a pathological phenomenon, i.e., that it is the result of the abnormalities of certain women. Just as some people are criminal by nature, some women, it is argued, are prostitutes by nature. Regardless of where or how such women might have lived, they would have turned to a life of sin.[17]

Kollontai's view was that the prevailing idea of an "inborn disposition" is false, and that prostitution is, "above all, a social phenomenon" born of economic circumstances. The view that prostitution exists because of "bad women" persists today, even if it is expressed in less biological terms. Much contemporary research into prostitution assumes, for example, that the causes lie in the personal, deviant history of individual women.[18]

The second implication of the idea of an innate sex drive is that it allows the possibility that the level of "drive" may be such that the individual has to satisfy it immediately, irrespective of the context. This is precisely the way in which male sexuality is sometimes seen within our society. Both male exhibitionism and rape are at times attributed to innate sexual urges that somehow overwhelm the male; both have been said to result from biological causes.

Male exhibitionism has been assumed to be biological by some authors, on the grounds that penile displays occur in several species of primates (such as squirrel monkeys). The suggestion is that human male exhibitionism also represents a penile display of similar form to that occurring in other primate species. The biological hypothesis does, however, provide problems of explanation since, among other primates, it occurs largely between males, in situations of hostility, while in humans it is most often done by men towards women. The authors of one paper advocating a biological hypothesis deal with this by assuming that the biologically determined display becomes "sexual" rather than hostile in the human male. Rather than considering the many reasons why men might behave in a hostile fashion towards women in our society, they persist in the biological hypothesis, but simply change what it represents. This allows them to conclude that "the fact that the human display is made almost exclusively to women makes a persisting *sexual* aspect of the behaviour highly probable".[19] Hostility, then, which is basic to the biological theory they espouse, can become converted to a sexual urge if necessary in order to make the theory fit the data. And, of course, if it is biological, then we can be assured that it is perfectly natural: exhibitionists are only giving in to their overwhelming biological urges.

Rape, too, is sometimes attributed to the dictates of biology. Men rape, we are told, because of this uncontainable sex drive. This kind of viewpoint has two significant effects: first, it conflates rape and sex, which serves to deny the *violence* involved in rape and sexual assault. Second, it has the effect of removing blame from the rapist; he commits the act because of his biology, so it is not his fault. The philosopher of the New Right, Roger Scruton, believes that feminism will inevitably fail because it can do nothing to change the innate sexual natures of women and men: rape is simply an outcome of men's insatiable sexual natures:

Men are the victims of an impulse which, left to itself, is one of the most destructive of human urges, and the true cause of rape, obscenity and lust—the lust that seeks, not to unite with another person, but to relieve itself upon her body.[20]

Sociobiology, too, provides biological justification for rape. If a man, or a male animal, rapes a female, then it may be because he is maximising his chances of spreading his genes among as many females as possible; if the female is not willing to assist him in this task, she is simply taken by force. Although conceding that human rape is "by no means as simple as" say, rape in mallard ducks, David Barash still puts it squarely in the biological camp:

Perhaps human rapists, in their own criminally misguided way, are doing the best they can to maximise their fitness . . . . Another point: Whether they like to admit it or not, many human males are stimulated by the idea of rape. This does not make them rapists, but it does give them something in common with mallards. And another point: during the India-Pakistan war over Bangladesh, many thousands of Hindu women were raped by Pakistani soldiers. A major problem that these women faced was rejection by husband and family. A cultural pattern, of course, but one coinciding clearly with biology.[21]

Whether attributed to an innate sexual desire, or to maximising the gene's chances, biological explanations effectively imply that a man is not wholly responsible for his actions—a view that is not acceptable to most feminists. Rape is, rather, an expression of male *power* over women.

In some feminist writing, rape and other sexual assault is explicitly associated with pornography, on the grounds that pornography frequently provides images of sexual violence against women which provide the cultural context in which it becomes more acceptable for men to rape. Those who would defend the right of people to buy or view pornographic material, on the other hand, often deny the existence of any such association, or suggest that the images of pornography provide alternative outlets for men's sexual urges.[22] What is significant about this latter view is that it is yet another form of biological determinism. The multi-million pound pornography industry is defended because men have an innate rapaciousness that can only be controlled by redirecting it. What is also significant is that the idea of redirection of rampant male sexuality explicitly denies the often extreme violence that characterises much present-day pornography to which feminists have drawn attention.[23]

(b) The naturalness of heterosexuality

The passive female/active male stereotypes inevitably lead to assumptions about heterosexuality. Heterosexuality is assumed in our society to be "natural", and natural heterosexuality is assumed to be founded upon those stereotypes. Above all, "natural" heterosexuality is assumed to be biologically based. But what about homosexuality? Cultural assumptions about homosexuality maintain the active/passive stereotypes:[24] it is also often assumed that homosexuality is itself biologically based, representing some kind of disorder of biological determination. To illustrate such assumptions, here is a quotation from John Money and Anke Ehrhardt, who have written extensively on human sex and gender acquisition, advocating a largely biological view. In this extract, they are referring to gay men:

Actually, such a person has an identity/role that is partially masculine, partially feminine. The issue is one of proportion: more masculine than feminine. Masculinity of identity manifests itself in his vocational and domestic role. Femininity of identity appears in his role as an erotic partner; it may be great or slight in degree and it is present regardless of whether, like a woman, he receives a man's penis, or, also like a woman, he has a man giving him an orgasm. It goes without saying that the ratio of masculinity to femininity varies among individuals.[25]

The equation is thus made between receptivity/passivity, and femaleness *or* the characteristics of gay men. The sexual acts themselves are defined by their passivity: "he has a man giving him an orgasm", for example. Moreover, gay men become defined by their passivity, and analogy to the feminine role, leaving gay men whose behaviour does not adhere to such assumptions out of the definition.[26]

Homosexual behaviour has never been widely accepted in Western culture, although it is only relatively recently that it has been attributed to specific individuals, and thence to inbuilt features of biology. Foucault has argued, in his *History of Sexuality*[27] that during the eighteenth and nineteenth centuries there was a significant increase in discourse concerning sex and sexuality, which in turn led to a multiplicity of definitions and categories. One consequence of this was that, whereas homosexuality had hitherto been viewed as a potential in everyone, different forms of sexuality now became attributed to specific kinds of individual. Once people can be defined as *a* heterosexual, *a* lesbian, or whatever, then it becomes possible to suggest that they might be so because of their biology.[28]

This process of categorisation has had several consequences.[29] In the first place, it helped to create an image of non-heterosexual sex as pathological, an image perpetuated by sexologists writing around the turn of the century. It is perhaps not surprising that those reformers, such as Havelock Ellis, who were attempting to increase bourgeois society's acceptance of homosexuality should do so on the basis that it was innate, and could not be helped.[30] Ellis went to great lengths to portray homosexuality as a harmless quirk of nature, something for which the individual could not be blamed. However, the assumption that homosexuality is biologically determined has continued into the medical literature of the twentieth century resulting in a number of attempts to change lesbians and homosexual men into heterosexuals, using techniques ranging from hormone therapy to surgery.[31] That these techniques do not normally work does little to alter the assumed biological determinism.

A second consequence of defining people by their sexual practice along the active/passive continuum is that it helps to maintain existing gender constructs. The popular stereotype of a lesbian or a gay man is of someone who is "less of" a women (or man) than their heterosexual counterparts. The lesbian is "less of" a real woman because she is, supposedly, more masculine and thus less passive. The assumption that there is a correct amount of maleness or femaleness, of which people can have more or less, does two things. In the first place it maintains the rigid boundaries of our concepts of gender, a point which I shall discuss more fully in Chapter Four. It does this by assuming that femininity and masculinity, femaleness and maleness, represent discrete catagories existing in individuals in definable amounts. This is evident from the way that Money and Ehrhardt write about gender in the quotation given above, in which they describe homosexual men as being "partially feminine". The second consequence is that by assuming that femininity and masculinity exist as *fixed* quantities (even if variable between individuals) Money and Ehrhardt clearly imply that these traits are inborn. It is then only a small step to infer biological determination.

These assumptions about the femininity or masculinity of lesbians and gay men are carried over into medical research, which frequently supposes some associated biology underlying the categories. Masculinity is attributed to lesbians, for example, so research often hypothesises an underlying biology having male-like qualities; femininity is attributed to gay men so the research supposes a biology that is more feminine or less masculine.[32]

A third consequence of increased categorisation is that the concept of heterosexuality itself becomes reinforced precisely because it becomes naturalised. Once individuals themselves are defined as intrinsically heterosexual, then heterosexuality can be seen both as biologically preordained, and thus as more "natural". This not only reinforces the idea that it *is* the only natural form of sexual expression, but also serves to reinforce what Adrienne Rich has called the "political institution of heterosexuality". By this she means the whole set of social, cultural and economic forces that serve to buttress the institution of heterosexuality to such an extent that it becomes, not a preference, freely chosen, but the only option for large numbers of people. This institution is, Rich suggests, the "beachhead of male dominance" that requires further analysis and challenge within feminism. She argues that feminism has not hitherto challenged it sufficiently because:

> The assumption that "most women are innately heterosexual" stands as a theoretical and political stumbling block for many women. It remains as a tenable assumption, partly because lesbian existence has been written out of history or catalogued under disease . . . partly because to acknowledge that for women heterosexuality may not be a "preference" at all but something that has had to be imposed, managed, organized, propagandized, and maintained by force, is an immense step to take if you consider yourself freely and "innately" heterosexual.[33]

Whether or not one agrees with Rich that the assumption that heterosexuality is innate undermines feminism's challenge to the institution of heterosexuality, it is undoubtably true that there is a widespread—and powerful—belief that heterosexual behaviour is indeed innate.

There are, then, a number of assumptions about the innateness of sexuality. Women's innate sexuality is held to be passive, receptive; men's, to be active, penetrating. The assumed innateness, somehow rooted in biological forces, ensures that sexuality remains that way, on the grounds that what is biological is assumed to be determining and immutable. Moreover, people who deviate from the norm of conventional heterosexuality are assumed also to deviate in the active/passive dimension. Lesbians are thus assumed to be sexually active and non-receptive (perhaps because they *are* non-receptive—to men). As I noted in the previous chapter, the ways in which biologically determinist arguments are applied differently to women and to men helps in the face of male aggressiveness.

I have argued in this section that the concept of innate sexuality supposes that this differs between women and men, and that this notion of different levels and types of inborn sexuality is used to justify male power over women. It is, of course, also a notion that can divide women. Women with disabilities, for example, are popularly assumed to have no sexual urges at all, innate or otherwise, a supposition which sets them apart from other women.[34] On the other hand, the alleged innate sexuality of black women has often been assumed to be far greater than that of other women, to the extent that they have been portrayed as having an "animal" lust for sex. The racism inherent in this mythology was evident during the period of slavery, in which black women's innate sexuality was frequently posited as an excuse for their sexual abuse by white slave-owners (and, indeed, by other white men).[35] But the mythology of black women's bestial sexuality continued long after the abolition of slavery, and continues to exist today. Bell Hooks, a black feminist writer, has described two effects of the myth. In the first place, it acts as an ideological contraint on interracial marriages, by "discouraging white men from seeing black women as suitable marriage partners. Whites condone inter-racial relationships between black women and white men only in the context of degrading sex."[36] Second, it maintains the belief that black women are little more than whores. Bell Hooks quotes from another black woman writer, Gerda Lerner, who wrote of the

... myth of the "bad" black woman. By assuming a different level of sexuality for all Blacks than that of whites and mythifying their greater sexual potency, the black woman could be made to personify sexual freedom and abandon. A myth was created that all black women were eager for sexual exploits, voluntarily "loose" in their morals.[37]

The image of a lustful black woman, eager for sex, is one that has similarly been exploited by the pornography industry.[38]

The supposition of innate sexuality thus has considerable implications for feminism. It can be used to legitimate heterosexuality, rape, prostitution, male exhibitionism, male promiscuity and the existence of pornography. With a few alterations to the supposed "levels" of this inbuilt sexual urge, racism can also be legitimated. And, of course, it serves to maintain gender stereotypes of female passivity and male activity. In the next section I will consider, briefly, the effects of biological determinism in another area of women's lives— work. Here, too, biological determinism has the effect of perpetuating women's subordination, just as it does with sexuality.

2. WOMEN'S WORK

Direct discrimination against women in certain types of paid employment may be justified with various arguments, many of which rest on the assumption that women are "by nature" somehow less suited to that kind of work. Biological arguments can also be found that expound women's suitability for labour within the home. The stereotype usually invoked by such arguments is one of women as physically weaker, somehow more frail, and intellectually less able, as well as being emotionally more suited to tedious, repetitive work.

In this section I shall look briefly at some instances of biological arguments about women's suitability for different kinds of work. As before, however, these arguments are often presented about "women" as a generality, although their power to affect women's lives is often highly dependent on other factors, such as class. If biologistic arguments are presented as reasons why women should not become bank managers, for example, then this is not likely to affect many working-class women. On the other hand, discrimination against women on the grounds of their biological potential for reproduction and the possible risks to them of working in dangerous industries may be more likely to affect the lives of working-class women.

One example of the class-specificity of biologically determinist arguments is provided by the kind of statements made during the later nineteenth century concerning the constraints imposed by women's biology. Many medical treatises at this time opposed education for women on the grounds that women were naturally physically weaker, as a result of the demands made on their reproductive systems; stimulating the brain through education could only result in energy being drawn away from the reproductive system, resulting in further weakening and enfeeblement. A particular target for such attacks were those women who were seeking entry into higher education, including the medical profession itself. The entry of women into medicine was opposed in, for example, this speech to the American Medical Association, by Dr. Alfred Stille:

Certain women seek to rival men in manly sports . . . and the strong-minded ape them in all things, even in dress. In doing so, they may command a sort of admiration such as all monstrous productions inspire, especially when they tend towards a higher type than their own.[39]

The constraints imposed by her biology on a girl's education were given at length by Dr. E. H. Clarke, a Harvard professor, who argued that menstruation imposed such stress on female physiology that the additional burden of brain exercise through study would necessarily result in poor health. He quoted a number of case studies of women whose health was irreparably damaged because, he claimed, higher education had arrested their reproductive development. He recommended completely sex-segregated education, combined with regular rest periods for girls:

A girl cannot spend more than four, or, in occasional instances, five hours of force daily upon her studies, and leave sufficient margin for the general physical growth that she must make . . . . If she puts as much force into her brain education as a boy, the brain or the special apparatus (that is, the reproductive system) will suffer.[40]

It was typical of much of this type of writing in the late nineteenth century that it ignored the fact that the majority of working-class girls of similar ages were working long and hard hours in factories—jobs that were presumably much more demanding of limited energy supplies than studying. Clarke, however, did note this inconsistency in the theory, but explained that factory labour was far less damaging than study to a woman because it worked the body, not the brain.[41]

It was primarily white, middle-class women, then, who were said to be weakened by education, and it was these women to whom the biologically determinist arguments of the time were directed. Other women could still continue the hard manual labour precisely because they were physically stronger, as Dr. Sylvanus Stall observed:

At war, at work, or at play, the white man is superior to the savage, and his culture has continually improved his condition. But with women the rule is reversed. Her squaw sister will endure effort, exposure and hardship which would kill the white woman. Education which has resulted in developing and strengthening the physical nature of man has been perverted through folly and fashion to render women weaker and weaker.[42]

By the mid-twentieth century, however, education for women

was, if not completely equal, at least accepted. During the last two decades, biologically determinist arguments about women's capacity for work have taken two major forms. First, arguments are sometimes put forward to suggest that, because of some biological factor, women are better suited to certain types of task; and second, arguments are put forward to oppose women's entry into otherwise male dominated fields.

Biological arguments about women's suitability for certain kinds of work operate in the following way. First, from the observation that women are often to be found doing different kinds of work than men, it is assumed that women must possess some special attributes that render them suitable for particular jobs. Second, it is then assumed that, if they possess such attributes, these might be related to some underlying biological feature of women. One example of a biological theory that has been used to "explain" women's preponderance in certain occupations is a hormonal theory proposed in 1968 by Donald Broverman and colleagues. They suggested that women were better than men at tasks requiring the rapid performance of already learnt repetitive tasks, such as simple calculations and typing, while men were better at what they called complex, "re-structuring", tasks, involving the inhibition of previously learnt tasks in order to learn new ones. These differences were, they suggested, due to hormonal differences between the sexes.[43] Corrinne Hutt, a psychologist writing about sex differences, similarly proposed that women's preponderance in secretarial work is due to their greater manual dexterity and "feminine facility . . for rote memory" attributes which, she argued, were the product of female biology.[44]

Similar types of argument have been proposed to suggest that, because of underlying biological factors, men are generally better at other skills, including those skills allegedly required for work in science and engineering. Starting from the observation that these are male-dominated fields, it is assumed that men outnumber women because they possess some special characteristic in greater quantity. A candidate skill is visuo-spatial ability, which is measured by a number of psychological tests,[45] and which, it is assumed, is a necessary skill for doing science. On at least some tests of spatial ability, men generally score higher on average than women, (although there is considerable overlap between them), an observation which has led some writers to assert that the sex difference is the product of associated biological differences. The most popular of such theories currently is that the sexes differ in brain organisation, which in turn determines their particular abilities. Now there are many reasons why these arguments are problematic. They ignore, for example, all the other factors, besides individual skills, that might influence a person's choices and success within a scientific career. They ignore, too, the fact that women are not as outnumbered in science as is commonly claimed; the difference is that women are more likely to be found in the lower-status technician posts than in the more prestigious research and teaching posts. Moreover, they ignore the fact that the evidence for significant sex differences in brain organisation, is to say the least, equivocal. And, of course, they assume that any sex differences in perceptual skills are caused by the biological differences: they do not normally consider the possibility that, for example, social differences in women's and men's lives may themselves contribute to any differences in skills or even in brain organisation.[46]

That such arguments are problematic has not, however, halted their proliferation. Janet Sayers, a feminist psychologist, has noted that this proliferation has occurred in the wake of the women's movement, and is hardly coincidental. She comments:

So germane do these findings about sex differences in brain organization appear to the current political debate about the justice of continuing sexual inequalities in professional life that they are now regularly singled out for coverage in newspaper reports of scientific meetings.[47]

—where, of course, their effect is to justify the continued domination of science and related fields by men on the grounds that it is rooted in ineradicable biological differences.

Women's biology is thus said both to predispose them to certain tedious, repetitive forms of work, and also to bar them from entering the more highly paid professional jobs. These sorts of biologically determinist assumptions clearly do not help to change the position of women in the labour force which *is* largely in low-paid, often tedious and repetitive, work. These arguments ignore, among many other things, the complex historical reasons *why* women have come to occupy their present position in the labour force: they simply assume women's role as historically static and biologically given.

As much as biological arguments are sometimes adduced which justify women's role within paid work, they have also been used to justify women's role in domestic work. Arguments abound that women "naturally" are suited to staying at home and being housewives. Around the turn of the century, for example, the idea of teaching domestic science in schools was being actively propagated, at least partly in the belief that "homemaking is the most natural and therefore the most desirable vocation for women".[48] The belief that women "naturally" should be, or want to be, homemakers and mothers is a prevalent one, and is often attributed to a particular version of human evolutionary history which supposes that the crucial determinants of human evolution have been male hunting of large animals and female gathering "at home". E. O. Wilson, a Harvard professor explained the significance for modern society thus:

In hunter-gatherer societies, men hunt and women stay at home. This strong bias persists in most agricultural and industrial societies and on that ground alone appears to have a genetic origin . . . . My own guess is that the genetic bias is intense enough to *cause* substantial division of labour *even in the most free and egalitarian societies.*[49] (my emphasis)

This example is typical of the genre, making inferences about human prehistory from what the writer perceives as social organisation in modern hunter-gatherer societies. Such arguments also make the inference that if something is thought to be a universal form of behaviour, then it must have a biological origin. At times the inferences are drawn more widely: thus David Barash refers to non-Western societies, irrespective of their type of social organisation:

If we assume that modern non-Western peoples give us some insight into prehistory (sic), we get a rather male chauvinist view of that time in human evolution: hairy-chested hunters and warriors all bloody and brave, bringing home the bacon and an occasional scalp, while the women dug roots, gathered berries and made children.[50]

To talk about "modern non-Western peoples" in relation to

prehistory is, of course, a massive distortion (as well as denying the cultural validity of a wide range of different human cultures, past and present). Moreover, we cannot necessarily assume that the habitat to which modern hunter-gatherer societies have become adapted is typical of the kind of environment in which the hominids (*Homo sapiens* and related species) evolved. But perhaps the most significant objection to the Man-the-Hunter view of human evolution is simply that there is little evidence actually to support it. That we can find the bones of large animals in the camp-sites of prehistoric times does not necessarily imply that the hunting of large animals was a major driving force in evolution. Nor does it imply that the supposed hunting of game exclusively by men was the cause of subsequent gender differentiation. Some feminist writers, opposing the Man-the-Hunter view of evolution, have noted that it is equally likely that male hunting was the *effect*, rather than cause, of gender differentiation.

Feminist theorists have generally argued against the view that male hunting was a major force in human evolution. Nancy Tanner and Adrienne Zihlman, for example, have argued that it is quite plausible (and as consistent with modern evolutionary theory) that females played a large role in selecting males in human evolution but that, rather than selecting men for their dominance and aggression, they selected those males that were more cooperative and likely to participate in child-rearing.[51] This viewpoint would imply that major selection pressures in human evolution were cooperation and sociability, rather than the competition and aggressiveness of the Man-the-Hunter story. It also implies that home and child-rearing may not have been the exclusive province of females in human history.[52] And if that is the case, it cannot be concluded that there exists some fundamental biological basis for women's domesticity, as is so often claimed:

women have almost universally found themselves relegated to the nursery while men derive their greatest satisfaction from their jobs ... such differences in male-female attachment to family versus vocation could derive in part from hormonal differences between the sexes.[53]

Note here how the assumptions of human evolutionary history have become translated into assumptions about "hormonal differences" between the sexes which supposedly determine respective gender roles. "Family" and "work" are assumed to be historically static phenomena, linked to biology through evolutionary time. That the family, work, and the relationships between them have all changed considerably, even in recent history, does not disturb the speculations of biological determinism.

Biological arguments, then, can be found to support sexual segregation in the labour market, and can also be used to legitimate policies encouraging women to remain at home. Biological arguments may also be used to defend occupational discrimination in another sense. It is well known that working in particular industries can pose enormous dangers to health, from accidents or exposure to chemicals, radiation, and other hazards. These dangers apply, of course, to anyone exposed to them, irrespective of gender, although there may be ways in which women and men are differentially affected by particular hazards.[54] If hazards pose health risks to adults, they may, obviously, pose even greater risks to the foetus during early pregnancy. Because of this, some factories have justified a policy which deliberately excludes all women of potentially childbearing age, a policy which in turn can induce a pressure for women to be sterilised, in order to protect their jobs. Jeanne Stillman and Mary Sue Henifin have described the pressure some women employees in particular American industries were under to be sterilised—or lose their jobs.[55] Apart from constituting direct sex discrimination, this kind of policy, based on women's role in reproduction, has two direct consequences. In the first place it averts attention from the fact that the work involved must pose health risks to whoever works there; if it is considered that women are at greater risk, that does not mean that men are at no risk. Second, it is *only* women who are seen as potential parents (and who can thereby be discriminated against). Yet many of these industrial contaminants may not only damage the developing foetus, but may also damage gametes (eggs or sperm). There have been few attempts, however, to protect potential fathers from chemical or radiation damage to sperm.

Women's biology can thus be invoked to defend discrimination in industrial jobs, just as it can be used to "explain" women's preponderance in certain types of work. In the final section of this chapter I want to turn to a third example of biologically determinist arguments in another area of concern to feminism—namely, violence towards women, which has sometimes been portrayed as emanating from biological, rather than social, causes.

3. VIOLENCE

I have already touched on one phenomenon which many feminists would see as explicitly involving violence against women; that is, rape. I did, however, consider it under the heading of "sexuality" largely because when biologically determinist arguments are adduced to explain it they do so on the basis of an assumed underlying sexuality. The argument is that rape exists because of men's insatiable sexual drive. Rape is not, however, the only form of violence against women that has been explained in biological terms. Another example is afforded by domestic violence.

Domestic violence by a man towards the woman with whom he lives is quite a common occurrence, and has a long history. Men had legal rights to beat their wives until well into the nineteenth century[56] and, even if it is no longer strictly afforded legal rights, there remains a consensus that what men do within their own homes is their own private affair. During the 1970s, however, public attention was at least drawn to the widespread existence of "wife-battering", as women's refuges were established throughout Britain.

Women enter Women's Aid refuges for various reasons. Some may have been threatened with violence and are frightened of the threat becoming real; others may have been victims of repeated assaults over many years. Whatever the complex reasons why these women find themselves in a violent relationship, the claim has been made that at least some of them do so because they are biologically driven into violent situations. This claim was made by Eriz Pizzey and Jeff Shapiro, who suggested that some women are "prone to violence", and tend to return to the same violent relationship after leaving a refuge, or seek another. The suggestion is that, in the past of such a woman, she herself was a victim of violent assaults, which at the time resulted in high levels of what are loosely called "stress" hormones. If the violence is prolonged, she starts to become addicted to them, to produce what Pizzey and Shapiro called "hormonal highs".[57]

Pizzey and Shapiro distinguished between what they call "adrenalin personalities" who become hooked on adrenalin surges during a moment of rage in which they may be committing acts of violence, and "cortisone personalities" who become hooked on cortisone surges while they are being attacked.[58] In both cases the hormonal "high" is said to induce an opium-like state of intense satisfaction.

This kind of argument is an extreme form of biological determinism, in which even the victim of violent assault has her behaviour blamed firmly on her biology: ultimately, then, *she* rather than her assailant is to blame. Pizzey and Shapiro's writings consistently fail to emphasise that what is being described is *male* violence towards women—they persistently refer to genderless "people", when describing the "cortisone personality", even though the personality being described—passive, masochistic—is based upon their description of the victims of assault: women.

Now there may be many social reasons for women finding themselves in violent situations (such as financial dependence), but these are ignored by Pizzey and Shapiro. The biological argument places the blame firmly on the victim, and even exonerates the assailant by its implication that, in becoming addicted to *his* hormonal highs he cannot help it. And it does more than simply remove blame. Pizzey and Shapiro use this "biology" as the basis for the supposition that, if someone's hormones are deranged in such a way that they get themselves into violent relationships, then we might consider the possibility of drugs to rearrange them:

> We hope to see pharmaceutical companies working to find a whole new spectrum of drugs that could be used to aid the internal work with the emotionally disabled ... in this period of drug-induced balance, intensive treatment can then be practicable, so that the person can learn to control his or her own chemicals.[59]

This is an important consequence of many biologically determinist theories. Not only do they serve to justify existing social arrangements, but they can also lend themselves to medical/biological interventions aimed at changing the underlying biology if this is considered to be at fault.

I have considered in this chapter several types of biologically determinist argument concerning gender. By supposing that gender differences are innate, they have in common the implication that those differences cannot be substantially changed. Moreover, some of these arguments have policy implications. As I have noted above, viewing women who have been victims of repeated violence as biologically driven is to place the blame firmly on the individual woman herself. The policy implications might then be, as Pizzey and Shapiro imply, attempts to change the woman's biology by means of drugs. That there are policies that follow from biological arguments is one of the reasons why biological determinism is political.

3 The Political Effects of Biological Determinism

If biologically determinist arguments about gender could simply be ignored, then they might be of no more than passing interest. They are, however, not usually ignored but are quite often articulated in overt defence of existing social inequalities. They are, too, sometimes proposed by feminists in an attempt to explain the pervasiveness of patriarchy. In this chapter I shall look at some of the responses people might make to these biological ideas of gender differences in terms of their political consequences. People can respond to them in, roughly, three different ways. First, they can accept a biological basis to gender at face value. I shall discuss this with reference to a number of writers whose biological arguments are apparently written in response to feminist claims, and also with reference to biological arguments within feminism itself. The second kind of response is simply to argue that whether or not biology is involved in the development of gender differences is simply irrelevant to feminism. And third, I shall argue for a rejection of biological determinism.

1. ACCEPTANCE OF BIOLOGICAL DETERMINISM

The notion that gender differences are somehow biologically in-built is a persistent one. It is also an idea that has proliferated during the 1970s and 1980s at least partly in response to the demands made by feminism. Steven Goldberg's book, *The Inevitability of Patriarchy*[1] was written for example as a biologically-based argument directed specifically at feminist demands for equality.

Biological arguments may take different forms. For some,

the biological substrate determines or limits *individual* behaviour, while social factors—society in general—acts at another level (for instance, arguments about women's suitability for particular jobs, discussed in Chapter Two). For other advocates of the biology-is-destiny view, human society and its organisation are themselves determined by the underlying biology. This is the view, for example, adopted by some writing from the far right of the political spectrum, such as the National Front in Britain. The National Front views what it terms liberal or Marxist attempts to alter society as misguided because the biology that underwrites that society cannot itself be changed. Here is one example of such argument:

we can conclude that social customs and organisation, or what we do, is very largely preconditioned by what we are, and more particularly by the process by which we came to be what we are. The fact that man is indeed the product of his genetic inheritance is again illustrated most forcibly in sexual behaviour and sexual differences. One only has to observe the degree to which male dominance and female passivity in sexual courtship obtains in the animal world, likewise qualities of male aggression and female domesticity, to understand their fundamental biological basis.[2]

The National Front is avowedly antifeminist, and uses this kind of biologistic argument to proclaim its belief in the "naturalness" of woman's place as wife and mother.[3] The article from which this quotation is taken goes on to announce that feminism is "puerile Marxist rubbish" on the grounds that gender differences are directly determined by hormonal differences which in turn "are governed by the sex chromosomes of our genes" (sic).[4]

It might be argued that relatively few people are likely to read, still less to be influenced by, anything written in the publications of the far Right. But biological arguments are expounded in various places, often with much wider publicity, and often claiming to be arguments against feminism. In the previous chapter, for example, I quoted from a newspaper article by Roger Scruton, entitled "The Case Against Feminism", in which he stated the belief that men do *not* significantly oppress women in our present society, as well as the belief that feminism is merely an ideology, serving to distract "the believer from the reality of his (sic) condition" and *fostering* male dominance.[5] He claims that feminism will not achieve much change (even if it were, in his opinion desirable) because there are fundamental, innate differences between women and men that no amount of ideology can ever transform.

During the late 1970s and the 1980s other newspaper articles have appeared designed, like Scruton's, to oppose feminism, and giving a variety of reasons for believing in the innateness of gender differences. Another newspaper report quoted, for instance, the "considerable displeasure" expressed by the women's movement over research which suggested that "sexism . . . is a natural, inevitable and permanent feature of personality". These findings, it claimed

challenge the view that sexual stereotypes are an invention of a male-dominated society and indicate instead that they arise, in part, from a biological programme, the legacy of millions of years of evolution which starts to unfold at birth.[6]

Newspaper reports such as this are noteworthy in two respects. First they often include some naive concepts of biology itself: it is a strange process of development, for instance, that begins only at birth! Second, and more significantly, they set up the biological arguments against what is portrayed as "the feminist position" according to which all gender-specific behaviour is environmentally conditioned. Now it is undoubtedly true that contemporary feminism has emphasised social conditioning, largely as a counter-argument to the prevailing beliefs in biological determination. Partly, too, feminist ideology was influenced by the stress laid on social construction by the Left during the 1970s.[7]

This technique of opposing "commonsense" biological arguments to social learning as "the" feminist position is not, however, unique to newspaper articles: it appears too in the pages of academic journals. One article taking this line appeared, for example, in the *Bulletin* of the British Psychological Society, in 1979. Entitled "The Sociobiology of Sex Differences", and written by Glenn Wilson[8], it caused quite a furore over its overtly sexist stance. At its outset, Wilson claims that social learning was *the* predominant theory of gender at the time—a debatable assertion—and that this hegemony was due to feminist "witch-hunts" which disallowed alternatives. Wilson's version of feminist theory was that "women have been taught by men to be submissive and to accept a secondary, supporting role, and that with appropriate counter-propaganda, they can be taught to be just like men". The view that he opposes to this is that a greater equality already exists between women and men than his version of feminism would imply, because "men and women are equal in the extent to which they are predisposed by their biological nature to behave in particular ways". Finally, he raises the question of the kind of social policy implicated by such determinism, and concludes that "there is a limit to the extent to which the feminist movement can override the natural inclinations of men and women by persuasion and political power".[9]

Apart from its biological determinism and blatant sexism, this kind of article is problematic for feminism, not least because of the way in which it portrays feminist beliefs. By setting up social conditioning as "the" feminist position, and then describing it in particular ways, the beliefs of feminism are ridiculed, and the counterposed biological position acquires the status of common sense. Consider the notion that "women have been taught by men", and could be taught something different. The idea that men have done the teaching to subservient women itself perpetuates the idea of woman as passive. Wilson does not discuss the other side of the social conditioning argument, which is that men are similarly taught to be aggressive, dominant, non-nurturant, or whatever; all that is merely taken for granted.

The major problem with such argument is, however, the way in which biological determinism appeals to common sense. Given the extent to which a belief in the "naturalness" of gender differences exists, it is relatively easy to persuade readers of the sense of biological argument, particularly if for good measure you caricature rather than argue against, alternative viewpoints. The political significance of articles such as these for feminism is, then, twofold. In the first place, like all biological determinism concerning gender, it serves to legitimate existing inequalities by naturalising them. Second, by portraying feminism in ways that are not likely to appeal to commonsense beliefs in "natural" behaviour, feminist arguments for greater equality are further undermined. We are thus doubly assured of the pointlessness of feminist struggles for a more just society.

The question of how society might deal with the knowledge that the basis of gender differences is innate was also raised by E. O. Wilson in his controversial book, *On Human Nature*. Wilson has frequently been criticised for his advocacy of biological determinism, particularly in his book *Sociobiology: The New Synthesis,* published in 1975.[10] *On Human Nature* was written partly in response to the publicity and fuss that surrounded the earlier book.[11] In the latter, Wilson outlines three types of policy that might be adopted by any society in response to the knowledge of fundamental, biological gender differences. It can do one of three things. It can (i) condition its members so as to exaggerate sexual differences in behaviour; (ii) train its members so as to eliminate all sexual differences; or (iii) provide equal opportunities but do nothing else. Wilson's responses to these three policy options are that he considers that option (i) can result in a society that could "be richer in spirit, more diversified, and even more productive than a unisex society. Such a society might safeguard human rights even while channelling men and women into different occupations." The regulation implied in option (ii) would, he suggests, "certainly place some personal freedoms in jeopardy". It is clear from these responses that Wilson feels that a sex-stratified society is desirable: it is also clear that he does not consider women's freedom to be jeopardised in our present society. As far as option (iii) is concerned, Wilson returns to the biological substratum: if completely equal opportunities were provided men would be "likely to maintain disproportionate representation in political life, business and science".[12] In short, whatever we might do to change gender inequalities we will be constrained by the dictates of our biology.

Whatever differences there may be in the way in which it is expressed, these writers share a belief in the underlying constancy—and determinacy—of the biological base. Gender differences exist fundamentally as a result of that biology, they suggest, and any social policy has to take this fact into account.

This, as Wilson implies, only allows a limited amount of social change.

The examples cited above imply that a degree of acceptance of biological determinism characterises anti-feminism. To a large extent this is generally true, and the arguments illustrated here have specifically addressed feminist issues in order to argue against them. Acceptance of the idea of biologically based gender differences also occurs, however, within feminism itself.

There have always been some advocates of equal rights for women who have maintained a belief in the primacy of the underlying biology, while simultaneously hoping for movement towards (limited) equal rights and opportunities. However, in recent years, several writers have espoused overt biological determinism as part of what they would claim is a more radical feminist politics. They start from the premise that feminine values are, in Western society, undervalued—a view that few feminists would dispute. However, in rejecting masculine values while rejoicing in female qualities, they run the danger of assuming that there is an essential female nature, an "essence of womanhood", which determines these qualities. In the end, gender differences according to this kind of vision, come down to biology again.

One of these approaches follows from the premise that male domination is universal, and so needs to be explained. A frequent problem in beginning with this premise is that male domination/patriarchy becomes portrayed as an ahistorical phenomenon with little cultural variation, as though the oppression of women in say, the Medieval European countryside, in subsistence agriculture in Africa, and in the affluent cities of advanced capitalism is essentially the same. But if that basic premise is accepted, then the universality requires explanation; one answer is to suggest that universal male domination is rooted in a biologically determined male aggression, which in turn is the bedrock of gender differences in all societies. From the camps of anti-feminism, this was the argument put forward by Steven Goldberg, although similar arguments can be found in feminism's own camp. Here, for instance, is Laurel Holliday, in a book entitled *The Violent Sex:*

> Male aggression as we know it today is not simply the product of culture, the legacy of patriarchal religion, or whatever doorstep that feminists have tended to lay the evil at, but rather it is the result of the decision to hunt large animals which men made at least a half million years ago. . . . What prevented early women from taking the male path to violence? Our biology, simply put.[13]

Holliday, and other feminists writing in this vein, assume that male dominance is everywhere and always the same. But if so, and if it is rooted in biology, then there is precious little that can be done about it. Feminists can either give up the struggle entirely, or withdraw into the feminist ghetto.[14] Holliday does at least suggest that some change might be possible, although her solution is basically an individualistic one, in which some men might be "persuaded" to overcome their biological roots and give up their privileges. How feminism is to achieve this goal remains unanswered.

Another approach is represented by the withdrawal—particularly noticeable in the U.S.A.—of erstwhile feminists from the radical politics that hitherto characterised their feminism. This withdrawal has been described as a move towards a "conservative feminism"[15]. Amongst other things, it forms part of an anti-feminist backlash aiming to oppose the "excesses of liberalism" within society. At its broadest, this backlash against liberalism has led to and been part of the rise of the New Right, whose agenda, particularly in the U.S.A., has been vocal in its condemnation of feminist ideals. It is, for example, anti-abortion, anti-equal rights, anti-gay, and pro-family, although opposed to the provisions of the welfare state.[16].

This backlash has also occurred within feminism itself, with some feminists beginning to espouse ideals with which many feminists within the movement would disagree. One plank of these ideals is a return to beliefs in a fundamental biological basis to gender, as a prerequisite for a re-evaluation of women's biology. For some proponents of this view, such as Jean Bethke Elshtain and to a lesser extent Betty Friedan, gender-based traits are to be valued, rather than undermined. Elshtain, particularly, rejects the prevalent feminist orthodoxy regarding social construction of gender, and locates the construction of gender firmly within the biological body. For her the biological basis, the "bedrock of who I am", is primary and irreducible. The focus on the irreducibility of the biological base allows these writers to disengage from the analyses that have been central to much feminist thought: as Judith Stacey has pointed out, they have overtly rejected feminist sexual politics, specifically denying for example, that "the personal is political". Elshtain's reason for rejecting this central tenet of feminist theory and practice is that she believes that it collapses boundaries between public and private life, leading to the erosion of both, and an end to privacy.[17]

The emphasis on the desirability of "female" traits and the assumption that these have an innate biological core is central to this new conservative feminism, although it is not unique to it. In later chapters I shall return to the idea of innate femaleness in another feminist context, namely, ecofeminism. What these contexts do have in common is a celebration of "femaleness", coupled with an implicit belief in its biological core. Acceptance of biological determinism can thus be found in both anti-feminist arguments and in feminist ones, a point to which I shall return in considering possibilities of rejection of biological determinism.

2. IRRELEVANCE

A second response to the idea that gender differences are innate is to respond by saying that it is not really a relevant idea for feminists to get heated up about. This is perhaps not a common response in feminism, although it was implied by Janet Radcliffe Richards, in her book, *The Sceptical Feminist*. In a chapter devoted to the concept of nature, she claims to reject the idea that women (or men) have an essential biological nature, yet at the same time she states a belief that we might ultimately know what human nature is like if we have investigated it in enough environments. Human nature is, according to her view, primary, underlying environmental or cultural variability: if we study it in enough situations, we will be able to ascertain its true nature. Richards concludes the chapter thus:

the knowledge we have of the natures of things *in no way dictates* what use should be made of the raw material. It does not dictate our values, and even within a set of values there may be enormous scope for different routes to be taken.[18]

The message of the chapter is that there may well be essential biological bases to feminine or masculine natures, but that this need not affect social policies. In other words, the knowledge of the essential natures is largely irrelevant to what we as a society decide to do about it. This is made clear earlier:

And suppose that men are naturally dominant because of the miraculous testosterone of which we hear so much these days. Why should feminists be reluctant to admit it, or anti-feminists think that it clinches their case? Even if men are naturally inclined to dominance it does not follow that they ought to be allowed to run everything. Their being naturally dominant might be an excellent reason for imposing special restrictions to keep their nature under control. We do not think that the men whose nature inclines them to rape ought to be given free rein to go around raping, so why should the naturally dominant be allowed to go around dominating?[19]

There are several points to make about this. Perhaps the most important is that feminists should be reluctant to admit it, since it is wrong. It is much less easy to correlate aggressive behaviour with hormone levels than is commonly supposed, even in laboratory animals, still less to correlate the supposedly universal human male dominance with these, or to go even further than correlation and assume causation.[20] There is simply no evidence to support the case that male dominance exists because of testosterone, or any other hormone for that matter. Richards' supposition allows a complex, and historically and geographically variable, phenomenon—"male dominance"—to be reduced to a simple biological cause.

Secondly, Richards' supposition assumes that there exists a biological base on to which environmental influences can be added; we can thus find out about the base by varying the superstructure.[21] Such additive models of human nature are common, but they are fundamentally flawed in one major respect: they do not readily allow for the possibility that the biology itself might be influenced by the superstructure. That such two-way influences can indeed operate is part of the argument proposed against the additive model in more detail in Chapter Five. If hormone levels might be changed by environmental influences upon that individual, then we never can know what the "basic biology" is, unadulterated by environmental variability; it becomes unknowable. What can be known however, are features of that individual's biology at any one time, in the context of her or his environment. Some of these features might vary little between individuals and so will be more predictable than those which vary much. Hormones, unfortunately for Richards' case, do tend to vary over time, and between individuals, in ways that are much less predictable—particularly in relation to ill-defined concepts such as "male dominance".

It is important to note that I am not saying that she claims biological determinism; she argues, rather, that *even if* there exists some hormonal determination it is irrelevant to the feminist case. What I am disputing is her suggestion that we can discover the reality of human nature by analysing it in many different environments, thus discovering the degree of variability due to the environment. Moreover, to assume that these methods can uncover the true base of human nature is also to assume the neutrality of science itself. The processes of science are themselves part of the larger society, and incorporate its values—however much we like to think of our science as objective and value-free—including its values regarding women, men, and even human nature itself. It is not clear how we are supposed to uncover true "human nature" in this way, unless we suppose that we are neither part of that human nature nor of science itself. Science is not neutral precisely because it is humans who do it.

The crux of her argument is, however, that biological bases are probably not relevant to feminist claims. This assertion is only valid if we suppose the existence of a core human nature, as I have just discussed. If there were such a thing we could indeed do little to change it and it would become largely irrelevant to the demands of women's liberation. We could analyse it; but we could never change it. If, however, you reject the idea of a basic human nature, and suppose instead that that nature is itself a complex product of social, historical and biological forces, then the question is far from irrelevant. If that "human nature" is the product of such complex interaction, it will itself be changed within different social environments, and will not be something whose essential nature we can understand by studying it in several different situations. In that sense, an understanding of how human nature might be *modified* is highly relevant to our plans for any social reorganisation towards a better society.

3. REJECTION

We can, of course, also reject biological determinism. As I noted in Chapter One, this was to some extent a response of feminism in the early days of the WLM. Feminists were concerned, rightly, both to reject biologically determinist notions and their implications for women, and to point to the enormousness of social influences in the construction of gender. In response to this concern, there is now a wealth of feminist literature outlining the various ways in which gender is constructed within our society, and its cultural and historical specificity. In this section, I shall deal first with the feminist emphasis on the social construction of gender. While this has been a dominant concern of feminist theorists, however, it is only the other side of the biologically-determinist coin. Like biological determinism, it is rooted in an assumed separation of the biological from the social domains, as I shall argue.

At one extreme is the view that gender is constructed through ideological representations.[22] While analysis of the ideology of women's oppression has been important to feminist theory, an emphasis on ideology alone as structuring sexual divisions is problematic, since it ignores both biology and the broader material conditions of women's existence.[23] Are we to conclude that biology is not at all part of our conception of gender, that biology remains in a sphere apart from our cultural representations of gender? At the very least, our concepts of gender derive from a basically biological division into two sexes, female and male, so in that sense biology can hardly be said to be completely irrelevant. The dangers of ignoring any role of biology in our zeal to stress social forces were summed up succinctly by Michèle Barrett who suggested that "we run the risk, if, as feminists we ignore arguments from the level of biology, of leaving the forces of anti-feminism comfortably encamped on this ground with their persuasive and popular arguments unanswered".[24] With those forces gaining fresh reinforcements in the 1980s, it is time we stormed the encampment, and attempted to analyse the significance of women's biology for their social status rather than simply ignoring it.

Biology is not completely ignored by all those who would argue for social construction of gender, however. Some feminists have argued that biology is relevant to the extent that women's biology influences women's social status only indirectly, by means of the way in which it is interpreted and itself constructed. An example of this would be the suggestion that menstruation affects women's lives principally through the way in which women's menstruation is viewed socially. Thus, in societies which have negative attitudes towards it—including our own—women's experiences of it will inevitably be negative. Put more broadly, the suggestion is that the ideas a society holds about women's biology lead to their social subordination.[25]

Now it is very likely that social and cultural beliefs contribute a great deal to women's experiences of menstruation and other biological events, as feminists have often argued.[26] There is, too, considerable variability between different cultures in the ways that menstruation is experienced,[27] further testifying to the importance of social beliefs. But stressing the significance of these does not mean that there is nothing else to the experience but social expectations. The experience of menstruation is, for many women, one of pain and distress that cannot simply be explained by recourse to ideology; it is also a biological event.[28] Feminist theory needs to take into account not only the ways in which our biology is interpreted, but also the very real ways in which our biology does in practice affect our lives.

One important point is that it may affect our lives in different ways. Taking time off work to cope with menstrual pain has a very different meaning to women working on piece-rates than the meaning it has for professional women. Indeed Janet Sayers has pointed out how the use of social constructionist views of menstruation has affected women of different social classes in different ways, precisely because it denies the biological reality of menstruation in women's lives. She notes that social constructionism serves the interests of middle-class women, for whom it has been useful to point to social construction, rather than menstruation itself, as limiting career possibilities. But the effect of this kind of argument on women working in industry is very different; and it can be argued that social constructionism is often used to serve the interests of the employing industry, rather than the women themselves. Sayers discusses attitudes towards menstruation during the Second World War, when full participation of women in the workforce was necessary, and notes:

> Rather than admit that some women did suffer with their menstrual periods and that they should therefore be given time off work on this account, it was urged that menstrual symptoms were often the effect of suggestion emanating from outdated menstrual taboos. Menstrual symptoms, it was implied, were not usually the direct effect of biology but were instead the effect of an unwarranted social construction of that biology.[29]

The effect of such beliefs is that women are denied the possibility of taking time off work, however great the discomfort and pain. Moreover, social constructionist views of menstruation have also led to the suggestion that industry might benefit if women were given hormonal drugs to relieve the symptoms.[30] As Janet Sayers argues, this is not only more to the advantage of industry than to the women workers, but is also liable to be detrimental to women, given the increasing evidence that hormonal drugs can be hazardous to health.[31]

It is not my concern here to criticise theories of social construction in detail, largely because the theme of this book is the biology that most accounts of social construction deny. While it is necessary for feminists to reject biological determinism as something which supports and extends existing ideology, it is also necessary for feminism to consider the ways in which women's biology actually and materially affects their lives. But if we reject biological determinism, and we reject the extreme forms of social constructionism, then what are we left with?

What we are left with is the need to acknowledge the importance of social factors in the construction of gender, while simultaneously admitting the significance of biology within the theory. But here a second problem arises. In formulating that statement I have necessarily adopted ideas of gender that consist partly of social factors, and partly of biology. As I noted earlier, that separation into the biological and social certainly characterises biological determinism, which seeks to use biological arguments to explain apparent universals, leaving cultural variation to be explained by social factors. It is also true of social construction which, in feminist theory at least, has emphasised sociocultural factors in gender to the extent that even biology becomes described in terms of social construction. Implicit in both these opposed types of explanation is a *separation* of the biological from the social.

The separation of the biological from the social is important to feminist theory in various ways, two of which I will consider here. First, it has implications for our theorising about the origins of the sexual division of labour; and second, it has implications for our understanding of how we acquire our sense of gender. Traditional assumptions about the sexual division of labour begin by assuming that it is based on fundamental biological categories, notably women's biological capacity for reproduction versus men's physical strength (and hence capacity for production in evolutionary history). It is this assumption which underwrites the predominant Man-the-Hunter story of human evolution to which I referred in chapter two, which assumes that women's biological reproduction contributed both to the development of a sexual division of labour, but also to the separation of the private, domestic realm from the public world. Ruth Bleier comments on the assumptions behind the Man-the-Hunter story of evolution, and notes,

These assumptions construct an evolutionary scenario that sees women as physically constrained by pregnancy, lactation and infant care to virtual immobility and evolutionary stagnation, and sees men as fundamentally unconstrained and creative, capable of bonding with each other, inventing weapons, and bringing home the meat each to his dependent domestic unit.[32]

In the previous chapter I referred to the fact that there is actually little concrete evidence to support this version of human evolution. But there are other, equally serious, problems with it. One significant problem is that the story is founded upon a second major assumption, that there are *universal* human social behaviours and characteristics. Thus it is assumed that, for example, women staying at home is a universal human characteristic, for which we might then seek evolutionary explanations. But it is not. Women's domesticity and the related separation of the public and private spheres are historically and culturally specific, being particularly characteristic of industrial capitalist societies.[33]

In her critique of the unfounded assumptions behind the Man-the-Hunter story Ruth Bleier stresses that, rather than women's relationships to biological reproduction being universal, cross-cultural and ethnographic evidence suggests that there is considerable *versatility* of women's productive and reproductive roles. She notes that it is, of course, women not men who actually do the childbearing, but argues against any inference that other social inequalities *necessarily* follow from this, stressing that,

This view unfortunately employs a fundamental assumption of biological determinist theories and reflects our own ethnocentric blindness to alternate modes of interpretation. It is important to see that, unlike breathing, for example, the biological capacity to reproduce does not necessarily mean that one *has* to reproduce or even be heterosexually active, nor does it dictate the social arrangements for child nurturance and rearing or determine how child rearing affects one's participation in other cultural activities. Whether or not we bear, nurse, or mother children is just as much a function of cultural, social, political, economical, and, no more importantly, biological factors as whether we are poets or soccer players.[34]

This suggestion is not, presumably, intended to imply that women have had choice about whether or not to reproduce since, at least within most present-day societies, women are in practice afforded little choice and do have to reproduce. What I assume is intended here is that the capacity to bear children does not *in itself* prescribe any other activities. As Bleier points out, "In some cultures, motherhood is irrelevant for the cultural definition of *woman* and for the significance of women's position and roles."[35]

In her analysis Ruth Bleier opposes the traditional assumptions about the sexual division of labour to feminist interpretations, arguing that the traditional account rests on unwarranted assumptions regarding human history and the existence of universals. Some feminist accounts do, however, seem to assume the existence of universals, particularly the existence of patriarchy. Joan Smith has pointed out that a number of feminist theorists argue for a dual systems theory of women's subordination, according to which women's oppression—at least in present-day Western society—arises conjointly from both capitalism and patriarchy.[36] One problem with dual systems theory, Smith argues, is that its proponents typically portray patriarchy as ahistorical, a portrayal which plays into the hands of those who would argue biological determination of the sexual division of labour. Feminist theorists may differ in the way that they see patriarchal control of women operating;[37] what they often have in common is the assumption that there are cross-cultural similarities in the ways in which women's subordination operates. Smith concludes:

Thus, for each of the theorists I have been discussing, (and they represent some of the most serious and interesting of recent feminist scholarship) female subordination cannot be reduced to or explained by the mode of production because it shares common and central features with female subordination as found in a variety of productive systems.... The assumption of male domination and female subordination rests on the author's assigning near universality to one or another social arrangement.[38]

And it is precisely this near-universality which, Smith suggests, places dual systems theory in a similar framework to sociobiology. If patriarchy existed unchanged over millennia then we might have to agree with Lionel Tiger when he concluded that "If male dominance extends over the whole species—and has existed for so long—we seem constrained by the law of parsimony to look first into the biological information and theory at our disposal for an explanation"[39]. But we are not so constrained, simply because, as Smith argues, patriarchy has not existed unchanged but is historically contingent.

Nonetheless Smith's objections to dual systems theory are valid, since any suggestion that there exists some universal phenomenon is likely to be met with biological determinism. Suggesting a near-universality to the experiences and subordination of women does come perilously close. It is certainly true that *if* we find phenomena which are virtually universal across cultures and history, then one source of explanation *might* lie in biology (although not necessarily so, as is so often assumed). But noting that women are, in all extant societies, subordinate to men is not *in itself* particularly interesting; if that subordination is to be changed, then we need also to know the particular forms it takes in any given society. The form that it takes will determine the forms of struggle against it.

When feminists have focussed on the existence of widespread subordination of women, rather than on the variability of its forms, they have indirectly maintained the separation of the biological from the social by emphasising universality. The existence of universal women's subordination has been attended to—with the attendant risk of biological determinism—rather than the variability that arises in different social, cultural and historical contexts. On the other hand, the division between biological and social is also maintained by those theorists, feminist or otherwise, who have ignored human reproduction in their analyses of historical change. The critiques of capitalism which ignore reproduction have thus maintained the division largely by leaving out human biology, while critics of patriarchy have maintained it by assuming greater homogeneity in female subordination than actually exists.

Mary O'Brien has suggested that one reason why reproduction is often left out is because there is a "strong historical tendency . . . to see reproduction as 'pure' biological process (which) carries the implication that reproduction is all body and without mind; irrational or at least prerational".[40] That which is pure biological process is assumed to be unchangeable, so biological reproduction falls outside the sphere of theories emphasising the significance of historical *change*. O'Brien, however, argues that reproduction should not be viewed as unchanging, but rather as dialectical process, which changes historically. She considers that changing history to have two nodal points, the first of which was changing male consciousness of biological reproduction, triggered by the historical discovery of paternity. The second is the present changes in "reproductive praxis brought about by technology. . . . Beneath these changes and, indeed, essential to the growth of the women's movement, is a change in the underlying dialectics of reproductive consciousness. The freedom for women to choose parenthood is a historical development as significant as the discovery of physiological paternity".[41]

Mary O'Brien has tried to avoid the dilemma of either ignoring biology, or of assuming it as given, by suggesting that the sexual division of labour arose not, as is often implied, because of the biological facts of reproduction, but because of changing male consciousness of these facts. She thus retains the feminist emphasis on reproduction as a key process in analysing and understanding women's subordination throughout women's oppression.

O'Brien's analysis is interesting to feminist theory in part precisely because she does attempt to move away from the dilemma. But the assumption, or implication, of female subordination as a universal continues to present problems for feminism, not only from the biological determinism of traditional versions of human history, but also from some feminist accounts which treat "patriarchy" as a transhistorical phenomenon. Either way, the existence of women's subordination is likely to be seen as the product of invariable biology.

The separation of the biological from the social in our theorising is also important to how we view the processes by which people acquire their sense of gender. The concept of biological factors as determining usually implies either that that factor at the present time determines the social or behavioural outcome (e.g. the idea that "raging hormones" determine women's irrationality), or that the action of that factor in the past determines present outcome. An example of the latter would be the idea that prenatal hormones determine adult homosexuality (i.e. via an effect on the brain). Implicit in both is the idea that the biology is somehow *primary*. On to this can be added the accretions of the social and cultural context, such as learning how to behave in gender-appropriate ways. In this view, biological and social factors may both act to contribute to a behavioural outcome, but they do so by *adding* to each other. The biology is primary, however, both in the temporal sense (e.g. biology acting before birth) and in the sense of it assuming greater importance by virtue of its implied irreversibility. Only the social factors can be subject to significant change.

"Gender", according to the additive view, emerges first from the action of biological factors, be they genes, hormones or whatever; and second, from the action of various social factors, such as learning about gender-differentiated behaviour. Much of the clinical research into prenatal hormone disorders and their relationship to gender operates with an additive model, assuming, for example, that if there are hormonal aberrations, then there will necessarily be aberrations of gender acquisition. Studies of the development of children who were genetically female but produced high levels of particular hormones (androgens, the so-called male hormones) thus sought evidence for masculinisation of behaviour—tomboyism. When this was found in some of these children it was ascribed to the action of the hormones, rather than considering any other possible factors.[42]

The problem with the additive model is just that: it does leave other possibilities out. What about the effect of parental expectations and attitudes towards a child who is clearly *known* to be hormonally abnormal? What about the child's expectations of her own behaviour? An alternative way of looking at the problem of how we acquire our sense of gender is to emphasise the extent of the interaction between any biological factors and the environment in which they are expressed, including such things as parental and social expectations. Interactions, of course, can occur at all stages of development, from the moment of conception. As these occur, they in themselves help to create a new environment in which the biology is expressed; at each stage, new patterns and interactions emerge. It is this type of approach to early development—human or otherwise—that I take in this book, and to which I will return in later chapters. The significance that should be noted here is that in adopting such an approach I am explicitly rejecting biological determinism and its associated additive model. What I am not doing, however, is rejecting biology: for too long biology has been rejected as irrelevant to feminist theorising, with its emphasis on social construction. What is needed now is some kind of integration.

The next chapter of the book leaves for a while the question of how we develop gender, in order to explore further what the implications are of biological determinism. So far I have considered only some of the implications for feminist politics of such arguments. In the following chapter I turn to the broader philosophical questions raised by biological determinism, and the problems posed to feminism by them.

4 Reducing Women: Feminism and Reductionism

The concern of previous chapters has been to outline what is meant by biological determinism, and also to illustrate its significance for feminist politics. In this chapter I will explore in more detail the meaning of biological determinism and its relationship to the additive model of development referred to at the end of the previous chapter. To do this I will introduce a related concept, that of reductionism. This term has been applied at various times both to scientific methodology and to certain kinds of explanation that predominate in science. The latter begin by seeing phenomena in the natural world as hierarchically organised, and "reductionism" applies to the assumption that phenomena in the upper levels of this hierarchy can ultimately be explained in terms of "more fundamental" events at a lower level of the hierarchy. In a sense, this is like explaining nature by going down to smaller and smaller bits of it. Thus, one example of a reductionist explanation in biology would be to say that an animal moves because of the action of certain muscles which themselves contract because of certain biochemical changes within them. A more extreme form of reductionism might take that even further, and relate the biochemical changes occurring in the muscle to events within the atoms of which the muscle is comprised.

I will begin this chapter by outlining what is meant by reductionism, and why the concept of reductionism has been both successful and criticised. In the second part I shall return to the theme of biological determinism, and relate it to issues raised by reductionist explanations, using some of the examples from previous chapters that purport to explain women's inferiority. The third part of the chapter will consider how reductionism helps to maintain some of the categories which feminism has questioned, notably those of gender. And finally, I will consider briefly some of the alternatives that have been put forward to reductionism.

1. WHAT IS REDUCTIONISM?

When biologists describe biology, they typically refer to "levels of analysis", which are hierarchically arranged. These levels correspond to our way of organising our knowledge of nature; thus, knowledge of living organisms is, according to the reductionist model, arranged so that whatever forms the unit of study at one level is only a small part of the subject of study at a higher level. Thus, at the upper levels, is the study of social groups. These in turn are made up of individuals, which form the basis of study at the next level down. These in turn are made up of organs, which are composed of tissues, which are composed of cells, and so on, right down to sub-atomic particles.

I will leave aside for the moment the question of whether or not these "levels" correspond to nature. What is important is that they represent our perception of the natural world, and the way in which we organise that perception. They are not, however, the only way of perceiving the world, as I shall argue later.

Reductionism is also sometimes used (though less commonly) to describe the methods by which science characteristically proceeds. In theory at least, these involve the analysis of one or two variables which are systematically varied, while other variables are experimentally held constant (or, if that is not possible, randomised). For instance, suppose that you wanted to study the effects of light on the growth of a particular plant. You might then experimentally vary the amount of light while keeping constant such potential variables as soil moisture content, soil mineral content, temperature, and so on. Some variables, such as the weather, or the earth's magnetic field, cannot readily be kept constant by the experimenter, who then has recourse to one of two approaches; either she or he must find out the magnitude of the variable in question and take it into account, or the experimental procedure must be made random in relation to it. Thus, if weather changes might influence the experiment, you might attempt to record weather conditions on each day of the experiment, and then interpret results in relation to them. Alternatively, you might design your experiments so that they are done randomly in relation to the weather—perhaps by carrying out the experiments at random intervals over a long period.

These methods of isolating variables and subjecting them to systematic experimentation have contributed greatly to the success of science; by carrying out experiments in this way a great deal has been discovered about the natural world, which has allowed us to sort out which variables might be significant to any natural event, and which not. Perhaps more importantly, scientific method yielded the power to *predict* natural events, a power that was put to use by the emerging capitalist system. Until quite recently, scientific method was viewed as largely progressive even if somewhat constrained and misused within contemporary capitalist society.[1] But even if methodological reductionism has at times been seen as progressive, it also works hand in hand with reductionism as explanation which, as I shall argue, is frequently far from progressive.[2]

The two work together in part because the very process of separating out the variables in experiments forces us to focus on those variables in isolation, with the result that complex interactions between variables tend to get ignored and we tend to interpret nature in terms of those isolated variables. To some extent, methodological reductionism—the process of controlling potential variables in experiments—operates within a "level". That is, the variables that a scientist controls are by and large those that are similar to or directly related to the variable under study. In addition some external variables, such as temperature or humidity, might be controlled. But the *assumption* of methodological reductionism is that other, "lower-level" variables either cannot be, or do not need to be, controlled. Take, for example, my own research interests, in the relationship between hormones and behaviour. Scientists working in this field might use procedures such as changing an animal's hormone levels by giving it an injection and then observing later changes in the animal's behaviour. Now this like many other procedures used in science, makes a number of assumptions, but the one that I want to consider here is that such a procedure assumes the constancy of the biological environment at lower levels. It assumes, for instance, that biochemical or even atomic changes that might be occurring after the injection are not particularly relevant to the outcome being studied, or at least that they have a simple, one-to-one relationship to the hormone treatment. Yet there is much that we do not know about what happens when we give injections. It is these assumptions that feed into reductionism as explanation; for if we assume the constancy of the biological environment at other levels, then the way is clear to interpreting any changes that we may observe solely in terms of (or reduced to) variations in hormone levels.

It is reductionism as mode of explanation, however, that is most often criticised, principally on the grounds that it impoverishes our understanding of the natural world. It also implies a high degree of biological determinism, and for that reason has formed part of reactionary politics. Central to reductionism is its insistence on chains of *causes,* running from molecular events right up to human behaviour or social organisation (see Figure Two). The notion of cause in science is complex, and is used in varying ways. It might, for example, be used in the sense of evolutionary change; thus, it might be said that new species evolved because of environmental changes to which they were better adapted. It might also be used for within-level explanation. This sort of explanation assumes that one event immediately precedes (and causes) another. We might say, for instance, that rising levels of particular hormones cause changes in the uterine wall during the menstrual cycle. But the sense of cause implied by reductionism is one that operates *between* levels.[3] That is, some event occurring among the molecules is assumed to cause subsequent events within cells, which in turn causes events at the level of organs, and so on. In this view events at, say, the level of the tissues can only be explained in terms of *preceding* molecular events. That is, the lower-level events assume priority, both in terms of the relationship between causes (that is, those at the lower levels are assumed to be the most primary or fundamental causes, from which control over higher levels flows), and in terms of

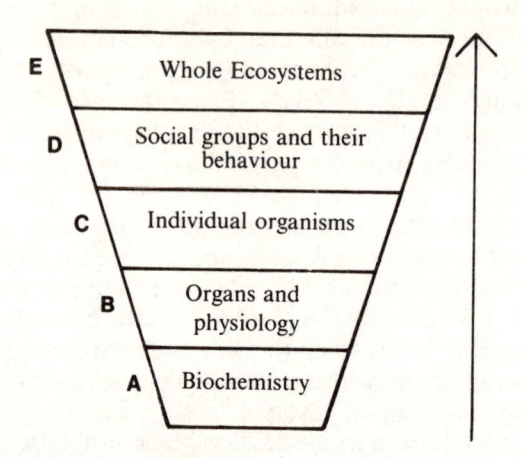

```
     E  ╲  Whole Ecosystems              ╱ ↑
      D  ╲ Social groups and their      ╱
          ╲    behaviour               ╱
       C   ╲  Individual organisms    ╱
        B   ╲  Organs and            ╱
             ╲  physiology          ╱
         A    ╲  Biochemistry      ╱
```

Figure 2: Some 'levels of organisation' in biology. The arrow indicates the direction of causes implied by reductionism; that is, events at level A are assumed to cause events in level B, and so on

the temporal sequence of events.

This type of explanation is certainly common in science, and for that reason is one with which most people are somewhat familiar. Some writers have even claimed that reductionist explanations are one of the ultimate *aims* of science, so that, one day, we should expect to be able to explain complex events at the organism or social level in terms of lower-level events. Eventually, it is implied, our explanations will get down to the level of the atomic particles themselves. E. O. Wilson, for example, suggested that eventually social structures, religious beliefs, systems of ethics, and more, might be explained by reduction to events at the level of the genes, while some molecular biologists expect that one day human behaviour might be explained in terms of biochemistry.[4]

So far I have principally been concerned with describing reductionism—albeit briefly—and have not dealt with the objections to it. What are these? Roughly, oppositions to reductionism have taken two forms; in the first place, there are objections phrased in terms of the impoverished understanding of nature that can result from assuming reductionist explanations. Secondly, there are oppositions couched in terms of the biological determinism that reductionism usually implies. These two approaches are not, of course, mutually exclusive, even if I have separated them for the purposes of discussion.

One significant argument used in opposition to reductionism is that reductionism does not adequately describe nature, that the functions of the organism, say, cannot be explained solely in terms of its component parts. By this is meant the idea that some features of the organism (those described, for example, at "higher" levels) cannot adequately be described only in terms of the underlying molecular configuration. By reducing phenomena down, it has been claimed, we lose vital information that is only meaningful at those higher levels.[5] The notable way in which information is lost is that, by reductionist reasoning, we lose sight of the fact that any phenomenon is *both* a unit *and* part of a larger totality. Reductionism assumes a chain of causality that does not allow something to exist simultaneously at different levels.[6]

Reductionism also fails to describe nature adequately by its assumption that there is one-to-one (or at least a simple) correspondence between phenomena at different levels. In this

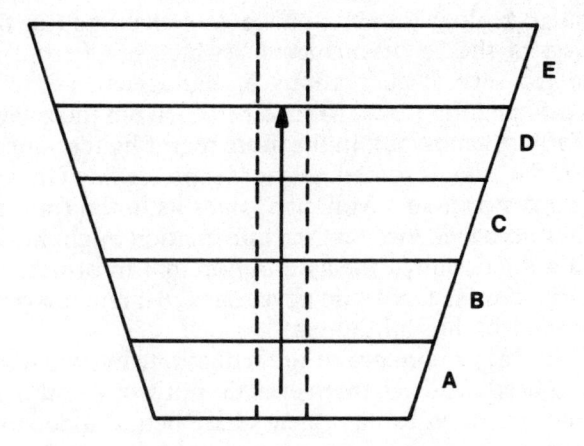

Figure 3: The assumption of correspondence. Reductionist science assumes that complex events at one level (e.g. rioting in inner city areas) is caused by some *corresponding* event at a lower level (e.g. brain dysfunction).

way, even very complex and ill-defined events or characteristics (such as "aggressiveness" or "nurturance" in human behaviour) become reduced to simple events at the molecular level (such as the action of particular genes) (see Figure Three). I shall return to this point a little later, in connection with the use of gender-associated categories. The point that I want to emphasise for now is that this assumption of correspondence encourages us to think no further than the chain of causation. And since that is a linear chain, we are not encouraged to think of complexity and interactions.

Reductionism and its assumptions are probably best illustrated by molecular biology, which is concerned with the study of the molecular functioning of living cells. From its development in the 1940s and 1950s, molecular biology has largely adhered to a reductionist programme, as one biologist made clear in 1950, in a lecture in which he argued for the use of the term "molecular biology":

It implies not so much a technique as an approach, an approach from the viewpoint of the so-called basic sciences with the leading idea of searching below large-scale manifestations of classical biology for the corresponding molecular plan.[7]

Molecular biology's reductionism was enshrined in the formulation of the "central dogma" (which has been a central dogma for several generations of biologists), according to which information flows in one direction from the genes to the body form (phenotype). In the more recent light of knowledge about DNA, this is sometimes now expressed as DNA makes RNA makes protein.[8] Although, since its initial formulation, there has been evidence that the information might not always flow unidirectionally,[9] the assumption that information flows outward from the DNA and never back to it remains central to mainstream biological thought.

Despite the dominance of the reductionist viewpoint, there has long been evidence that genes do not work in this simple, deterministic, way. Rather "genes" are better understood not as directing operations but as participating in complex interactions, subject themselves to influences from their environment, and participating in changing that environment. In other words, genes do not act apart from the cellular environment (or even the wider, non-cellular environment) in which they are found. In the 1950s, while the reductionism of modern molecular biology was gaining ground, there were few dissident voices. But dissidents there were, voices arguing a different view of genetics to the orthodox one. One of these was Barbara McClintock, whose work and views of nature have been described by her biographer as exemplifying much that science *could* be—but currently is not.[10] Her work on cytogenetics led her to a belief in the interrelatedness and connectivity of cellular events, rather than in DNA as the "master molecule". She emphasises the variability in the ways that genes appear to act, concluding that, "According to this view it is organised nuclear systems that function as units at any one time in development".[11] Organised systems, but not determining genes. Evelyn Fox Keller, writing about McClintock's work, stressed how different were McClintock's views from the dominant themes of molecular biology at the time:

During the decades when the cell was becoming a relatively straightforward machine to most biologists, to McClintock it was opening up in complexity. In lieu of the linear hierarchy described by the central dogma of molecular biology, in which the DNA encodes and transmits all instructions for the unfolding of a living cell, her research yielded a view of DNA in delicate interactions with the cellular environment—an organismic view . . . No longer is a master control to be found in a single component of the cell; rather, control resides in the complex interactions of the whole system.[12]

Over the next thirty years or so, molecular biology has come to a greater acceptance of McClintock's work, and an emphasis on the complexity and embeddedness of cellular events. But a belief in the notion of a fixed "genetic programme" still persists, in at least some areas of biology. Reductionism is remarkable for its tenacity.

If reductionism has tended to obscure the complexity of which McClintock wrote, then it does seem reasonable to conclude that our understanding of nature is necessarily impoverished by it. This is perhaps most obvious when the reductionism is applied to human behaviour and society (though our understanding of the rest of nature is no less impoverished—simply less obvious), as it is in some human sociobiology. Sociobiologists thus sometimes write of genes as though they were unequivocally "directing operations", subject to no influences save the random processes of natural selection. At its extreme, this takes the form of writing of the entire organism as though it was merely a vehicle for making more DNA.[13]

Apart from assuming a linear sequence of causes running from the bottom up, reductionism also assumes a reality to the "levels" of analysis with which it works. "Levels of analysis" are however, merely the observers' device for classifying and understanding the complex world around. Biochemistry classifies the natural world in different ways—and by asking very different kinds of questions—from, say, physiology or ecology. But these spheres of human understanding do not *necessarily* have any counterpart in nature; the different levels might instead be thought of as representing arbitrary dividing points along a continuum. For me at least, different levels of explanation are just different ways of describing the world, having no clear-cut counterpart in nature. Even the organism itself does not live in splendid isolation but is constantly interacting with, and changing, its environment. On the other hand, some writers opposed to reductionism have taken the view that the levels do indeed correspond to reality. Steven Rose argues, for example, that levels do have meaning in nature, but that the problem is one of emphasising that a phenomenon can be simultaneously a unit, and also part of a larger whole. That is, combating the problems posed by reductionism takes the form not of opposing the hierarchy of levels, but of opposing the associated assumptions of unidirectional cause. Individual units, be they cells or organisms, cannot be assumed to have priority over the group of which they are part if they are seen as simultaneously being both. That may be how, ideally, we should look at any biological unit: but as soon as we begin to study it in any way—using modes of study defined precisely *by* those hierarchical levels— then we abstract the unit from its context. By so doing, it becomes in practice impossible to see the unit as part of a larger totality.[14]

It is interesting to note that one writer who has argued for the existence of levels in nature, Paul Weiss, was instrumental in helping to define those levels on a hierarchical basis. He notes how, on assuming chairmanship of the biological division of the American National Research Council in 1951, he recategorised the administrative divisions of biology, and introduced the hierarchical classification of levels with which we are familiar.[15] Prior to that, the principal classifications were based on forms of life (e.g. botany, zoology, entomology, and so on). We can only wonder how real the concepts of hierarchical levels seemed to the many generations of biologists before that. The consolidation of our ideas of levels—the ways we have of organising our knowledge of nature—over the last thirty years can thus be thought of as facilitating the separation of any unit from its context. Its context becomes defined by, and is the proper business of, another level.

Reductionism, then, can be said to lead to only a particular kind of understanding. It has, of course, yielded potentially useful knowledge and as a research strategy has proved enormously successful in making predictions about nature. But it has, by its very methodological power, led us away from attempting to understand the *complexity* of nature. There are other kinds of objections to reductionism, however, such as those which emphasise its consequences for biological determinism. These I shall explore in the next section.

2. REDUCTIONISM AND BIOLOGICAL DETERMINISM

Reductionism's hierarchy of levels and associated causes carries with it an implied biological determinism. To take an example used in earlier chapters, a complex social phenomenon, such as violence, towards women, is said to be associated with hormonal abnormality. It is clearly implied that this is seen to be causal (hence the suggestion that we might give appropriate drugs to cure it; these would alter the biochemistry, and hence shift the causality). *Even if* it could be shown that there was indeed a hormonal change associated with the violence (which is doubtful), then to assume that this is causal is to imply that other possible factors are less important. And that, as I have argued, is what biological determinism does; it assumes that the biology is primary, thus having a far greater determining role than any other, social, factor.

What I did not do in the previous discussion, however, was to consider the question of the time-scale over which the determinism is assumed to operate. Since it does influence the nature of the reductionist assumptions made, it is important to consider it further here. Put roughly, there are three kinds of time-scales in biological explanations. First, there is a time-scale that operates in terms of immediately preceding causes—the kind of reductionism that I have discussed above. That is, it assumes that event A at a lower level precedes event B at the next level, and so on. The actual time-scale may be milliseconds, as in the case of nervous transmission, or it may be days or weeks, as in the case of hormonal control systems. The second sense of time-scale concerns the individual development of the organism. Here, causes are seen to operate over a rather longer period. One example of this kind of explanation would be the suggestion that exposure to particular hormones during early (foetal or neonatal) life will effectively "switch off" the parts of the brain that control cyclicity in female mammals.[16] This is what is assumed to happen during the normal development of male mammals, with the result that their hormone output as adults is more or less constant. So here events during foetal life are thought to cause irreversible changes in the brain of the animal that are only manifest much later in life (i.e. after puberty). The third sense of time-scale in biology is of course, evolutionary time. Here, the causes are seen to be changes in the genetic material, which may occur for a variety of reasons. These occur in, say, a few individuals, and might confer some advantage to these over the rest of the population, so that these individuals survive and breed better than others. The change then spreads through the population, over a very much longer time-scale than the two previously considered.

Now although the timescales are vastly different, what these different types of explanation share is an assumption of the *priority* of the lower levels in the explanation. Thus within the literature on hormones and development it is widely assumed that the hormones are prior, and causal to, the changes in later life. On the evolutionary time-scale, it is the *individuals* and their changed genetic complements, that are assumed to be more significant, prior to the population as a whole. The assumptions made about the causal chain are illustrated graphically in Figure Four.

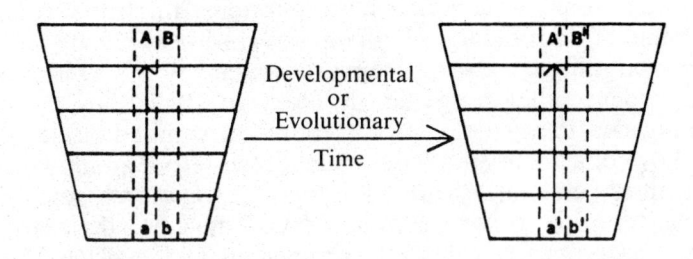

Figure 4: Reductionist explanations also assume a constant relationship between levels over time. That is, a' and b' are assumed to be causes of A' and B' in much the same way as a, b were causes of A, B in the past.

Let me bring this rather abstract discussion back to some of the explanations that have concerned feminists. In doing so I hope to show why reductionism can be criticised at more overtly political levels. The first example is premenstrual tension. A prevalent view of premenstrual tension (PMT) is that it is caused by a hormonal imbalance, particularly of the hormone progesterone.[17] It is assumed that the sometimes dreadful mood changes of which women have complained are determined by these abnormal hormone levels. So strong is the determinancy assumed to be that hormone abnormalities have successfully been used as grounds for defence in court cases, and the women involved have been acquitted of manslaughter.[18]

This is an example of the first kind of reductionism. It assumes immediately prior causes, running up the reductionist hierarchy. Thus, deranged hormones are said to cause changes in fluid balance which cause changes in the brain which cause mood swings which cause social unrest. No consideration is made—or indeed was made in the court's interpretation of events—of the other contributory factors, such as diet, anxiety, sleep patterns, drug use, income, housing, and many more. If any of these are held to contribute, it is only in a peripheral way; the central culprit is the hormone. And no consideration is given, either, to the possibility that the hormone production itself might be altered by other factors, such as life-style, or diet.

Apart from its reductionist assumptions, this story is an example of what Georgio Bignami has called "ex juvantibus" logic—arguing backwards from that which helps.[19] Although the evidence that progesterone levels in PMT sufferers is deranged is, to say the very least, equivocal, some advocates of the hormonal theory have found that progesterone administration does sometimes help sufferers. The logic then runs: if progesterone helps some sufferers, then it must be a deficiency of progesterone that caused the problem in the first place. This is rather like arguing, Bignami points out, that if a blow on the head stops complaints about an ingrowing toenail, then brain hyperactivity caused the complaints (or perhaps even the ingrowing toenail!)[20] Arguing backwards, however, does not prove the case.

An example of the second kind of reductionism is the suggestion that adult homosexuality results from a hormone imbalance in foetal life.[21] On the basis of many animal experiments which have demonstrated that early exposure to hormones can permanently alter the frequency of sex-differentiated behaviour patterns in adulthood, it has been supposed that what gay men must have suffered from is exposure to a "feminising" set of hormones. I shall come on to the category assumptions being made here a little later. This sort of experiment is often based on "bad" science, even within its own terms,[22] but more to the point, it clearly assumes that this early hormone exposure has been causal. The reasoning is also retrospective, in that the hormone "abnormality" is only assumed on the basis of the men's adult sexual behaviour (despite many efforts, it should be noted, no evidence for abnormality of *adult* hormone levels in lesbians or gay men have consistently been detected).[23] All sorts of factors are omitted here, including: (i) the possibility that, whatever the putative hormone pattern is, it could occur in a variety of people—including in the early development of many heterosexuals. The association with homosexuality is only inferred, not proven. The suggestion that early hormones have effected a "feminising" change is made on the basis of tests of hormonal competency in adults (i.e. the magnitude of the response to a test injection). Thus, (ii) the possibility that lifestyle might affect the response is ignored. It might be altered, for example, by time of day, people with different life-styles having different hormonal peaks and troughs. It might be affected by stress, diet, alcohol consumption and so on. Indeed, so many are the ignored variables, that I have a sneaking suspicion that if the experiments were repeated in a genuinely *blind* fashion so that the experimenters did not know who was who, and the subjects did not know the purpose of the experiment, no differences would be found.

An example of reduction in evolutionary arguments is the suggestion that genes for spatial ability exist, and have evolved particularly in men because they were useful for hunting.[24] Individuals with good spatial ability, it is argued, are more likely to catch game. Since they are then less likely to starve to death, the gene begins to spread through the population. It is, of course, interesting that this explanation presupposes the Man-the-Hunter story, as well as presupposing a sexual division of labour in early hominid history. The gene for spatial ability has thus been useful to men, but not to women, in the past and is now responsible for men's greater spatial abilities. Among other things, what is never clear about explanations couched in terms of genetic determinism is precisely how the supposed gene's effects manage to be translated into their complex behavioural products. How, for instance, does a gene for (female) "coyness" get expressed? Or a gene for (male) philandery? What is the gene supposed to do? Even within orthodox molecular biology, all that genes do is to organise the manufacture of proteins. It is a very long way from a protein molecule to *Playboy*.

These various types of argument, assuming very different time-scales, have in common that they assume reductionist causal sequences. Over the evolutionary time-scale, it is the success of a particular gene which allows it to spread through the population, and cause change at that level; on much shorter time-scales, it is the individual molecules that cause changes in the person. Previous chapters have shown the significance of biological determinism for feminism, whatever its time-scale. What this section set out to do was to show how such explanations are thoroughly grounded in the mode of explanation—reductionism—that lies at the heart of science. In the next section I want to consider some other ways in which reductionism is relevant to feminist concerns.

3. REDUCTIONISM AND FEMINISM

In part, reductionism is of concern to feminism because of the biological determinism that it implies. There is another way, however, in which reductionism is relevant to feminist theory and that is that it can serve to *reinforce* the categories by which we classify the world about us. That is, reductionism assumes that, however we divide up the threads of life at one level of analysis, these categories *also* apply at other levels of analysis. If, then, the categories at a higher level are ones that feminism might question—such as categories related to gender, or to sexuality—then we need to consider how they fare when reduced to other levels.

The starting point of concepts of gender is that they are founded upon a biological division into male and female, the two sexes necessary for sexual reproduction. Gender refers, however, to the social construction of attributes arising from that initial division; masculinity and femininity, men and women. These are generally assumed to be equally dichotomous divisions, such that people are either masculine or feminine, either men or women. Although a moment's reflection would make most people agree that human beings are not always so easily classified, there is a prevailing assumption that these dichotomous concepts do at least correlate with the initial biological division. Now as far as "women" and "men" are concerned, the correlation with sex categories of female and male is nearly always accurate: most women are biologically female, and most men are biologically male. There are exceptions such as hermaphrodites, or surgically altered transsexuals, but the generalisation holds for the great majority of people. Femininity and masculinity do not correlate so neatly with biological sex however — and indeed, different individuals may display "femininity" or "masculinity" at different times depending upon the circumstances.[25] The behaviour ascribed to gender, then, does not correlate with biological sex particularly well.

The assumption that masculinity and femininity are dichotomous is sometimes taken further and it is assumed that there is a uniquely "masculine" biology associated with masculinity, and a feminine one with femininity. The either/or division into male and female is something that seems to be projected as a rigid dichotomy both on to the concept of gender, and back on to the biology. To take one example, both biological articles and popular accounts of biology refer repeatedly to such things as "male" and "female" hormones, which are supposedly associated with maleness or femaleness. A "masculine" man is, according to his supposition, one who is blessed with lots of "male" hormones. The either/or projection does not work very well, however, since the sex hormones do not divide themselves up in such a simple way: there simply is no one hormone, or even class of hormone, that belongs uniquely to one gender or the other.[26]

Other dichotomous classifications are also frequently mapped on to that of gender. One such is the dichotomy between heterosexual/homosexual, to which I referred in Chapter Two. Dichotomous concepts like this presuppose that people *can* be neatly divided into one or the other category, and this in turn leads to the supposition that simple biological factors can be found that cause those categories. Although research into sexual behaviour has generally shown that rather few people can exclusively be defined as "homosexual" or "heterosexual" throughout their lives, the prevailing assumption is that everyone can be neatly packaged into one or other category. A subsequent assumption is that, once packaged in this way, the packages can be tied with other genderised assumptions. Among gay people it is those who more obviously flout society's accepted criteria of sex-appropriate behaviour that are likely to be labelled as homosexual; a common stereotype, for example is that men behaving in "feminine" ways are, or might be, homosexual, while "masculine" men are expected to be heterosexual. "Feminine" women are similarly assumed to be heterosexual, while "masculine" women are likely to be lesbians. These assumptions are carried over into medical research, as I noted earlier, which in turn reinforces popular belief.

Whether or not the search for putative biological correlates to homosexuality succeeds is not relevant here. What is relevant is that the biomedical literature addressing the question of how people become homosexual is predicated upon multiple assumptions about gender and its supposed biological roots. In short, the existence of homosexuality becomes explained in terms of the assumed biological dichotomy, as Figure Five summarises. Homosexuals are assumed to have an abnormality of gender, which in turn is referred back to an assumed abnormality of sex at the biological levels. The reductionism, by which the behaviour (homosexuality) is reduced to some facet of biology, then operates within the dichotomous categories of sex. This kind of reduction *within* the category boundaries that may be applied (even if not

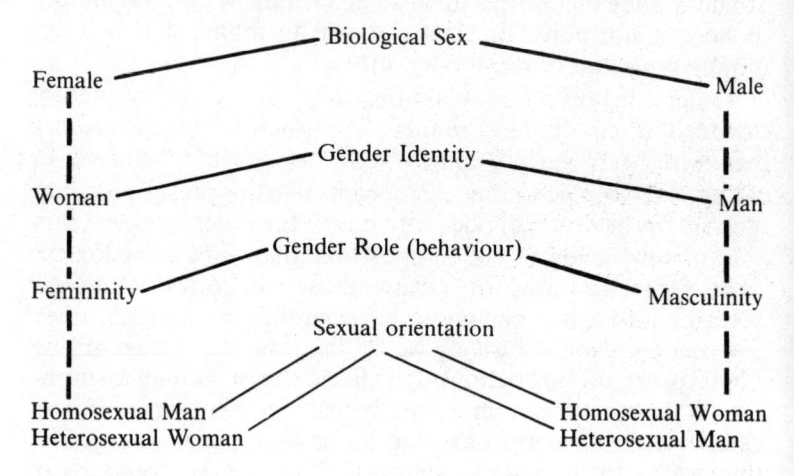

```
                    ── Biological Sex ──
Female ──                                  ── Male
  │                                          │
  │                  ── Gender Identity ──    │
Woman ──                                   ── Man
  │                                          │
  │              ── Gender Role (behaviour) ──│
Femininity ──                              ── Masculinity
  │                  Sexual orientation        │
  │                                          │
Homosexual Man                            Homosexual Woman
Heterosexual Woman                        Heterosexual Man
```

Figure 5: Assumptions about sex and gender. Western society tends to stereotype gender as a dichotomy in the manner shown here. Each of the categories shown here is assumed to be dichotomous, and also assumed to map onto other categories.

accurately) serves to reinforce those categories. It does this in two ways. First, the more phenomena that are assumed to be synonymous, the less likely we are to question the boundaries of the original classification: if "homosexuals" are said to have a definite type of biology, then we are less likely to ask questions about the validity of the divisions into homosexual versus heterosexual types of people. Second, reduction within categories serves to reinforce precisely because it naturalises: if our definitions of gender, sexual preference, or whatever, are seen to have *biological* roots, then they are likely to be seen as more natural, and by implication more desirable or unchangeable. The logic with respect to sexual preference runs as follows. Homosexuality is often considered to be unnatural, abnormal (that is, the initial assumption is normative); biological bases to homosexuality are then hypothesised; some biological factor is located that seems to correlate with a gay life-style, and this is then assumed to be causal, representing a deviation from "normal" biology. Normal biology then becomes defined as the opposite of this, so that normal biology—and thus heterosexuality—become seen as more natural. Written out baldly like this, the logic is clearly circular. It does, nevertheless, underwrite much of the medical literature on topics such as homosexuality.[27]

Reductionism, then, not only makes assumptions about causality in its explanations of natural events: it also makes the associated assumption that the categories by which we organise our perception of the world at one level necessarily apply at other levels. If we all agree on the categories in the first place, that assumption may not be particularly problematic. The categories of gender are, however, immensely problematic for feminism, and when they are carried over to other levels of analysis simply because it is assumed that they apply everywhere then the problems are likely to be multiplied. Femininity, masculinity, homosexuality, or whatever, simply do not map on to some underlying biological terrain which then has primacy over them.[28]

4. ALTERNATIVES TO REDUCTIONISM

There have been various attempts to propose alternatives to reductionism, to try to avoid the problems outlined above. It is usually claimed that the alternatives provide better, more realistic, descriptions of the natural world. Yet reductionism is surprisingly resistant to such attacks, and continues to be the *modus operandi* of the sciences. Before outlining some of these alternatives, it is worth reflecting on *why* crude reductionism persists even in the face of apparently viable alternatives. There are, I would suggest, two major reasons for the persistence of reductionism as a mode of explanation: first, reductionism and the associated concept of nature as mechanism have proved not only useful to the development of capitalist science, but also relatively easy to understand. Reductionist explanations are thus vindicated because more people are likely to accept them. Second, alternative modes of explanation are not always considered even to be part of science, so that reductionism often remains unchallenged in terms of the science that it serves.

The first point is that reductionism has served capitalism well. By emphasising the partition of nature into its component parts, reductionism can be said to foster an ideology of control over those components, which has in turn contributed to capitalism's exploitation of nature: if the world is viewed as consisting of an aggregation of bits, some of which can be directly exploited for financial gain, then the overall effects of exploitation are likely to be overlooked. The effects on the global ecosystem of capitalism's piecemeal exploitation of resources bears witness to this.

Reductionism offers apparently easy, and often commercially exploitable, solutions to many problems. If some derangement in a biological or social system is detectable at one level, then changes in a lower level are frequently sought. Because it is assumed that there is a chain of causes from the lower levels upwards, it is consequently assumed that changes in the lower level will lead to changes in the higher. That this had led to some patently absurd claims has often been noted. One well-known example is the claim that, since stimulation of one part of the brain is known to influence aggressive behaviour in at least some kinds of vertebrate animals, then a cure for human ghetto violence might be to remove that part of the brain from riot leaders.[29] The violence is assumed to stem solely or largely from the brain; the reductionist answer is thus to remove the troublesome bit of the brain. But whatever the absurdity of some of its claims, the utility of reductionism has been that it isolates causal factors within the individual (be that organism, cell, or whatever) which might then be subject to manipulation—by surgery, drugs, and so forth. It is this application of *ex juvantibus* logic that has led to ready commercial exploitation.

A second reason why reductionism has been so persistent is that its proponents often use the tactic of demolishing alternative models as unscientific—and, by implication, less true. Now there are, of course, many non-scientific ways of describing the world, such as through religion or mysticism, but here I am not primarily concerned with these. What I am more concerned with is the claim that alternative frameworks occurring within science are in fact "unscientific".[30] Alternatives to reductionism commonly emphasise the interconnectedness of phenomena, and point out that "the whole is more than the sum of its parts". This is sometimes taken to mean that the whole possesses properties which cannot necessarily be predicted from a knowledge of the separate parts' properties, which in a sense transcend those of the component parts. The implication is that the transcendent properties of the whole may *not* be directly explicable in terms of chains of causes operating upwards from the component parts. It is this possibility of indeterminacy, of not being able to define preceding causes, which is liable to provoke the claim of not being scientific. It is salutory to remember that similar debates to these occurred in earlier decades of this century concerning the new atomic physics which, with its concerns with the indeterminacy of atomic structure, was breaking the causal rules.[31] Indeterminacy has, however, remained part of quantum physics, which in turn has forced a reappraisal of assumptions about cause and effect—at least in that branch of science. In biology and the behavioural sciences, however, the reductionist assumptions about chains of causes linger on.

Despite its tenacity, however, there are things that reductionism cannot explain. It does not really explain, for example, how divergent biological forms arise.[32] The extreme reductionist answer is to say that a species' characteristic form (or shape) is the product of information encoded in the DNA—one species' DNA is not the same as another's, and so different forms result. But this is not enough. At most, DNA encodes for protein structures; it is not at all obvious how this process of encoding brings about the processes by which biological form is generated. Moreover, the reductionist model assumes that the *differences* between forms arise from differences in the DNA—yet no consistent relationship between the two has been shown.

Given the problems posed by reductionism, some writers have—as Barbara McClintock did—tried to view nature in different kinds of ways. One common response in opposition to reductionism's assumptions is to stress "holism"—that is, to emphasise that the whole can only be understood properly as a whole, and is not likely to be understood as a conglomeration of bits. Discussions of holism in biology tend to emphasise relations between integrated elements, putting stress on the operation of the whole system, rather than on the individual elements themselves. There have been various expressions of such a view, differing in the ways that relationships within a system are described, but having in common that they stress the functions of the whole system and its irreducibility to component parts.[33]

Reference to "holism" is often made in the context of opposing reductionism in general, or mechanistic science in particular. "Holistic" views of nature are often emphasised, for example, by people concerned with environmental issues, for whom a holistic approach is seen to be more in harmony with, and integrated with, the rest of nature. In similar vein, the reductionism inherent in much orthodox, allopathic, medicine is often counterposed to "holistic medicine", by which is meant the various forms of alternative medicine, such as homeopathy, acupuncture, herbal medicine and so on. Within feminist writing, such a holistic approach to nature and to the human body has been strongly stressed. It is often seen as particularly, even essentially, female, as Jill Raymond and Janice Wilson suggest:

Allopathic medicine takes power over and from the body and replaces it with drugs, whereas holistic medicine restores the body's own powers of healing.... We see the holistic healing arts as female-principled and allopathy as male-principled. The female-principled medicines respect the cycle of life and death, whereas the ultimate power of the male-principled medicine is to control life and death.[34]

It is certainly an attractive idea to oppose reductionism's excesses by pointing to its mirror image. What is not always made clear, however, is just what is meant by a "holistic" viewpoint. For some, "holism" puts emphasis on interactiveness, relatedness, embeddedness—an emphasis which is little different from the one that I shall argue in the next chapter. For others, however, "holism" means an inversion of the chain of causation: instead of causes seeming to operate from the bottom up, they now operate from the top down. In this sense of holism, causal precedence is given — as it is in reductionism — to certain levels of analysis; in holism's case, however, these are the higher, rather than the lower, levels. Thus holistic medicine might imply that some shift in the body's balance, at the level of the whole organism, causes changes in, say, cellular biochemistry or the functioning of a particular organ. To some, this inversion of notions of cause is preferable; by asserting the primacy of the whole, human dignity—in its wholeness—is not lost. On the other hand, inverting the pyramid does not, as some have argued, *necessarily* get away from the assumption that phenomena at different levels can be straightforwardly mapped on to each other, so that events at level A determine events at level B in some way, and so forth.

It is this assumption about the relationship between events at different levels that has led to the paradoxical suggestion that holism in this second sense is actually reductionist.[35] This arises because the organisation at any one level is assumed to impose order on the component parts, and hence on the next lowest level. Arthur Koestler described this relationship using the analogy of language structure: it is, he suggested, the "deep structure" or syntax of a language which is primary and which imposes order on the structure and sequencing of the individual words, and it is learning these grammatical rules which comprises the most significant part of language acquisition by young children. Once the rules are learnt, then other words—more component parts—can be added.[36]

Order in this model is thus seen as something which, at least at the lower levels, is derived from the structures of the higher levels: using the language analogy, the order of words and sentences derives from the grammatical structure of the language. Where this view is "reductionist" is that, like bottom-up reductionism itself, there is no capacity for organisation to appear *within* a level, nor for influences to operate in two directions at once. Order is either imposed from above, or from below. But to continue the language analogy, order and meaning do not only come from the grammatical rules; indeed, language is dynamic and living precisely because it does not always obey rules. Poetry, for example, frequently uses words in ways that do not obey rules of syntax but which create new meaning, new symbolism; in this case the meaning, the order, derives in part from the "bottom up" (the words themselves) and in part from the "top down" (the syntax), and new meaning is created out of the relationship between the two.

Top down models also do not allow for the possibility of order arising spontaneously at any given level; it is assumed to arise from above. But the interactions between component parts may themselves impose some self-organisation on the system, independently of other levels. The detailed structure of a living cell, for example, emerges from the complex interactions between its various components; it is highly ordered, yet in dynamic equilibrium with its environment and within itself. It is self-organising, since its order is largely a product of its internal processes. Reductionist explanations of that order would reduce it to, say, the activities of particular genes; while holistic interpretations would imply that the order and organisation derive from "higher" levels, such as tissues, organs, or the whole organism itself.

Although holism has been posited as an alternative, in radical opposition to reductionism, neither are wholly satisfactory. I have already referred to the problem of assuming that the heirarchy of levels common to both reductionism and holism represents real distinctions in the natural world. The notion of cause in both type of explanation is similarly problematic. The way in which the notion of cause is commonly used in science implies a linear correspondence between particular events, and it also implies that one event more or less immediately precedes another (at least in the first kind of timescale considered earlier). If A is thought to cause B, then we usually assume that A occurred shortly before B did, whether our framework of interpretation fits a reductionist or a holistic model. What this assumption tends to diminish is the richness of complex interactions occurring both within and between levels. Both event A and event B are embedded in a tangle of other events, preceding them, occurring simultaneously, or occurring just after, events which may be interdependent, or independent of one another. They may be haphazard, or organised. It is just this complexity of the living world which provides us with enormous intellectual challenges, not least because it is immensely difficult to begin to think in terms of constantly changing and interacting systems. If they are constantly in flux, how on earth do we define the rules?

A second problem with both reductionism and holism is that both tend to assume that there is a similar, if not synonymous, relationship between levels over development time. That is, both assume that the relationship between putative levels at one time in the organism's developmental history is similar to that at an earlier stage. But the relationship between levels is itself a function of the processes of development, and cannot necessarily be assumed to exist unchanged. During early development from the fertilised egg, for example, the emerging structures and the relationship between them change dramatically before they develop into the organ systems of the fully formed animal. Consider, too, the relationship between the individual animal and the next "higher" level, that of social organisation. The question then is: is this relationship always constant, as reductionism and holism tend to assume? I would suggest that it is not. Take the example of an individual member of a "solitary" species; that is, an animal which spends most of its time on its own. It is part of a population of such animals, and there will inevitably be some limited social contact at certain times of the year for breeding. For most of the year, however, social relationships—the stuff of the social organisation level of analysis—are distant and determined largely by mechanisms of mutual avoidance. But the animal did not necessarily begin its life in such a social network; for many animals, life begins in a closer-knit social community. Mammals, in particular, begin life with very close physical and behavioural contact with their mothers and with any siblings.

That is, the relationship between the individual and its social context has changed, particularly over its developmental history.

Even for relatively social species, the relationship between an individual and its social context changes dramatically. There is a sense in which the individual mammal, say, shortly after birth can only be understood as part of a group which interacts almost as one with the mother. As it grows up, however, it becomes separated, begins to lead a life of its own, and becomes part of different social networks. The dynamics of these changing relationships between individual and social organisation become lost in the rather static descriptions of rigid hierarchies of "levels".

What is frequently done within the reductionist framework is to look at development backwards, from the adult, or final form. Thus, to take one example relevant to the themes of this book, the reductionist viewpoint would take as a starting point the existence of, say, sex differences in adult behaviour. It would then seek a potential biological factor that is dichotomised, so that the existence of two adult forms might be traced to the dichotomised biological factor. In the sex/gender differences literature, the dichotomised biological factors are usually the sex chromosomes, or sex hormones. (In practice, the sex hormones are not nearly as dichotomous as is commonly supposed). Over developmental time, the assumption is that the adult differences emerged due to the influence of some similarly dichotomous factor early in development, which are then assumed to effect some irreversible change in the organism.

One example of this is to focus upon the existence of sex differences in behaviour in adult animals, such as laboratory rats, and then to ask questions about the possible role of hormones, either in the adult itself, or in the very young (just born, or foetal) animal. There is now a large body of research literature documenting the various ways in which exposure to hormones during early life can effect changes in the adult expression of behaviour and it has generally been assumed that it is the nature of that early exposure that leads to sexual differentiation.[37] That is, exposure to one type of hormone "mix" results in male-type patterns of behaviour (and a male external genital anatomy), while exposure to another type results in "female" type patterns.[38]

I will deal in more detail with ways of interpreting these kinds of findings in the next chapter; suffice it to say for now that the assumption of hormonal causes of sexual differentiation is a reductionist one. The sex differences are attributed to alterations in the structure and hormone sensitivity of the brain, in turn resulting from the early hormone exposure. Holistic interpretations, particularly with regard to experimental animals, are far less common in science. It might, for instance, be considered a more holistic interpretation of the origins of adult sex differences to focus instead on the social context of early life. Some sex differences in adult behaviour might thus be affected by the social experiences of the animal or person in its early life. This would be "holistic" in the sense that causes are assumed to operate from the social context to the individual, shaping its infant behaviour in ways that in turn influence its behaviour in a social context when adult. This sort of explanation is less likely to be found, in part because of the reductionist assumptions in science, and in part perhaps because it is less straightforward to study empirically. Nonetheless, there is now evidence from animal studies that—among rats at least—there are social differences in early life that might contribute to the development of adult sexually differentiated behaviour.[39]

Neither the reductionist nor the holistic account is sufficient, however. To continue the example of sex differences in behaviour, it is not enough to point to the existence of hormones or differences in social experience, since these coexist. Each may influence the other, and may in turn influence the behaviour of the individual concerned at any moment in time. If mother rats discriminate between their offspring by sex, as experiments have shown,[40] then this may well be because the mother is responding to the hormonal differences of the pups.[41] How, then, do we separate the effects of the hormones from those of social experience?

When behavioural development is studied in the laboratory, all that is usually studied is one or a few such influences and their effects during tiny fragments of the individual's life. We simply do not know much about the complexity of influences on that individual over its whole life, and how these have interacted in the past or interact now. What we are studying in fact is the structure of particular components of the behaviour of an individual organism, a structure which has developed from the structure of their behaviour in the past. And, of course, that structure in the past of a rat includes its responses to influences from many sources, including hormones and mothers.

Holism has been proposed as a radical alternative to reductionism, an alternative espoused, too, in some feminist writing. As an alternative, however, it runs up against many of the same problems that reductionism does as a way of explaining the world, which in turn limits its radical potential. Using the example of genderised behaviour in our own society, it is no more helpful to interpret gender in "control-from-above" (holistic) terms than it is to locate it in biological bits of individuals. A crude kind of control-from-above explanation of genderised behaviour is to say that it is ultimately caused by patriarchal social organisation—an explanation which diminishes the individual and denies any significance to her or his individual developmental history. The reductionist model does not help much either, since it denies the significance of the social organisation and roots the individual's behaviour firmly in biology. And that biology, of course, is a static, history-less one.

There have been attempts to resolve the dualism of, on the one hand, the individual and society, and on the other, the individual and her/his biology. To some extent, the remainder of this book revolves around the dilemmas posed by reductionism versus alternatives, and attempts to step towards their resolution in feminist theory. In the next chapter I will consider some ways of looking at gender development that posit a form of interactionism in which "biology" and "society" are not seen as mutually exclusive, existing on different levels, but are held to interact in some way in the production of gender. From there, I will turn to the relationship between women, gender and nature that has been forged by reductionist thinking within science, before turning in the final chapter to the question of a feminist science and whether or not such a science might provide other radical alternatives to reductionism.

5 Developing Gender

At the end of Chapter Three I noted how prevalent is the view that human nature can be understood as resulting from the addition of our biological and social selves. This is the age-old nature/nurture dichotomy, which supposes that all, or most, traits can be understood as being so much innate, and so much learnt. To acknowledge that both biology (nature) and culture (nurture) might be important in our development is, it must be admitted, an advance over extreme views which suggest that behavioural traits are *either* due to instinct, *or* to social conditioning. It is currently quite fashionable in the behavioural sciences to assert that the nature/nurture dichotomy is long since dead. If it is, then the ghost is very much alive and well: Chapters Two and Three outlined a number of instances of it. Even if academic journals attempt to avoid the dichotomy, the popular press continues to present it in stark either/or terms. *The Sun* in 1979 ran a series of articles on premenstrual tension, in which readers were asked "Is premenstrual tension caused by physical factors—or is it all in the mind?"[1] Nature, or nurture?

It is perhaps not surprising that the popular press continues to dichotomise nature and nurture in this way; apart from its conceptual simplicity, it also makes for good journalism to present complex arguments as a straightforward opposition. The suggestion that intelligence is largely an inherited trait has often been portrayed in the press, for example, as a simple opposition to the view that it is "only" inequality of opportunity that limits some human potential. Put thus, the reader is forced into assuming one or other stance; there is no middle ground.[2]

While the popular press portrays this in sharp opposition, it is not alone in perpetuating the view that human nature is moulded according to an additive effect. The additive model of human nature, with a primary biological base and social or cultural contributions added on, is still the dominant one in the academic literature. In Chapter Two, for example, I referred to the suggestion that the scarcity of women scientists and engineers results from women's lesser spatial abilities. There are a number of biologically determinist theories which purport to explain the rather greater proportion of men who do well on tests of spatial ability. The observation that such skills can be improved with practice is simply assimilated into the theory by supposing that the effect of the biological factors is primary; practice can only improve skills within limits set by the biology.

Despite considerable evidence which does not readily fit a straightforwardly deterministic model,[3] the idea that sex differences in spatial skills are the product of biological differences continues to thrive. Years of research into sex differences in such skills have thrown up contradictory and often negative results. Yet the biological view persists. One commentator rather cynically observed that the reasons for this persistence lay in:

The pay-offs, as it were, for adopting the genetic hypothesis . . . a clear cut, largely immutable sex difference to play with; a reinforcement of the hereditarian approach to human abilities; a justification for current sex discrimination in education and employment; and a validation of forty or more years of psychological research.[4]

One important reason for the strength of the additive view of human nature with its implications of biological determinism is that it fits comfortably with the ideals of liberal individualism, which have dominated Western politics and philosophy for over three hundred years. The liberal tradition has particularly emphasised rationality—the human capacity to reason—as a foundation for human society and for moral principles. This is assumed to be an essential part of individual human nature, which is somehow prior to the society of which that person is part. This underwrites definitions of what constitutes "humanness": for liberal philosophy, the capacity for reason is the prime justification for categorising a being as human, rather than anything else.

Although liberal philosophy does not always make explicit the idea that a capacity for reason may be innate (and indeed at times may deny it),[5] that reason may be part of the *essence* of human nature does tend to follow from liberalism's assumption of the priority of individuals over society. In this sense, individualism is a necessary precondition for the additive viewpoint. Alison Jagger, in a discussion of liberal feminist views of human nature, points out that, according to liberal logic:

> individuals could exist outside a social context; their essential characteristics, their needs and interests, their capacities and desires, are given independently of their social context . . . the metaphysical assumption of human beings as individual atoms which in principle are separable from social molecules does discourage liberals from conceiving of rationality as constituted by or defined by group norms, let alone as being a property of social structures.[6]

Jagger also points out that, while maintaining a belief in reason as a human essence, contemporary liberalism, including liberal feminism, actually ignores the potential of human biology. Reason, paradoxically, is both an unchanging essence and also that which removes us from biological continuity with other species and into the unique world of human culture. It is the liberal assumption that human beings are essentially self-sufficient entities which, for Jagger, denies the significance of biology in human development. She notes that:

> As soon as one takes into account the facts of human biology, especially reproductive biology, it becomes obvious that the assumption of individual self-sufficiency is impossible. Human infants resemble the young of many species in being born helpless, but they differ from all other species in requiring a uniquely long period of dependence upon adult care. This care could not be provided by a single adult; in order to raise enough children to continue the species, humans must live in social groups where individuals share resources with the young and temporarily disabled. Human interdependence is thus necessitated by human biology, and the assumption of individual self-sufficiency is plausible only if one ignores human biology.[7]

The additive model presupposes an immutable, underlying biology—the essential human nature—on to which social and environmental effects are added. In the additive view of the individual's development the biological factors have primacy, both temporally and in terms of the relative weighting given to the two components.

Yet there is much evidence—as I implied in the previous chapter—that the additive model in general, like the spatial ability hypothesis noted above, is not an accurate way of describing the development of organisms. Its persistence, despite the evidence, underlines its utility to the prevailing individualistic philosophy. The rhetoric of the individual and individual liberty goes hand in hand with a rhetoric of an inner core of essential nature. At the heart of Western society is the privacy of the individual and the family which remain sacrosanct and relatively untouchable by the concerns of the state, a division central to the right wing of political thought. The British right-wing ideologue, Ian Gilmour, wrote for example of the "strict demarcation between public life which is the concern of the state, and private life which is the concern of the individual and the family", while at the heart of the individual lies the untouchable human nature.[8] Note how, whether we are asked to consider the relationship between the human nature of the individual in her or his immediate environment, or between the individual-in-a-family and the larger society, the relationship is always an additive one.

The advantages of the additive model to certain political philosophies may help to explain its continued existence, but simultaneously there is a considerable accumulation of evidence against it. In order to attempt to explain some of this interactive models have frequently been proposed, to allow for reciprocal effects. In very general terms, these propose an interaction, rather than an addition, between, say, biological factors and environmental ones. Thus, a female gender identity might be said to result from the interaction between a female biology and societal expectations.

Now there are a number of ways in which the concept of interactionism has been used. While my concern in this chapter is to focus upon processes of development, it is important to note that ideas of interactionism are not unique to developmental studies. Ideas of interaction can be found, for instance, on each of the three time-scales noted in the previous chapter. Perhaps the most prevalent use of interactionist concepts on the immediate time-scale is to describe mind-brain relationships. In attempts to circumvent the obvious problems that arise from mind-body dualism, interactionism has been proposed to account for ideas of reciprocal causation: mind affects body and vice versa. The argument is that it is more meaningful to describe the interaction between mind and body than to suppose that mind is somehow a separate phenomenon from the body in which it occurs.[9]

Interaction in the sense of fairly immediate causation can also be used to describe immediate behaviour. It would be an interactionist explanation, for instance, to suggest that depression might result from the interaction of internal biological events, such as biochemical changes in the brain, and external events, such as a recent shock.

At the other end of the scale, interaction may be emphasised over evolutionary time. The common, neo-Darwinist, view of evolutionary change is that change emerges as a result of chance mutations, some of which confer advantages. Those individuals having such advantage are more likely to survive and reproduce, with the result that the advantageous mutation spreads throughout the population. An alternative is to stress that change occurs through the interaction of the organism with its environment; as a result of the active engagement of a population of organisms with their environment, the characteristics of that population may change.[10]

That is not a common idea, admittedly, and most people adhere to the idea of chance mutations. Still, it does provide an instance of ideas of interaction in an evolutionary context. But the most relevant use of interactionist ideas for the theme of this book, is their use over the developmental time-scale—the idea, for example, that a person's development is a production of an interaction between her/his biology and the social environment in which the individual develops. Such views have the merit that they attempt to move away from naive assumptions of nature/nurture, taking into account reciprocal effects occurring throughout the developmental process: as one writer discussing the development of gender differences observed, "commitment to an interactionist model prevents an exclusive focussing on either biological or social factors".[11] Recent (i.e. 1970s onwards) research into the development of gender differences has tended to use this kind of approach, seeking to establish multicausality, and reciprocity.

Do ideas of interactionism help in overcoming the problems of the additive model? They have often been advocated as a plausible solution to overcome the dichotomy, nature *or* nurture. It is clear that individuals and their behaviour do not act in ways that can readily be explained as one or the other, so in that sense interactionism does provide an advance. To take one example: we know that hormones, say, can affect behaviour, but we also know that behaviour can affect hormones, in humans as well as other animals, so any explanation of behaviour will have to take such instances of reciprocity into account. The additive model, with its implications of a primary, determining biology cannot account for reciprocal effects.

Although interactionism has been proposed as a better alternative to the additive model, it has also come up against difficulties. It is seriously limited in two ways. First, when used in the developmental sense, it still tends to treat present behaviour as a dependent—and thus still determined—variable. That is, behaviour is seen somehow as the outcome of the interaction between biology and environment in that organism's past. The organism is thus frozen in the present, and its behaviour now does not necessarily enter the interactive process. This use of interactionism is applied, for instance, to some accounts of gender development. Thus, McGuiness argues that perceptual differences between infant girls and boys interact with cultural influences to produce adult sex differences in behaviour.[12] Viewed in this way, "adult sex differences" become seen as something relatively fixed, rather than themselves interacting in particular contexts.

The second limitation is that, while often counterposed to nature/nurture dichotomies, this form of interactionism still has built into it *potentially* separable components of nature and of environment. The difference is simply that the relationship between these is no longer held to be a straightforward additive one, but is at least multiplicative. "Biology" and "environment" may interact, but they remain essentially distinct. In part, this separateness arises from the assumption of reciprocal causation itself. If we consider that there is reciprocal causation, then we have to consider, at least as a logical possibility, that one component of the interaction can exist without the other. "Interactionism", suggested Charles Taylor, writing about mind-body relationships, "by envisaging mental and physical events as causes of each other ... allows that it makes sense to enquire whether after all a given mental event does not have physical causes or consequences, even if a case of this kind is never discovered".[13] As Taylor observes, the notion of disembodied thought that follows from this logical possibility is somehow not a very credible one!

I want now to bring this consideration of additive and interactive models back to the themes of the book and feminist theory. The additive model, as I have emphasised, poses problems for feminism. First, it presupposes that "biological" and "environmental" factors can in theory be simply separated, thus allowing some degree of biological determinism. If it is argued, say, that 70 per cent of gender-specific behaviour is socially conditioned, then that leaves 30 per cent that might be assumed to be biologically determined and hence resistant to change. This is the kind of argument implied, for instance, by E. O. Wilson, in *On Human Nature,* when he considers how society might be organised: even if equal rights were in theory assured, he suggests, there would remain a (30 per cent?) tendency to return to our present gender roles simply because of the underlying biological constraints.

A second problem for feminism with the additive model is its significance for liberal individualism. While to many liberal feminists the idea of individualism and individual liberation may be of primary importance, this remains problematic for many other feminists, for whom the needs or aspirations of the individual do not necessarily take precedence over what is perceived as the common good. Feminist emphasis has generally been on relationships between women (and between women and men), which are seen to have primacy over the individuals themselves, whether the relationships are seen as unifying (for example, the notion of "sisterhood") or potentially divisive (such as social class). This is contrary to the emphasis in the liberal tradition in which individuals and their essential natures take precedence over social relationships.

Liberal individualism also places emphasis on reason in a

paradoxical way, as I noted above; reason is both an unchanging essence and that which removes us from the biological domain into human culture. Alison Jagger observed that this emphasis denies the significance of human biology in a way that is of particular significance to feminism, since she points out that the assumption of individual self-sufficiency is only feasible if we ignore the interdependence of humans, particularly the dependency of infants.[14] At least in the context of present care-giving arrangements, which are almost entirely in the hands of women, to do so is to ignore a large part of women's role in human reproduction in its widest sense. Thus, the additive model, with its implications for the significance of the individual, both overemphasises biology in general as a separable component part of the individual's nature, and underemphasises the significance of women's biology in relation to wider social relationships.

Interactive models of gender are relevant to feminism in that, as noted earlier, they do attempt to move away from the focus on purely biological factors. According to the interactionist position, gender, or women's position in society, cannot be understood solely in biological terms. With that few feminists would disagree. Feminists might disagree with it, however, for its maintenance of the potential separation of the biological, even if the biological component is no longer seen as uniquely determining. Consider the following suggestion, made in the context of discussing an interactionist view of gender: "Adopting an interactive approach, one of the more meaningful questions we can ask is how a genetically influenced trait is expressed in the range of environmental conditions in which it may develop".[15] This is indeed a meaningful question within the interactionist framework; by looking at the trait in question across a wide range of environmental conditions and seeing how it is expressed, we might begin to understand how these environments have interacted with the biological components of the trait to produce the observed variations. But what happens if the various environmental conditions produce a degree of uniformity? In this case, we would have to conclude that the biological component(s) are relatively unchanged by the interaction, that they are, in effect, relatively determining.

This is where problems might arise for feminism, and it is a consequence of the potential separability of the components implied by interactionism. It has often been pointed out that, while there is considerable variability in the ways in which it is organised, one phenomenon appears to exist almost universally. Wherever you look, male domination of society occurs in one form or another—the social structure loosely called patriarchy. So one consequence of adopting this kind of interactionism is that you are led to the conclusion that the phenomenon of male domination, for all its superficial variability of form, is a deeply conservative arrangement in the face of environmental variability, and so must reflect some underlying biological trait. This conclusion is unlikely to be acceptable to most feminists, for whom the widespread existence of patriarchy (howsoever defined) is a problem that needs to be explained, not reduced to a component in a minor interaction.

This sort of problem arises because, as I have already indicated, interactionism implies that the biological and social components are *potentially* separable, even if they affect each other reciprocally. Thus, the only way in which it can explain relative uniformity in the face of social variability is to assume a relatively unchanging biological component. I referred to one instance of this kind of argument in Chapter Three, where I discussed Janet Radcliffe Richards' suggestion that we could discover what human nature was "really" like if we could study it in enough environments.[16] It is not, however, necessary to invoke biological determinism to explain relative uniformity, as I shall argue later.

Another area in which interactionist models present problems for feminism is the study of gender differences, particularly the advocacy of a concept of *androgyny*.[17] In psychological studies this is taken to mean the co-existence of "femininity" and "masculinity" in personality structure. In the psychological literature on androgyny there is an approximate consensus that feminine and masculine traits often do occur in the same individuals, and that their co-existence is the product of an interactive developmental process.[18] Moreover, the feminine and masculine may themselves be interactive.[19]

During the 1940s and 1950s, psychological testing scales were used which assumed that femininity and masculinity were opposite ends of a spectrum, implying that the two were mutually exclusive.[20] This assumption came in for criticism, on the grounds that most people have a bit of both, and this led to the suggestion of methods of measuring "androgyny"—that is, the extent to which someone possesses both kinds of trait.[21] Since then, the notion of androgyny has been taken up extensively in the research and literature on sex role acquisition. Androgyny is, however, a concept that has a much longer and more varied history than can be found in recent journals. It can be traced back at least to classical times,[22] and was clearly developed in the alchemical traditions of Medieval Europe, which emphasised the conjunction of the feminine and masculine as an ideal form.[23]

Androgyny is an idea that had initial appeal for contemporary feminism, but has more recently been criticised. The basic criticism is that, like other variants of interactionism, it retains an essential duality, however much the component parts interact. The second, and more overtly feminist, criticism is that androgyny obscures the fact that "femininity" and "masculinity" are not simply alternative ways of being; masculinity brings benefits in contemporary society that being feminine does not. It is simply not true, as some advocates of androgyny have implied, that the sex role system of masculinity versus femininity oppresses both sexes equally. This inequality has always been recognised by at least some feminists within the WLM: the manifesto of the New York Feminists written at the beginning of the current movement, in 1969, stated that they had:

discarded the notion generally accepted by popular feminism that the sex-role system defines the oppression of women or that our enemy is the male role. The inadequacy of the sex-role theory of oppression becomes obvious when one considers its implication: that both men and women are oppressed by their respective sex-roles. Which is comparable to: both slaves and masters are oppressed by the slave system. By adopting this theory the women's movement has managed to skirt the issue of power and its relationship to oppression.[24]

Nonetheless, despite criticisms of it, the notion of androgyny, both as a description of human personality and as some sort of ideal state, lingers on within feminism.[25] It has a heuristic appeal, in that most people feel themselves to *be* both "feminine" and "masculine" in different ways, a fact which has long been recognised within psychoanalysis.[26] But there is a danger of the notion becoming prescriptive simply because it retains an underlying duality. If we argue that everyone has these traits, interactively or otherwise, and we have arbitrarily labelled them according to gender, then we are likely to infer that one trait is more *appropriate* for one or the other sex. In other words even if masculinity and femininity are held to coexist and to interact in all individuals, it is hard to get away from the notion that, for instance, femininity is somehow more suitable for females. The processes of "interaction" do not get away from the essential qualities of femininity and masculinity, which are held to be features of particular individuals—and they certainly do not sever the links with the social roles to which women and men are subject. In the form of interactionism I have discussed, they remain distinct, and having essential characteristics.

If "interactionism"—at least as I have described it—fails us, then what are we left with? What I shall argue in the rest of this chapter is that while interaction is indeed an important concept for understanding behavioural development it is in no way as straightforward as is sometimes implied. In the first place, the interactions are multiple and complex and cannot readily be reduced to "biology" versus "environment". Secondly, it is necessary to emphasise that any interactive processes occurring in the present are necessarily the products of interactive processes in the past—both the past of that individual organism and the past of others of its species. And thirdly, we have to consider the problems arising from the duality that remains in the forms of interactionism that I have outlined.

I shall look at some of these points below, in relation to an example I used in the previous chapter, that of sexual differentiation in rats. I am doing this not because I think that rats are particularly relevant to humans (!)[27] but because in some ways it is easier to grasp the complexity by looking at some other species. It is also arguably easier for me to present the complexity in animals, given my familiarity with them. But before attempting this task, I want to dwell on the third consideration above, that of the implied duality. How can this be overcome? In one sense it cannot, at least within the constraints implied by the levels of analysis discussed in Chapter Four. The duality under discussion is, of course, that between the individual's biology and the environment, including the social context. Insofar as individuals and their social context are studied and understood at different "levels" within the hierarchy, they will always retain a distinction.

However, the model of interactionism discussed so far also implies a fixed, static dualism, and it is that which is problematic. By way of example, think of a layer of oil on a layer of water. There is no doubt some interaction at the interface between the two, some molecules of either moving across, as it were. But on the whole the two remain distinct, however much we may try to mix them up. This is the way interactionism looks at the relationship between individual biology and environment. Not only do the component parts not mix, but neither can significantly change the other. In other words, the essential characteristics of each part of the duality remain unchanged. What I want to argue, on the other hand, is that interactive processes in development *do* involve change and transformation. This is the point about how relationships between levels can change during development, made in Chapter Four. The duality, embedded in the hierarchical levels by which we classify our perceptions of the world, is constantly being changed and transformed just as the ingredients of a cake become transformed in the process of their interaction during baking.

I would argue that the duality will remain, but we must recognise that it is a by-product of our attempts to classify rather than being fundamental to nature. Looking at individuals developing in their social context is somewhat like physicists looking at electrons, who have had to accept that an electron can be both a wave *and* a particle, depending upon the preconceptions of the observer. If the observer wants to ask questions about electrons and their wave-like-ness then she /he has to ask questions about waves; if the observer wants to find out about an electron's particulateness, then questions have to be asked which address the electron as a particle. Answers then depend upon the observer's decisions in the first place about the kind of question to ask; it is this which has led to the realisation—at least in atomic physics—that the human observer cannot be said to stand, objectively, outside the system, but is intrinsically part of it by virtue of that initial decision. Much the same applies to our study of organisms; the dualism results from the kinds of questions we can ask. Yet at the same time that very dualism is being changed at the very moment that we ask the questions, since the "biology" and the "environment" will be in constant interaction.

This raises an important point that I have hitherto avoided—and that is, the extent to which we can talk about *change* in biological factors. Obviously, various factors change over developmental time, particularly in the very young organism. But what does it mean to say that the biology is undergoing change now? We tend to think of a person's biology as rather static; after all, someone's body is a particular shape and size, and these features are part of the way that that person is perceived. But that biology is not static. The most obviously labile feature of individual biology is to do with internal biochemistry, the internal chemistry of our cells, our hormone systems, and so forth. These are certainly subject to environmental modification: what we eat, for instance, can influence the internal milieu. Human hormone balance can be altered by, for example, stress, sexual activity, or the proximity of other people.[28] The ways in which our brains work are relatively labile; we can go on changing some components of brain function through learning throughout our lives; even in cases of brain damage, the brain shows a remarkable capacity to recover lost function. By contrast, organ structure—anatomy—does not seem to change very much.

The fact that organ structure does not seem to change, however, does not mean that it is in fact static. The various tissues of the body are constantly undergoing growth and are in constant interaction with their various environments; even bone shape can be slightly altered depending upon the muscular stresses to which it is subject. What is remarkable is that, despite this constant flux, organ structure remains relatively uniform over time. The inevitable question then to ask is, why? Given the constant turnover of tissues, why is organ structure constantly conserved?

The reductionist answer is inevitably that the information about organ structure is encoded in the genes—not a satisfactory answer, as it says nothing about how such information is supposed to be translated from organising individual proteins to building up the structural relationships between various parts of the body. A more satisfactory answer is to say that the conservation arises from the constraints imposed by the physical structure of the whole organism, by the structural relationships between the various parts. Thus, even while the biology can be transformed in the sense of constantly being subject to environmental changes, there is little apparent change because the structures are constrained physically by each other, like houses in a terraced row.

The extent then, to which change is *apparent* depends upon the way in which we approach it—the levels of analysis, if you will. Moreover, the ways in which different components interact or are capable of change vary considerably. This is another reason why it is not enough to say that "biology" and "environment" interact: of course they do in a very general sense. What we have to try to understand—and it is an enormously difficult task—is the varying ways in which they interact and how the components become changed in those processes of interaction.

Let me return to the example of rats that I used in the previous chapter, as a way of exemplifying some of the complex interactions involved. In the 1930s it was discovered that early exposure to hormones can alter the patterns of behavioural sexual differentiation; if, for instance, you castrate a male rat at birth, it grows up behaving in ways that are somewhat similar to those of females.[29] Since then there have been a plethora of studies of effects of hormone manipulations on later development. Even if it is not always made explicit, the framework within which this line of research has progressed is that hormones in early life are the prime determinants of adult patterns of sexual behaviour. To a large extent this assumption still holds, and the existence of sex differences in behaviour in adults is frequently attributed to perinatal hormonal effects. Now it may well be true that hormones exert a large effect. The problem is not there, but with the exclusive focus on hormones from the individual's own testes or lack of them which dominated research for several decades. More recently, however, that myopic focus has begun slowly to break down, and the picture is becoming far less clear. I have tried to summarise some of the complexity in the diagram (Figure Six). On the left-hand side is a diagram representing the unit of the pregnant female with all the offspring *in utero*. Rats, at least, have large litters, so there are likely to be several males and several females. The whole unit is subject to outside influences—odour, other rats, diet, noise—all or any of which may affect her and/or foetal development. If, for a moment, we focus on an individual foetus and its hormones (as the research had predominantly done), then what factors might affect that? The answer is probably rather a lot of them, but few have been studied. We do, however, know that maternal stress can alter pups' hormonal and subsequent sexual development;[30] and so can the sex of the littermates lying next to them in the uterus, presumably because some hormones produced by each pup will cross the placentae to reach the next adjacent pup.[31] And, of course, exposure to various poisons might affect prenatal development. Even before birth, then, it is difficult to separate the individual pup and its hormones from a network of complex processes.

The next part of the diagram refers to life after birth in the first two or three weeks while the pups are still suckling. I doubt very much if it is complete, even in terms of research that has been done, but it indicates some of the complexity. In the middle—perhaps arbitrarily—is the individual pup and its internal milieu, including its hormones. One significant change to earlier assumptions is that it is not only the presence or absence of testes that is significant for development, since ovarian and even adrenal hormones can also be influential.[32] Maternal behaviour also has a significant effect. Mother rats, as I noted in the previous chapter, discriminate between female and male offspring in ways that have implications for later behavioural (and possibly physical?) development.[33] Infants may also be affected by maternal physiological changes, including hormones, via changes in the composition of maternal milk. Many hormones, for instance, can pass readily into milk, with possible consequences for the newborn.[34] Mothers also respond to pups in other ways, such as responding to their ultrasonic calls.[35] Pups in turn respond to the mother, orienting towards her odour, particularly around the nipples[36] but also

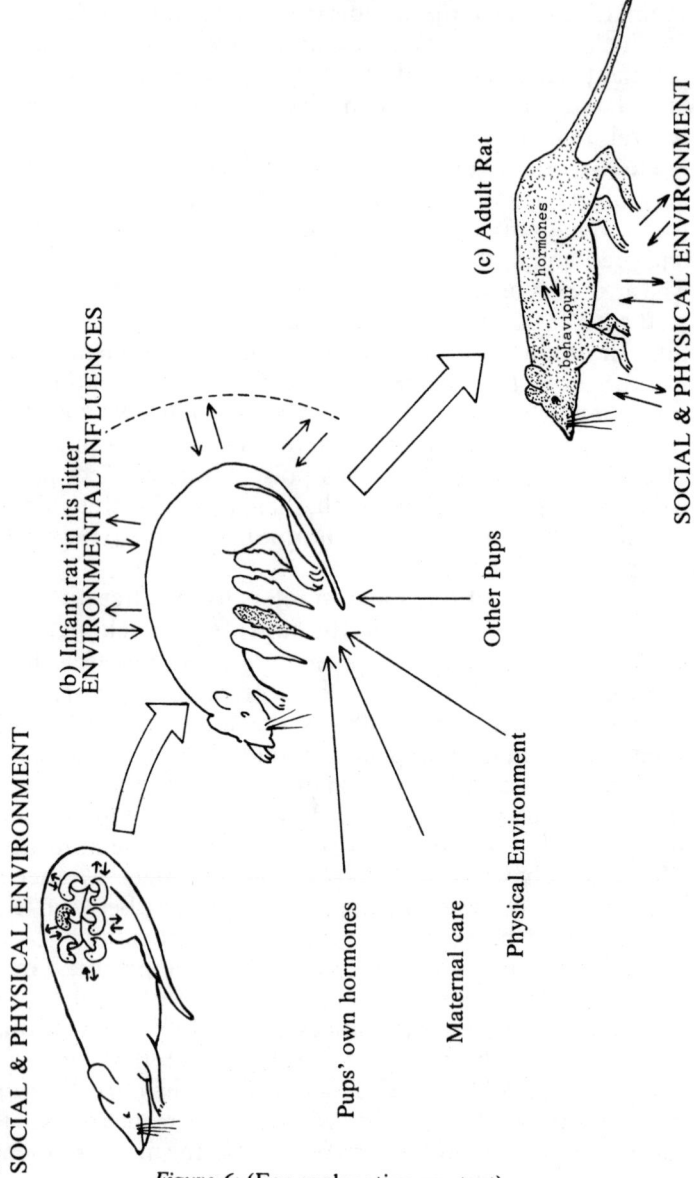

Figure 6: (For explanation see text).

more generally to her body odour.[37] Pup development can be affected by the presence of other pups, and by their sex.[38] And all of these interactions themselves occur in a social and non-social environmental context, which in turn can affect the interactions.

Thus far I have suggested that individual factors such as hormones are not rigidly determining, and have stressed that we need to think in terms of complex, ongoing, interactive processes in which the factors on which we focus can be thought of as themselves subject to change. All well and good, but it rather leaves the feeling that we cannot see the wood for the trees. Two immediate problems face us when we try to understand development in this complex fashion. The first is empirical. At least a reductionist framework does suggest some reasonably straightforward ways of investigating development, such as tinkering with hormones. How on earth do we investigate the enormous rag-bag of interactions? Things are easier to look at than interactions. The second problem facing us is how to deal with uniformity, particularly in relationship to behaviour. Given all the multifarious interactions—social or otherwise—outlined above (and the rest that I have missed out), why does development appear to proceed along lines that do have some predictability? Why don't all these interactions lead to a huge array of possible outcomes?

I have to confess that I do not know the answer to the first question. Science has thus far proceeded using methodological reductionism, and that is, by and large, the framework within which we ask nature questions. It does, however, make the study of very complex interactive processes very difficult simply because it dissociates the component parts. Perhaps the very method of constraining and controlling variables may not allow us to study nature adequately in terms of continually changing dynamics. In short, once we have removed ourselves from the level of theoretical abstraction in order to begin to *do* biological research in a more progressive way, then we may be doomed to failure simply because of the ways in which we do science. This objection has some validity, but is rooted in the assumption that our present scientific methods are both optimal and unchanging. When the theories of quantum mechanics necessitated a revision of the ways in which the atom was conceptualised, so new methodological approaches had to be considered. It is only when biology begins to take seriously the need to develop different theoretical frameworks that the appropriate methods will be developed. So, while I cannot give an answer to the question of how to study it yet, I would suggest—perhaps with some complacency—that the methodology may well evolve as biological theory evolves.

The second problem is more germane to this book, however. Why, for instance, do adult sex differences emerge with such regularity in the face of such complexity in the social life of young rats? And underlying that question, of course, lurks the much more difficult one . . . what about human gender? But I will play safe for a moment, and continue to think about rats. Clearly, if regularity emerges, there must be some kind of constraint on development.

One useful way of conceptualising developmental processes was suggested over thirty years ago, by Waddington.[39] He pictured the processes of development using the analogy of a ball rolling down a slope in which there are valleys (these are shown by the interconnecting lines in Figure Seven). At the top

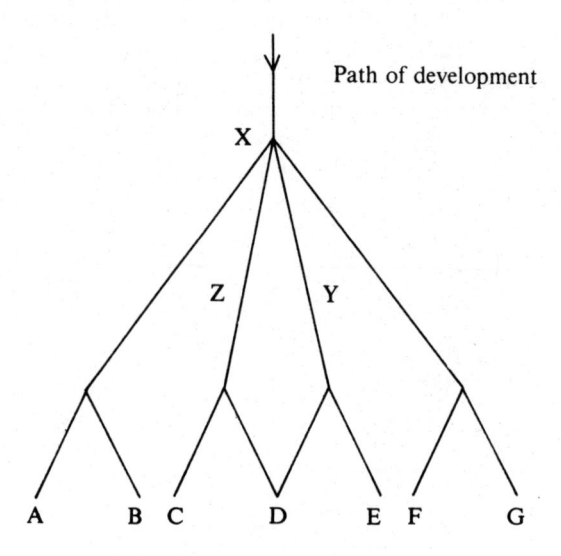

Figure 7: (For explanation see text).

of the slope, the ball potentially could end up in any location at the bottom. As development proceeds (that is, as the ball progresses down the slope) its "choices" become more and more determined until it lands up in one specific location at the bottom. The hills in between the valleys comprise constraints on the system, such as physical constraints.

Using Figure 7 as a basis, there are seven locations at which the ball may end up: A-G. Note that location D has two paths leading to it; that is, there may be more than one developmental path to the same end. Moreover, organisms are capable of returning to the same path of development if that path is perturbed (e.g. developing animals will quickly return to normal patterns of weight gain after a brief period of starvation). Consider the seven locations as representing arbitrary points on some equally arbitrary continuum in behaviour, such as the propensity to show mounting behaviour. Obviously, males generally show this behaviour more readily than females, so one end of our arbitrary scale can be called "masculine" (A). Most females do show mounting in some circumstances, but some more than others and generally less than males. We can designate this at the other end of the scale at G. C then represents males who show rather less mounting than A, and G represents females who show the least mounting. D represents a level of mounting which either males or females could show—so for this behaviour at least, there is more than one path to the same end.

What are the constraints on the development of this behaviour? Clearly, since females do it too it is not something which is uniquely determined by sex, even in our rats. On the other hand, females tend to do it less often. One constraint on this during behavioural development is that females and males obviously have somewhat different genital anatomy, with the result that females probably receive more genital stimulation from being mounted that males do.[40] They might then learn that this is rewarding, and subsequently behave in different ways (such as by showing less overt mounting). In more general terms, what would supply constraints on the development of behavioural systems, would include processes of learning.

There are inevitably anatomical constraints on development too, in that mounting behaviour probably relies for its expression on sensory feedback from the genitals. If a rat were born without genitals then I doubt very much if it would bother to mount anyone! In that sense, hormones probably provide constraints earlier during anatomical development, in that the development of the reproductive tract in either a "female" or a "male" direction is a process strongly influenced by hormones.[41]

Waddington originally used his model to describe processes of anatomical development, but it can just as well apply to behaviour. The idea that development might proceed along paths that become further and further constrained and that are capable of correcting perturbations might seem to argue against the interactions discussed earlier. On the other hand, it does lend itself to thinking about how development tends to lead to regularities. The two ideas are not necessarily as incompatible as they may seem, however, since we could conceive of processes of interaction as potentially altering the landscape down which the ball is rolling. Interaction with the environment might, as it were, change the shape of the valleys so that the ball is biased more in one direction than another.[42] We could well reinterpret some of the experimental findings from infant rats in this way, instead of assuming direct determination of the outcome. Exposing an infant rat to hormones might be said to alter the balancing points through which behavioural development has to proceed—the whole interacting system has to be shifted as a result. Suppose, for example, that hormones are experimentally present when our metaphorical ball reaches X. The ball which would have gone down valley Y is, as a result, constrained to go down Z. It could still end up at D. This would be like imagining a genetically female rat exposed to certain hormones *in utero*. These hormones have a "masculinising" effect on the size and structure of the external genitals; Z corresponds to the anatomical path down which genetic males might normally go, but down which our hormonally treated female now goes. But in the end, depending upon other factors during development at later "points" in the valley, the effect may not necessarily be any different from that found in some untreated females; both may end up at D.

Where does all this get us? I would argue that the development of an organism represents processes of complex interaction, processes in which the interacting parts become changed. But, at the same time, there are constraints upon those processes; it is quite clear that not all outcomes are possible. The constraints may be obvious ones, such as having the necessary anatomy to carry out some behavioural act (e.g. animals without wings cannot fly); or they may be not at all obvious. The study of how animals develop behavioural sex differences is about both uncovering the complexity (within the limits of our existing methodology) and understanding how that complexity is simultaneously constrained to produce regularity.

So much for rats: what about humans? Human development in a genderised society is infinitely more complex (we suppose) than rat sex differences. Given the variability between human societies in what is considered to be gender-appropriate behaviour, then the balancing point between the interactiveness of development and the constraints upon it must be at the interactive end. There are various theories about how we acquire gender identity, varying in the extent to which they stress interaction. During early development, it is argued, children become aware of the existence of gender and of physical sex differences. Although there is disagreement about the processes whereby this occurs, the various theories agree that children eventually learn about gender-appropriateness and incorporate it into their sense of self.[43] What the theories do tend to do, however, is to assume that, once acquired, gender is a fixed attribute of individuals. Like the form of interactionism I considered earlier, this sort of approach assumes interactive processes during early development, which result in a person's gender, the dependent variable.

I would suggest that gender should not be viewed in this way. What I would argue instead is that gender is something which human beings constantly reconstruct throughout their lives, both with respect to themselves and to other people around them. That is, gender is itself part of interactive processes, rather than being a fixed property of individuals. Among other things, this constantly reconstructed sense of gender could include more directly awareness of the biological self. One problem with prevailing theories of gender acquisition is that adult biological experiences, such as menstruation or childbirth, are not thought of as influencing self-perception of gender. Because it is assumed to be constructed early in life, the only biological component that has been included in theories of gender is the structure of the genitals. Yet I cannot accept that adult biological processes have no impact upon our perception of ourselves as women or men. The biological changes of puberty occur long after gender is assumed to have been largely acquired, according to existing theories. Apart from the biological experience, such changes have huge social significance, which itself alters the ways in which people view their physical selves. As a result, an integral part of a woman's identity of herself *as a woman* is her experience of the biological changes that go with that, as well as the social meanings attached to these.[44] Thus, adult gender identity, as woman or man, can only be understood as the present, dynamic point in a continually evolving process which, I would argue, includes the real lived experience of our biological selves as well as the social meaning and economic context of our lives.

Consider the example of menstruation. From the age of menarche, women experience menstruation approximately monthly for roughly four decades. With each cycle come biological changes. But these are made sense of, understood—and thus experienced—in the context of cultural evaluation of women and their biology. The biological events themselves interact with the environmental events of women's lives; neither are constant or static. "Gender" then becomes the way in which we understand the meaning of that whole interaction, not just its social context. If, then, gender is viewed in these terms it necessarily cannot be fixed since that whole interaction will inevitably change and be given different meanings at different points in women's lives and in different cultural contexts.

The way in which I am using the concept of gender here refers, of course, to the notion of gender a person applies to her or himself. There is another sense of gender, and that is to refer more broadly to social divisions—hence, "gender divisions"—in society. Since this term does refer to social divisions the concept of gender on which it relies is inevitably not quite the same. On the other hand, what else are gender divisions if not the collective experience of gender? Experiencing gender means not only experiencing our individual bodies and their functions in a social context, but also the shared social assumptions that derive from individual experiences.

Feminists have often been criticised for utilising what is essentially a biological division by their insistence that women in general do have some shared experiences, particularly at the biological level. Biology in this sense becomes something of an unchanging essence, possessed by all women and which thereby underlines our commonality. I would agree that women do have something in common biologically, at least at a trivial level; that is, nearly all women menstruate, and most become pregnant and go through childbirth. But that biology is not an essence, and may not always be the unifying principle that we are sometimes led to believe. A woman's biology, and her experience of it, do not exist in a social and political vacuum, but in a society which is criss-crossed by social divisions of all kinds in addition to that of "gender". These in their turn can affect women's experiences of biological events, and can possibly affect components of the biology itself. It is at the level of the lived experience of our biology that both the similarities and the differences between women become manifest. By way of example, consider the differences in the social views of upper- and working-class women in the mid-nineteenth century. Both (usually) menstruated, and in that sense, had something in common. Upper-class women were, as I noted earlier, treated as potential invalids for whom menstruation was supposed to be an insufferable burden, placing untold stress on their delicate frames. Menstruation, they were told, could not safely be combined with the strain of studying. Working-class women by contrast were presumed to have little trouble with menstruation—and, indeed, had to overcome any physical problems that they did face in order to earn their money. The biological events of menstruation were common to all women in one sense, but the ways in which they were experienced probably differed widely.

Having said that our experience of our biological selves should be considered in thinking about gender, I am in no way saying that I think that gender is largely a product of biological experience. The way in which we evaluate gender in a capitalist patriarchal society is rooted firmly in the social inequalities that characterise such a society. What I am saying, however, is that our concepts of gender should not be seen as purely social phenomena, but should admit biological experience. Perhaps more importantly, they should not be seen as something fixed and unchanging but as something that is continually being reconstructed. Our theories of gender construction need to take this possibility into account, rather than seeing gender as something acquired for ever in childhood.

What about the constraints discussed above? There is a sense in which admitting that biological experience can affect our experience of gender carries the implication that there will always be some kind of gender differentiation; after all, women but not men, menstruate and so forth. This might be considered some kind of constraint. However, gender differentiation does not have to mean gender division in the hierarchical sense in which we now understand it. And, of course, we cannot at present say anything about how that gender differentiation might be experienced—including the experience of biological events—in a different society. Looking at gender in this way allows that we can admit to experiencing our biological being, while seeing that as embedded in complex, interactive processes. These processes can change during the lifetime of the individual and can change between individuals over historical time, as the social and historical context of individual lives change. Our biology, however, does not determine anything.

6 On Female Nature

In this chapter I turn to another gender-related dichotomy, that of nature versus culture, a distinction which has become central to Western ideas about the natural world and about humanity's place within it. "Nature" is often regarded as somehow disorderly, chaotic and intractable; by contrast, our concept of "culture" has come to include the capacity for human mastery over nature. Science, too, is implicitly part of that distinction, for it is science that has long promised to give up mastery over our environment, to force nature to yield up "her" secrets. In the twentieth century, indeed, concepts such as "progress" and "culture" have become almost synonymous with those of science and technology.

Yet, despite our familiarity with it in the West, the nature-culture dichotomy is by no means as universal as is sometimes supposed. I shall begin this chapter by considering the ways in which the dichotomy arose, in relation to its association with gender. As I noted in Chapter One, the nature-culture dichotomy has historically been associated with gender in the sense that nature is usually thought of as female, while "culture" is considered to be much more of a masculine domain. An important connection for feminist analysis is thus the link between this conceptualisation of nature as female, and the oppression of women.[1] Not only is nature commonly thought of as female, but also women are somehow seen as closer to nature, and hence more likely to be dominated by the dictates of the "natural" instincts. In the first part of this chapter, I will outline recent feminist accounts of the rise of the nature/culture dichotomy. It is not, however, only women who suffer because of this dichotomy, and in the second part of the chapter I want to relate this historical development to contemporary concerns within the Women's Liberation Movement about the exploitation of nature and the environment as a whole.

The nature-culture dichotomy is so prevalent in contemporary Western thought that we tend to take it for granted without seriously beginning to challenge it. We tend to conceive of nature as somehow being "out there", something which humans can influence, rather than something of which we are part. It is important, then, to begin by reminding ourselves that this rigid dichotomy is in fact not so rigid after all: not all societies, for example, actually recognise a fundamental distinction between nature and human culture. Many societies thus see their culture as embedded in, and a significant part of, nature: the latter in turn may be portrayed as living in harmony with human society rather than being distinct from it.[2] This view of human society as embedded in living nature has, at times, inevitably come into conflict with the Western notion of nature's subservience to culture, perhaps most forcibly in the context of imperialist expansion. The beliefs of the Native American Indians thus conflicted with beliefs of their oppressors: one Sioux chief remarked, noting how nature itself changed with European conquest:

We did not think of the great open plains, the beautiful rolling hills, and winding streams with tangled growth as wild. Only to the white man was nature a wilderness and only to him was the land infested with wild animals and savage people. To us it was tame... Not until the hairy man from the east came and with brutal frenzy heaped injustices upon us and the families we loved was it wild for us. When the very animals of the forest began fleeing from his approach, then it was for us the Wild West began.[3]

Nature to the Sioux was thus not something wild or untamed, utterly opposed to human culture, but was something *in* which human society was felt to exist. Perhaps because of her alleged unpredictability, woman in the Western notion of nature versus culture is held to be part of that untamed, intractable nature. But, just as the opposition of nature and culture is not seen as such by all human societies, so the idea of woman as being embedded in nature is not culturally universal. Indeed, cross-cultural data tend to suggest that, rather than woman being "in" nature, women and men should both be seen as mediators between "nature and culture, in the reciprocity of marriage exchange, socialising children into adults, transforming raw meat and vegetables into cooked food, cultivating, domesticating, and making cultural products of all sorts".[4]

Furthermore, the nature-culture opposition as we now know it is not only culture-specific: it is also historically specific. In Medieval times, the idea that the earth was a living, sentient being with which humans could coexist rather than dominate was prevalent,[5] and even by the eighteenth and nineteenth centuries, long after the initial rise of modern science, the distinction was not inevitably one between an intractable nature and an utterly opposed human culture. Ludmilla Jordanova, writing about the history of these ideas, has stressed that the two were not conceptually in opposition at this time, but were thought of in terms of a dialectical relationship between the two that is, as culture changes nature, so it is itself transformed, and vice versa.[6] This emphasis on the reciprocity of nature and culture is much less evident today: "nature" has become subdued, and subordinated to culture, with little power to effect change. And, as this dichotomy hardened, so too did the associated stereotypes of gender.[7]

In part, the dichotomy between nature and culture and its association with gender stems from the ancient idea of a Great Chain of Being, which was the dominant theological view of organisms and nature for many centuries.[8] According to this, creation was arranged such that God was at the top of the chain, below him were the angels and other heavenly beings, then European man, then woman, and then the various species of animals known at the time, followed by the plants and so on, in a linear hierarchy. As Europeans spread out from the centre of the world that they knew, other human races that they discovered had to be fitted into the Chain—but always below European man who thought of himself as the pinnacle of earthly perfection. The notion of this scale, like that of the Ptolemaic universe[9] persisted: indeed, it persisted with little change well into the eighteenth century.[10]

Linear scales can, of course, be arbitrarily broken at any point into two parts, thereby creating dichotomies. Given that the Chain was, by definition, hierarchical, this in effect creates a division into a higher and a lower part. In this way, men could be portrayed as nearer to God, while women were closer to brute creation (i.e. nature). So much so, indeed, that Thomas

Aquinas gave much thought in his twelfth-century *Summa Theologica* to the vexed question of whether women had a soul at all!

All human societies use some form of classification in order to understand their world, and most use some form of binary system, with little or no overlap between the categories.[11] Ours is no exception, and there are many dichotomous classifications that we commonly use to structure understanding. What is noteworthy, however, is that many of them—at least in Western culture—are also hierarchical. Consider the following dichotomous pairs:

nature	culture
woman	man
non-European races	Europeans
animals	humans
working-class people	upper/middle class

What the items on the left have in common is that they are, or have been, associated in common parlance (and sometimes in scientific writing) with proximity to nature. In the nineteenth century, for example, much was made in eugenicist writing of the "lower classes" being unable to overcome their animal natures, and thus breeding like rabbits, or of the animal qualities of people of other races. According to one writer:

The careless, squalid, unaspiring Irishman, fed on potatoes living in a pig-stye, doting on a superstition, multiplies like rabbits or ephemera; the frugal, far-seeing, self-respecting Scot passes his best years in struggle and celibacy.[12]

Similar juxtaposition of the "lower classes" with animals, and hence with "nature", was employed by Lloyd Morgan, the animal psychologist, writing in 1885:

In every group of animals there should be lowly forms which have remained stationary while their fellows were becoming the winners in life's race; just as we see the poor, the weak, the unenlightened, and the unsuccessful living on beside the rich, the strong and the highly cultivated and the successful. And these lowly forms should retain features which are embryonic in the more highly developed forms; just as the less favoured individuals among us are apt to be childish and undeveloped.[13]

While many such dichotomies might be demonstrated in Western thought, it is important to note that associations tend to be made on one side of the dichotomy; thus, non-white people are associated with proximity to animals and to nature, an association all too frequently made in contemporary racist writing. I noted in Chapter Three the use made by defenders of slavery of the idea that black women had "animal-like" sexual passions; the proximity of black people to animals/nature is forcibly underlined, by the stress placed on slave breeding in antebellum America. As one (white) southern observer commended. ". . . as much attention is paid to the breeding and growth of negroes as to that of horses and mules. Further south, we raise them both for use and for market. . . A breeding woman is worth from one-sixth to one-fourth more than one that does not breed."[14]

In the way that these dichotomies remain strong in Western thought, the idea of a "Chain of Being" is clearly a persistent one. Even if it is less fashionable now to talk about "higher" and "lower" races of humanity, the notion that the living world can be divided by an evolutionary "scale" into higher and lower forms remains very prevalent, even in biological writing.[15] The Great Chain of Being may not be as central to our thought as it was to many in Medieval times, but it lingers on.

However, even in Medieval times, many kinds of ideas coexisted, just as at any time in history, and the Great Chain of Being was not the only way of conceptualising nature. Some ideas extant at any one time may wither and die, while others gain rapidly in credibility, eventually becoming the dominant ideas of the time. Still others fight a long-drawn-out battle. While the ideas inherent in the Great Chain of Being have indeed been significant in the history of Western thought, they have coexisted with other ideas about nature that were less compatible with the notions of hierarchical chains of creation reaching down from the omnipotent deity to the bowels of the earth. For instance, while the early Christian church was struggling to establish the idea of an omnipotent male god, there coexisted beliefs that the origin of creation was not male, but hermaphrodite, embracing both male and female principles in the universe. These beliefs coexisted with the gendered hierarchy promulgated by the Christian church for many centuries, and indeed were incorporated into some Christian writing—though the latter was condemned as heretical by the dominant church.[16]

Related to such ideas was the belief that the cosmos represented an organic unity, imbued with a feminine spirit.[17] Within this, the earth was seen as a nurturing mother, sensitive and alive, and capable of responding to human action; moreover, she was the living matrix that gave birth to all living things, including human beings. This belief was, it would seem, widely held during the Medieval and Renaissance periods. One significant consequence of it was that, if humans and all other living things are born from a living, breathing, and sentient earth, how then could tearing that earth apart on any large scale be justified? In some ways, it has been suggested, this belief acted for a time as a moral restraint, limiting such activities as mining for precious metals, on the grounds that it was akin to tearing into the living flesh of Mother Earth.[18] Veins of metal ore were portrayed in some writing of the time as equivalent to the Mother Earth's veins, which she had hidden deep so that her resources could not be exhausted by human greed.

These moral restrictions began to change, however, as human need—or greed—for metallic ore and other resources increased. The belief in a living, sentient Mother Earth began to give way to a more mechanistic conception of the cosmos. The rapidly expanding market economy of the early sixteenth century helped to create a new, more exploitative relationship with the earth and its produce: mining for minerals, for example, increased rapidly to meet expanding market needs, and crops were no longer grown principally for the use of small local communities, but increasingly for surplus production. Increasingly, too, technological interventions were employed in order to conquer the earth further, to extract more and more. Land not currently in use for agriculture or similar purposes came under pressure, and means were rapidly devised to reclaim it. If the land could be changed to meet the needs of the expanding market, then it mattered little what effect the changes had; as ecosystems were altered, animals, plants and many people were dispossessed of the land that had for centuries sustained them.[19]

For some time, though, this exploitative vision of nature coexisted with other, more organic and holistic, philosophies which emphasised the unity and harmony of the whole and of humanity's place within it. Writers such as Giordano Bruno (1584) and Thommaso Campanella (1602) wrote utopias extolling such organic philosophies;[20] these utopias, moreover, contained ideas that today we would call socialist, and for which their authors were respectively burned at the stake and imprisoned. Such cooperative philosophies, like their advocates, lost out in the end to the scientific, mechanistic view: not only was the latter actively encouraged by the emerging bourgeoisie, since it provided legitimation for their exploitation of natural and human resources, but there was considerable repression of whose who, like Campanella and Bruno, held alternative views.

That there have always been dissenting voices raised in opposition to the mechanistic view of nature is a theme to which I shall return in the next chapter. My concern here is to consider the changing ways in which nature "her" self has been portrayed, in opposition to human culture. Views of nature were changing dramatically during the period in which Campanella and Bruno were writing their utopias, giving way eventually to a conception of nature as "that realm on which mankind acts, not just to intervene in or manipulate directly, but also to understand and render it intelligible"[21] It has been suggested that this change led to two distinct positions: first, nature could be that part of the world that humans have already understood and mastered. But, second, it was also that part of nature that represented disorder and unreason—that which has not yet been penetrated and understood. To both of these are corresponding images of woman as nature. In the first place, Ludmilla Jordanova argues, women increasingly became seen as the repository of natural laws, swayed, for example, by the natural rhythms of menstruation and childbearing; but in the second place, they were seen as labile and unpredictable, just as wild, uncontrollable nature.[22]

Carolyn Merchant has also referred to this double-sided image of woman and of nature:

> The images of both nature and woman were two-sided. The virgin nymph offered peace and serenity, the earth mother nurture and fertility, but nature also brought plagues, famine and tempests. Similarly, woman was both virgin and witch: the Renaissance courtly lover placed her on a pedestal; the inquisitor burned her at the stake... Disorderly woman, like chaotic nature, needed to be controlled.[23]

One method of control that operated over several centuries was, Merchant suggests, the accusation and subsequent trial of large numbers of women on the grounds of witchcraft.[24] Slowly, the views of nature that emphasised cooperation and harmony came up against more and more challenges from the mechanistic world view. Where nature had once been seen as a living organism so, during the seventeenth and eighteenth centuries, it became increasingly seen as a machine, whose inner workings could be understood in terms of mechanical analogies. The human body, too, came to be seen as operating according to mechanical laws.[25] This change of perception went hand in hand with the rise of empiricism as a philosophy; that is the idea that, ultimately, we can only have knowledge of the world through the direct mediation of our senses.[26] Empiricism emphasises the largely passive role of the human observer, while mechanism lays stress on the mechanistic functioning of the observed nature. The result of such emphases has been an increasing belief in "objectivity"—the belief that we, the human observers, can dispassionately stand outside the things that we observe. Concomitantly, the subjectivity of both the observer and the observed has been lost.[27]

The rise of the mechanistic world view went hand in hand with dramatic changes in the nature-as-female metaphor. Where once nature had been seen as living, as the mother of creation, by 1700 the metaphor had changed to one of dominion and enslavement. It has been pointed out that this metaphor carried often aggressively sexual overtones, implications that female nature needed to be subject to rape-like force,[28] to enable men (sic) to tear her secrets from her. Discussions of the sexual metaphor commonly make reference to the writings of Francis Bacon, sometimes called the "father of modern science". In his perhaps aptly-named *The Masculine*

Birth of Time Bacon wrote of the need for the human mind to conquer nature by gaining knowledge about her: "I am come in very truth leading to you Nature with all her children to bind her to your service and make her your slave". Bacon appealed to all "true sons of knowledge" to "penetrate further", and thus find the way into her "inner chambers". Female nature was, in the face of such masculine prowess, coyly submissive.[29]

This emerging image—of nature as both a mindless submissive body, yet also a darker, disorderly character needing to be made submissive—provided the legitimation for the further exploitation of the earth made possible by rapidly expanding capitalist economies. But it did more than that: according to Carolyn Merchant:

> Not only did this new image function as a sanction, but the new conceptual framework of the Scientific Revolution—mechanism—carried with it norms quite different from the norms of organicism. The new mechanical order and its associated values of power and control would mandate the death of nature.[30]

The processes of the exploitation of the earth and the "death of nature" increasingly became consolidated during the nineteenth and twentieth centuries as a result of the emphasis on the mechanistic world view; and accordingly alternative, more harmonious views of nature came less and less to influence history. Above all, "nature" became increasingly opposed to "culture".

FEMINISM AND THE NATURE-CULTURE DUALITY

Given that the nature-culture duality has become associated with gender, it is not surprising that it has also become a topic of interest to feminism. Questions of how different cultures interpret concepts of gender, and of "nature" and "culture", have been discussed extensively by a number of feminist anthropologists, and there has been much controversy over the universality or otherwise of nature-culture oppositions.[31] However, I want here to consider the opposition of nature and culture in relation to twentieth-century science, and how contemporary feminism interprets this relationship.

Insofar as nature, including women, emerged in opposition

to culture, including science, then women's relationship to science is caught up in the values of the nature-culture duality. Most significantly, those values include gender, and it is no accident that science is seen as intrinsically masculine, not only in terms of who does science, but also in terms of the very values it espouses.[32] This "masculinity" of science has often been seen as one fundamental reason why women often opt out of science subjects at school; that "masculinity" is in conflict with the femininity to which women are stereotypically expected to aspire.[33]

The femaleness of nature, and its exploitation by scientific culture, has been a source of inspiration to some feminists, and has given rise to what has been dubbed "ecofeminism". Ecofeminism claims to be a marriage between the values of Women's Liberation and those of the ecology movement, and has gained considerably in strength during the early 1980s, particularly in relation to the various peace campaigns. In the remainder of this chapter I want to turn to three ways in which the changing ideas of nature and of culture discussed so far have become the focus of concern in ecofeminism. The first of these is a concern for exploited nature as a whole, expressed typically as a concern with environmental issues. Second, there is a concern for the plight of animals of other species and our relationship to them, which can be seen to have arisen historically from the mechanistic ideas already discussed. Third, is a belief that feminism, because of its commitment to "female" values, might provide some sort of salvation from the excesses of science as we now know it. This last is a belief which I shall criticise, since it is founded upon ideas of the intrinsic "femaleness" of nature, and of femininity as both intrinsic to women and fundamentally desirable. This kind of belief is little different from the ideas of biological determinism of which feminists have also been critical, as I shall argue.

At the beginning of the scientific revolution, the new science was hailed by some as a bringer of progress, a knowledge that would enable humanity to conquer nature and her disorder. That image of science as progressive has persisted, and there is still profound faith that "science" will ultimately do all kinds of wondrous things, perhaps even discovering that dream of the Medieval alchemists, the elixir of life.[34] It is, of course, true that twentieth-century science has brought us discoveries and inventions that have often been beneficial, such as the discovery of antibiotics, insulin to treat diabetes, and so on. But there has, during this century, been increasing awareness that science is not a smiling benefactor, but is Janus-like.[35] The other face of twentieth-century science is the one that produced nuclear bombs, pollution and wholesale destruction of the environment. It would be hard to define science as "progressive" if you were a Vietnamese villager on whom napalm was dropped or an Indian villager witnessing yet another drastic failure of a "scientifically improved" crop, or someone living close to Seveso or Bhopal.[36] You might also be extremely doubtful, if you were "Mother" Nature herself.

The rise of mechanism has served, as we have seen, to legitimate an exploitative view of the natural environment. Not only do we destroy vast tracts of land for commercially profitable enterprises, often with little direct benefit to humankind, but we extract from the earth what are essentially non-renewable resources such as coal, gas or petroleum, while returning to the earth little more than poisons. This was the context in which environmental concern grew, particularly in the late 1960s and early 1970s, when the need to struggle against things like environmental pollution became increasingly apparent within radical politics. This was also the context in which contemporary ideas of women's liberation were born.

Environmental issues have tended to have a doomsday quality, focussing on the risk of global catastrophe. At the beginning of the 1970s this took the form of predictions that the earth would soon run out of available resources or would become drastically over-populated.[37] In the 1980s the focus has more to do with the risk of nuclear war, and this latter focus has facilitated particularly the amalgamation of feminist and ecology politics.

To some extent, however, a concern with environmental issues has also become more broadly fashionable, a trend which might be said to devalue their radical potential. André Gorz has pointed out, in his book *Ecology as Politics*:

Ecology is like universal suffrage on the 40-hour week; at first, the ruling elite and the guardians of the social order regard it as subversive, and proclaim that it will lead to the triumph of anarchy and irrationality. Then, when factual evidence and popular pressure can no longer be denied, the establishment suddenly gives way—what was unthinkable yesterday becomes taken for granted today, and fundamentally nothing changes.[38]

He goes on to argue that the ecological movement should not be "an end in itself, but a stage in the larger struggle"—not least because of the power of contemporary capitalism to take on board arguments about ecological concerns and simply adapt itself to them.

Despite such adaptation, it has been claimed that more people are now aware of escalating militarism and threats of nuclear war, thus contributing to a groundswell of resistance. This groundswell has close connections with feminism, as Susan Griffin observed in her foreword to a collection of essays on feminism and ecology. She notes that the book is:

. . . a document of change. It is a cry of protest against the devastation of the earth. It gives evidence of a social movement whose size and depth we have only begun to imagine. It records a transformation in consciousness. And that this book has been edited and written by women is not irrelevant to this transformation. For women have long been associated with nature. And if this association has been the rationalisation of our oppression by a society which fears both women and nature, it has also meant that those of us born female are often less severely alienated from nature than are most men.[39]

"Ecofeminism" has thus begun to stress the associations between feminism and the broader exploitation of the environment, and to connect these to the association of nature and women. This association is stressed not only in terms of the nature-culture duality, but also in terms of women's connections to nurturing life through their role in reproduction. Ynestra King, an American ecofeminist who helped to organise a large meeting in response to the meltdown at the nuclear power station at Three Mile Island, emphasised this by asking:

Why women? Because our present patriarchy enshrines together the hatred of women and the hatred of nature. In defying this patriarchy we are loyal to future generations and to life and this planet itself. We have a deep and particular understanding of this both through our natures and through our life experience as women.[40]

That this association between women, nature and reproduction brings ecofeminism very close to arguing a form of biological determinism is a point which I shall argue a little later in this chapter.

Within ecofeminism, the opposition to militarism and the commitment to the broader peace movement are inevitably central in the face of nuclear proliferation. But it is also much broader than that, embracing a variety of ways in which nature is under threat. Women have been involved in struggles to protect the living environment against despoliation in many parts of the world. Anita Anand has described, for example, how a group of women in a remote village in northern India successfully resisted attempts to fell the forest around them, which for them was not only home, but resources: she described how the women were "doing an unusual thing. Hugging trees. They were resorting to Chipko, which means to hug, to prevent trees from being felled. With their arms wrapped around the tree, the women and children cried: 'the forest is our mother's home, we will defend it with all our might' ".

Feminist concern may extend not only to the environment in general, but also to specific kinds of organism within it. As I noted above in considering the continued viability of the idea of a Great Chain of Being, our society maintains a dichotomy between humankind and other animals. Although much is made at times of the similarities between us and other animals, humans are generally considered to be more important and superior to all other animal species. This division into humans versus the rest of nature had a long history of theological justification, followed by a justification in terms of ideas of mechanism; in turn, it has contributed to the exploitation of animals—in laboratories, in intensive farming, in the fur trade, and so forth—that many people find unacceptable. This exploitation too has been connected to ecofeminism.

One of the significant changes accompanying the scientific revolution was, as I noted earlier, the categorisation of nature in terms of mechanism; nature was to be understood, for many eighteenth-century writers, in terms of machine analogies.[42] As the scientific revolution progressed, the view of nature as dead inert matter—mere mechanism—become dominant over the view that humans could coexist harmoniously with other forms of life. For animals this meant that, being *part* of nature, they were consigned to the category of machines. What distinguished humanity from the rest of brute creation was the possession of a soul. This dualism did not allow for sentimental feelings towards animals: following Descartes' suggestion that animals were nothing but mechanism, one seventeenth-century woman is reported to have objected most strongly to the prospect of a dog as a pet on the grounds that "we want only rational creatures here, and belonging to the sect we belong to we refuse to burden ourselves with these machines".[43]

This view of animals as machines became absorbed into the values of the emerging sciences. During the eighteenth and nineteenth centuries, for example, many physiological experiments were conducted on living animals—long before the days of anaesthesia. The screams and howls of the tortured animals were assimilated to the concept of mechanism: the howls were merely the grinding of machinery. Even with the advent of clinical anaesthesia, little changed in the physiology labs: dogs and cats were still being nailed to boards and eviscerated while still alive. Indeed, some nineteenth-century physiologists, such as the Frenchman François Magendie, seemed positively to revel in the infliction of pain in experiments and demonstrations.[44]

In the face of such obvious cruelty, it is scarcely surprising that opposition to vivisection and other forms of animal cruelty grew during this period.[45] Significantly, this opposition was linked in the minds of many people to other forms of oppression, such as slavery and the oppression of women. Jeremy Bentham, the utilitarian philosopher, wrote in 1780:

> Why should the law refuse its protection to any sensitive being? The time will come when humanity will extend its mantle over everything which breathes. We have begun by attending to the condition of slaves; we shall finish by softening that of all the animals which assist our labours or supply our wants.[46]

Feminism and animal rights became explicitly linked in the late nineteenth-century. In her account of feminism during this period, Olive Banks has described how many feminists involved in the campaign for moral reform[47] were also involved in anti-vivisection campaigns, their interest being:

in part an expression of their concern for the weak and helpless. . . Moreover the anti-vivisection movement appealed particularly to women who were not only heavily represented in the membership but were even prominent in the leadership. Indeed Frances Power Cobbe, one of the most active of the anti-vivisectionists, was also an enthusiastic feminist who believed in women's suffrage as a means of raising the moral level of society. For her, feminism and the anti-vivisection movement were part of the same crusade.[48]

They remain part of the same crusade for some contemporary feminists, who see connections between the ways in which women and animals are subordinated in their proximity to exploited nature. One feminist writer suggested that "Perhaps the sympathy that many women feel towards animals is recognition of the mutual victimisation of both women and animals by men", and went on to observe that membership of many ecological or anti-vivisection groups is "made up predominantly of women".[49] Sympathy, however, may not be enough and it has also been argued that feminists *must* recognise and be aware of the suffering of other animals if they are to achieve the overthrow of patriarchy:

But if while aiming for this change (the overthrow of patriarchy) we do not become aware of the sufferings of non-humans, then I feel we will not have understood the concept of liberty. If we struggle to free ourselves, without realising that we are also crushing the most oppressed and exploited creatures on the planet, we can only fail.[50]

The concern for animal rights is thus seen as a logical extension of the more general feminist concern for nature or for less privileged human groups, all of whom are seen to share some features of oppression within patriarchal society.

So far I have outlined some of the ways in which the nature/women connection is maintained in the writings of contemporary ecofeminism. Ecofeminists have pointed to the exploitation of the environment that occurs with increasing frequency today, and have likened it to the exploitation of women. They have similarly drawn connections with the exploitation of animals. A concern for the fate of nature in general and of animals in particular is, I would agree, a valid concern for feminism. It does, however, present problems, with some of which I take issue. I would certainly agree that we need to consider carefully the question of how we use other species of animals, which is a theme I raise again in the final chapter when discussing the issue of a feminist science. On the other hand, this tends to be written about as though there are no fundamental points of disagreement. One problem I have with some of the writing in this vein is that it tends to suggest solutions that are largely based on individual choice, such as choosing vegetarianism.[51] Presumably if the whole world population did so, then humanity would exploit fewer animals; on the other hand, individual choices are not likely to effect much change globally. Perhaps a more significant problem with the discussion of our exploitation of animals is that "animals" often becomes synonymous with certain species of animal; this raises the vexed question of whether, if we deny the arbitrary division between humans and animals, we can or should erect such a division elsewhere. If it is wrong to kill an animal for its fur, then is it equally wrong to kill a slug because it is eating our vegetables? In practice, we do draw lines, and even most animal sympathisers are more sympathetic to vertebrate animals, especially mammals, than to invertebrates. While I agree with the general claim that the question of animal oppression in our society is related to other forms of oppression,[52] I also suspect that feminism will have to tackle the question of that arbitrary division. Among other things, that division will necessarily have to be confronted in the establishment of ideas of a more "feminist science".

Apart from the issue of animal rights, however, much ecofeminist writing seems to me to present problems of dualism, despite claims to the contrary. It is dualistic in the sense that it helps to perpetuate the nature-culture duality with which this chapter has been concerned. It does this by positing women's affinity with nature and the environment in relation to women's "special" attributes, writing about these as though they are essential, unchanging female characteristics. It is undoubtedly true that in contemporary society women are on average more likely to be nurturant, affiliative, and life-loving, but these qualities need not spring from some mysterious female essence. Writing about women's cooperativeness and so on as though they are eternally feminine traits is to invoke a form of biological determinism.[53] And once women's connections with nature are portrayed in this way, the female nature versus male culture dualism becomes fixed.

This is not to say, however, that ecological concerns are not of particular significance to women. The pollution of the environment can, for instance, be seen as of special concern to women because of women's role in reproduction. The connection here is that pollution can damage the unborn child, which can thus bring women particular anguish, through miscarriage or through giving birth to a malformed child. In this sense environmental issues are very much women's issues. In a poem entitled "A Micronesian Woman", Rosalie Bertell describes the anguish of a woman in the aftermath of radiation effects following the months of longing for her baby to be born:

My baby, the fruit of my womb—it had no face for me to kiss

Unheard my songs

No eyes; no hands

A bunch of grapes

My baby, the fruit of my womb—its heart beat furiously then stopped[54]

The risk of hazards to the foetus was similarly important to feminists organising in the aftermath of the explosion at the chemical works in Seveso, Italy. The dreadful tale of bureaucratic incompetence and deliberate lies that followed the explosion has been well documented, including the problems faced by pregnant women exposed to the highly toxic dioxin that was contaminating the atmosphere.[55] Abortions were difficult to obtain, and women had to face the often horrifying consequences of dioxin exposure. The Seveso feminist collective explains:

At the... dispensary, a woman confronts the psychiatrist, saying: "But what if I give birth to a deformed child?" The psychiatrist replied: "Come now madam, don't you know that abnormal children are often happier than other children?"... A Seveso woman gives birth to a dead child without a brain. Doctors declare that dioxin has nothing to do with it. Any woman who wants a legal abortion has to go through unbelievable tribulations... This is how Maria Chinni died... she did not go to the dispensary with its reactionary gynaecologists. Maria was the sole breadwinner for herself, her sick husband and two children. She tried to induce an abortion by swallowing a substance that was supposed to poison the foetus. Dreading the legal consequences of her action, like all the women in her situation, she was only taken to hospital when already in a coma.[56]

Insofar as women are indeed the reproducers of life, those who bring life into the world, then women should be concerned about any potential contaminant. The danger of assuming biological determinism lies not in recognising the special concern to women arising from their reproductive role, but in assuming that women innately have special qualities arising from that role. These special qualities of women are sometimes counterposed to the death-loving qualities of men. Simone de Beauvoir made such an opposition in *The Second Sex,* in which she referred to women as the sex that brings forth life and to men as the sex which kills.[57] This kind of opposition is, more recently, taken even further by Mary Daly who argues, in *Gyn/Ecology* that patriarchal society is wholly necrophiliac, loving to kill, in various ways, both women and nature.[58]

Not all feminist writers would agree, of course, that the dualism resides in innate, determined qualities. Ruth Wallsgrove, for example, wrote about the masculine contempt for life as a product of male socialisation:

I believe that in controlling women for material benefits men have come to despise the one indisputable difference between men and women—the reproduction of human beings in women's bodies—as part of the ideology of male supremacy. Reproducing children necessarily entails caring and a respect for life; and in despising reproduction men have come to be contemptuous of caring, and careless with life. The ultimate in contempt for life is war: it's very "manly" to kill without anger, without even noticing.[59]

Nevertheless, the implication remains in some ecofeminist writing that "nature" is women's special concern because of women's inbuilt sympathies. While it might be comforting to think that characteristics that most people would agree are desirable, such as cooperativeness and nurturance, are biologically determined, it remains a dangerous thought. It is dangerous partly because, as we have seen, biological determinism is frequently used to justify women's oppression in various ways. It is also dangerous because the other side of the coin is that men's capacity for aggression and warfare might, by implication, also be biologically determined. And, as I have argued throughout this book, the implication of that is that it cannot be changed.

Yet, despite the limits to change implied by the biological assumptions, ecofeminism has been said by some writers to herald change. The mechanistic view of nature outlined in this chapter has always had opponents, and in one sense, ecofeminism can be seen as the latest source of opposition. But it has also been portrayed as more than simply opposition. In the next chapter I will turn to some of the ways in which mechanism has been opposed, and will outline some of the views put forward by two writers who consider ecofeminism to provide some sort of salvation, a hope for the future.

7 Feminism as a Herald of Change?

Feminism's opposition to the exploitation of nature is perhaps not surprising in view of cultural associations between women and nature. It is not, of course, only contemporary feminism that has opposed such exploitation; the mechanistic science that is now dominant in our culture has had philosophical and political opposition from its inception, emerging but slowly from competition with other, more organic and holistic views of nature. But gain ascendancy it did, not least because it served the interests of those in power. In this chapter my major concern is to address the recent suggestion that the conjunction of ecology and feminist movements in the 1970s and 1980s is bringing change in that mechanistic world view. Those who have made that suggestion, such as Hazel Henderson and Fritjof Capra,[1] see evidence of dramatic ideological change accompanying this conjunction which, they believe, heralds hope for the future—hope, that is, of a more peaceful and harmonious relationship to nature and to each other.

Whether or not there is any evidence of such a change arising out of feminism is a question that I shall address later in the chapter. I want to begin, however, by considering briefly some of the historical background to the ideological changes emphasised in ecofeminist writing. My reason for doing this is to show, albeit briefly, that the ideas currently receiving attention do have historical antecedents; they have not arisen *de novo* in the context of contemporary ecological concerns. This is not to say, of course, that the ideas of earlier epochs or the opposition to them are the same as those of today. My intention is simply to indicate that those ideas to which we might now take exception do have a history of opposition. Given that history, one question which might be addressed is why—if Henderson and Capra are correct about the conjunction of ecology and feminism—should significant ideological change be occurring *now*? Why have earlier forms of opposition failed? The latter is a particularly difficult question and is one that I possibly cannot answer. Nonetheless, it should be borne in mind when considering the notion that we are presently witnessing an ideological revolution.[2]

Current ecofeminism—and particularly the ideas put forward by Henderson and Capra—generally takes exception to presently dominant ideas of mechanism, fixity, and competition. Instead it tries to argue an anti-reductionist, anti-mechanistic viewpoint emphasising, for example, cooperation in nature rather than competition, change and transformability rather than fixity. In the previous chapter I noted how the exploitative vision of nature that emerged with mechanism coexisted for a time with other, more organic philosophies—philosophies that also argued for transformability, cooperation and harmony with nature. Why, then, did mechanism finally emerge triumphant? Or, why did the alternative philosophies lose out in the end? One possible answer is to suggest that the mechanistic framework offered answers that were somehow more true than their predecessors. Certainly, the new scientific method associated with the rise of mechanism offered considerable predictive power that gave it great advantage over the mysticism often associated with its rivals. In that sense, it was more "true". But a more significant reason why mechanism won was that its predictive power facilitated greater and greater exploitation of nature: as Carolyn Merchant notes:

The philosophy that the world was a vast machine made of inert particles in ceaseless motion appeared at a time when new and more efficient kinds of machinery were enabling the acceleration of trade and commerce . . . . Mechanism substituted a picture of the natural world which seemed to make it more rational, predictable, and thereby manipulable.[3]

In other words, seeing nature as merely mechanism allowed it to be exploited more directly.

Not only did the mechanistic philosophy serve to justify nature's exploitation by the classes in power, but also the alternative philosophies were, during the seventeenth century associated, in the minds of those holding the power, with the various dissident (and thereby potentially dangerous) groups of the period. It has been argued that the processes of rapid economic development accompanied by the English civil war contributed to the formation of such dissident groups, many of whom were propertyless and saw their dissidence in terms of some sort of class struggle.[4] The social order generally advocated by such groups was largely one of social equality and classlessness, gender equality and non-hierarchy. Moreover, their view of humanity's relationship to nature was largely founded upon the organic, holistic interpretation deriving from Medieval organicism. They saw nature in terms of its relationships rather than machine analogies and, ultimately, in terms of its transformability.[5] One historian of the period has argued:

that the philosophy and methods of the Hermeticists and other occult schools of the civil war era were based on a dialectical approach to reality. That is to say, entities and relationships were not viewed statically, but as in a perpetual process of development. This perpetual development was seen to occur primarily because every entity and relationship, in itself, was inconsistent, contained within itself its own opposite.[6]

How different this was from the mechanistic world view that saw nature as a series of mechanisms, fixed and winding down like clocks! The struggle was not, then, entirely one between sets of ideas, but also between the people who held them. Mechanism became supreme, and remained so, because it served the interests of the propertied classes; and organicism was actively suppressed because it was espoused by political radicals advocating the abolition of class and property ownership. Isaac Newton was apparently aware of this tension between the opposing viewpoints and who held them and, although his earlier work was greatly influenced by the mysticism and organicism of the alternative frameworks, his later writing began to emphasise the stability of nature implied by the mechanistic view. Possibly this showed his shrewdness rather than any change of mind, indicating "Newton's greater awareness of just how dangerous were the social implications of the hermetic aspects of his philosophy".[7]

Mechanism thus grew up with considerable opposition, opposition which was associated, just as it often is now, with political dissent from the prevailing social order. The view of nature often associated with such dissenting groups was one in which the wholeness and complexity of the natural world was stressed, in which humanity's part was more cooperative than exploitative. Ideas of the transformability of nature, rather than its fixity, were, too, part of the organic world view, in which change was held to be a significant part of the workings of the universe.[8] "Reality was thus defined", notes Carolyn Merchant, "in terms of activity and process. Cosmic unity was maintained through the coming together and dissolution of opposites." Such philosophy "emphasised the harmony of the whole, pointing out that an organic whole is more than the sum of its parts".[9] The holism and anti-mechanism stressed by contemporary ecology movements is clearly not entirely new.

The beliefs in mechanism and fixity that served to justify economic expansion during the seventeenth and eighteenth centuries did, however, meet with problems in the nineteenth century in the form of theories of evolution. Evolution implied a concept of change. In the sense that it implied that historical change was possible, and that therefore immutable mechanism could not be relied upon to justify existing social organisation, then Darwinian theory could be seen as in principle working against ruling-class interests.[10] On the other hand, Darwinian evolution was in practice accommodated to the ideology of hierarchy implied by the Great Chain of Being: evolution could then be viewed as movement towards perfection. Perfection, in turn, became construed as white, middle-class and male. This was, of course, the interpretation of evolution that gave rise to social Darwinism, with its emphasis on "survival of the fittest", the superiority of men over women, of Europeans over other races, and of the educated middle class over the "teeming hordes of degenerates" among the working class.[11] Perhaps not surprisingly, it is the emphasis on competition and evolution towards perfection that have come down to us as popular concepts of evolutionary theory. Images of "nature red in tooth and claw" abound in popular nature books as a result. Competition has also become the cornerstone of right-wing rhetoric, in which competitive "human nature" is portrayed as the basis of selfishness and greed—as well as of capitalism itself. "The growth of a large business", wrote John D. Rockefeller in 1900, "is merely the working out of a law of nature and of God".[12] A competitive human nature, coupled with ideas of survival of the fittest, increasingly became central to capitalism's defence of its own existence.

All of these ideas have had their opposition. Perhaps the most familiar are the criticisms of the eugenicist ideas contained in social Darwinism.[13] But Darwinism did not only engender notions of competition; some critics of social Darwinism attacked prevalent notions of competition by using evolutionary ideas in alternative ways. Writing in 1889 about Darwinism and its relationship to socialism, D. G. Ritchie took issue with some popular notions of the time concerning Darwinism and suggested that cooperation might evolve at the social level out of initial competition—in other words, that cooperative behaviour was a more advanced or more highly evolved form:

International arbitration and economic cooperation are as yet small beginnings, but not smaller than the first germs of representative government. So far as we have yet got, neither arbitration nor cooperation have done for society what their advocates hoped, but they may be the first "variations" which, if they prove their fitness, will bring into being a new species of civilised society.[14]

An alternative form of opposition to competition took the form of arguing that competition simply was not as central to the balance of nature as Darwinists often supposed it to be. This was the line taken, for example, by the anarchist Peter Kropotkin, who published his book *Mutual Aid* in 1902. In it, he argued that cooperation between animals was actually more important in enhancing the survival of the species than was competition, and stressed:

how false is the view of those who speak of the animal world as if nothing were to be seen in it but lions and hyenas plunging their bleeding teeth into the flesh of their victims. One might as well imagine that the whole of human life is nothing but a succession of war massacres. Association and mutual aid are the rule with mammals.[15]

Opposition to the prevailing orthodoxy of science, and to mechanism as an explanatory framework for the universe, clearly has a history. The emphasis placed by ecology movements upon cooperation, holism, transformation and so forth derives not only from opposition to contemporary exploitation and despoliation of the environment, but also from earlier ideas of the universe as an organic whole. The dominant mechanistic views became dominant, however, at least partly because of the ways in which they served class interests (and inevitably the interests of men), and it is thus not surprising that the strands of opposition have tended to come from people also opposed to the existing social order. In this sense, current feminist opposition to the structure and assumptions of twentieth-century science has a logical and honourable history.

Contemporary feminism has, as I noted in the previous chapter, become associated with ecological and holistic views of nature, and it is in this conjunction of feminism and ecology concerns that some writers have seen hope for, or even evidence of, progressive social change, a vision to which I will now turn. Carolyn Merchant, for instance, in her book *The Death of Nature* concludes her analysis of the oppression of both women and nature with the suggestion that:

> The conjunction of conservation and ecology movements with women's rights and liberation has moved in the direction of reversing both the subjugation of nature and women .... Today the conjunction of the women's movement with the ecology movement again brings the issue of liberation into focus .... Socialist feminist and "science for the people" groups worked towards revolutionizing economic structures in a direction that would equalize male and female work options and reform a capitalist system that creates profit at the expense of nature and working people.[16]

The problem with this conclusion is that she neither suggests how such change might be achieved[17] nor suggests what the evidence is for a *reversal* of previous subjugation. Many other feminists would not agree that the subjugation of either women or nature showed any signs of reversal: indeed, with the rise of the "New Right" in Western politics and increasing escalation of the arms race, there is more evidence that the subjugation of both is being augmented.

The genre of feminist writing on which I based the discussion in the previous chapter has emphasised the ostensibly "feminine" values of nurturance, cooperation and non-hierarchy if we are to achieve a more just and humane society. Some writers have taken this further and, like Merchant, have suggested that Western society *is already* moving towards such an ideological shift. In this shift, these writers see hope for the planetary future.

One significant source of a shift in values is seen to lie in science itself. Even if much of biology has remained steadfastly reductionist and mechanistic, at least some areas of physics have had to move away from such assumptions: once you enter the realms of the atom, nature is no longer so predictable or manipulable. Some of the contributors to the feminist anthology *Reclaim the Earth* refer, for example, to this shift of values in physics away from the deterministic model of Newtonian mechanics towards a conception of nature that follows from contemporary quantum physics, in which uncertainty and unpredictability are stressed.[18] Moreover, contemporary quantum physics has had to contend with the rather disturbing idea that the observing human cannot stand passively outside nature, but inevitably interacts with the atomic world being studied. One of the *Reclaim the Earth* contributors, Lin Simonon, notes that the Newtonian world view has:

been superseded by the recognition, through quantum physics and the development of the science of ecology, that our universe is an interplay of dynamic natural forces, energies which flow, bounce and weave their way through reality. We now see ourselves as part of nature, part of a wonderful, intricate, fragile yet resilient web of interconnections. This view is non-linear, non-hierarchical, multi-dimensional, curved, organic and feminine in foundation.[19]

Hazel Henderson writes similarly about the hope for the future emanating from what she terms the "coming synthesis of Eco-philosophy and Eco-feminism". She writes about how a number of ideas are emerging that imply a less deterministic vision of nature, suggesting that:

We need no longer bound our imagination with the dismal deterministic view of a universe winding down like a closed system. In fact, Cartesian science's search for certainty, equilibrium, predictability and control is a good definition of death. We should happily embrace the new view that uncertainty is fundamental, since it also implies that everything can change—for the better—in a twinkling of an eye.[20]

Hazel Henderson also sees alternative ideas emerging from "the world's ethnic and indigenous people, from subsistence cultures and traditional wisdom; from the world's women and from the rising female principle, whose nurturant energies can be seen in the new breed of gentle-men".[21] These ideas are, she implies, evidence that progressive cultural change is occurring: although there is opposition from the New Right and other sources to feminist demands, these are unlikely to overcome the rising culture. She suggest for example that:

Fear overcomes the Politics of the Last Hurrah, Reaganomics, and the Moral Majority's attempts to put women back in the kitchen, gay people back in the closet, blacks and hispanics back at the end of the line. Yet the genie will not go back in the bottle. The cultural revolution has already occurred . . . .Even more terrifying for the old patriarchs and their female dupes is the knowledge that the whole culture is "up for grabs".[22]

Another, similarly optimistic, writer who has described the "rising culture" and the influence on it of feminism is Fritjof Capra. In his book *The Turning Point*, he argues that a new age is emerging from a number of transitions which he believes are currently taking place. Among these he includes the decline in fossil fuels, which he believes will mark the transition to a "solar age, powered by renewable energy from the sun; a shift that will involve radical changes in our economic and political system." The second transition he believes is occurring is what may be termed a "paradigm shift"—a "profound change in the thoughts, perceptions and values that form a particular vision of reality".[23] For Capra, this includes a decline in the belief that scientific method offers the only reliable way of understanding the world, and in the belief that the universe is deterministic. Like Hazel Henderson, he bases this upon a consideration of the shifts that have occurred in contemporary physics, which he suggests will undermine, if they have not begun to do so already, the deterministic, mechanistic, model of nature.

The third transition that Capra notes is the influence of feminism, which he believes is contributing to the "slow and reluctant but inevitable decline of patriarchy . . . . Today, however, the disintegration of patriarchy is in sight. The feminist movement is one of the strongest cultural currents of our time and will have a profound effect on our further evolution".[24] Capra refers to the rise of forces of anti-feminism as part of the

declining culture. They are in the process of disintegration. The social movements of the 1960s and 1970s represent the rising culture, which is now ready for passage to the solar age. While the transformation is taking place the declining culture refuses to change, clinging ever more rigidly to its outdated ideas; nor will the dominant social institutions hand over their leading roles to the new cultural forces .... As the turning point approaches, the realisation that evolutionary changes of this magnitude cannot be prevented by short-term political activities provides our strongest hope for the future.[25]

It is undoubtably tempting for feminists to think of feminism as one of the strongest cultural currents of our time, capable of bringing about dramatic cultural change; and to think of anti-feminism as a mere force of reaction against this rising tide. But there is, unfortunately perhaps, no evidence to suggest that any such cultural change is occurring; if anything, the forces of anti-feminism seem ever more entrenched and the gains of women's liberation have begun to recede. Moreover, the kind of vision expounded by Henderson and Capra is essentially a passive one, in which humans have no agency.[26] Eventually, it is implied, the repression achieved by anti-feminism will be swept away by the irresistible force of cultural change. Feminists need, it would seem, to do no more than persuade everyone else by power of argument of the wisdom of the solar age.[27]

But this is not what the Women's Liberation Movement is about. While it is, partly, involved in challenging patriarchal ideology—and thus acting at the ideological or cultural level—it is also about political action, active struggles to achieve change, the change that comes from human engagement with history. Indeed, it is basic to the beliefs of WLM feminism that ideological change *alone* is not likely to be brought about in the absence of more active political struggle.[28] This necessity is just as true for ecofeminism and the peace movement as it is elsewhere in the women's liberation movement: the attempts to blockade the air bases at places such as Greenham Common is one example. Waiting for feminist cultural change is unlikely to remove the missiles.

The most fundamental criticism I have of this kind of vision is, then, that it implies a largely passive shift in values and implies also that this shift is already taking place, and owes much to the impetus of feminism. I have to confess to finding this kind of optimism rather hard to swallow in Britain in the

1980s, at a time when many of the gains made by women during the 1970s have been eroded. I can find little evidence for Hazel Henderson's assertion that "the genie will not go back into the bottle. The cultural revolution has already occurred". The passivity implied in such a vision is also dangerous; not only is there the suggestion that the New Right is fighting a "rearguard action"—with the implication that they are accordingly losing ground to the "rising culture"—but when political action is suggested it too is dangerous in its naivety. Consider, for example, the suggestion made by Henderson following her statement that "the whole culture is 'up for grabs' ":

> it (the whole culture) could shift fundamentally in less than a generation *if* women simply took back their reproductive rights, endowed by biology and Nature. All that women would need to do to create a quiet revolution is to resume the old practice of concealing the paternity of their children . . . . Thus, male-dominated families, institutions of inheritance, property rights in wives and children would be undermined. Accumulation of great landholdings and estates would be less likely. Land trusts and different, more consensual democratised families and social groups might emerge. Children, in whatever group setting they were raised, would have rights as persons, rather than being "legitimised" by a marriage contract . . . . Already, the nuclear family is becoming a lost cause.[29]

Apart from the rather large assumption that property rights and so forth would necessarily be democratised by the denial of paternity, the suggestion for action hinges on a very big "if". We could see, Henderson suggests, dramatic changes very rapidly *if* women concealed paternity. Perhaps we would—although I somehow doubt that the suggestion is a viable one. Apart from the wishes of individual women living in particular relationships who might be unwilling to conceal paternity, such action is probably more likely to result in an intensification of women's oppression than in its amelioration. It certainly ignores the possible effects of reproductive technology which could well be used to ensure paternity.[30]

However, although these alternative visions can be criticised for their assumptions and political passivity, they *are* presented as radical alternatives, as utopian visions, and in that sense there may be things that we can learn from them. The final chapter of this book is concerned with another kind of vision, that of creating a "feminist science" and there is, I would suggest, much that might be of value to such a vision in these holistic and ecological alternatives. They do also indicate some features of the kind of science towards which we might wish to strive. In the remainder of the chapter I will consider some of the features of the suggested "paradigm shift" that a more "feminist science" might wish to retain. Although presented as a novel paradigm shift, it will be evident that—in some senses at least—these features bear resemblance to the earlier forms of opposition to mechanism with which the chapter began.

The first component to which several authors refer is the paradigm shift that has occurred in contemporary physics, which they see as the prototype for similar changes that will occur in other branches of science. Classical Newtonian physics (and, indeed, classical science in general) makes certain assumptions about the world. It assumes, for example, that we can describe objectively the things of which nature is made; that we can eventually specify the causes, at lower levels, of specified events; that what we are describing has an abstract and possibly timeless reality "out there", apart from us. As physicists began to explore the atomic and subatomic world in the early years of this century, however, they found that these time-honoured assumptions began to fail them. As Capra explains: "physicists faced, for the first time, a serious challenge to their ability to understand the universe. Every time they asked nature a question in an atomic experiment, nature answered with a paradox, and the more they tried to clarify the situation, the sharper the paradoxes became".[31] What they found instead was that, at the level of the subatomic world, it simply was not possible to define unambiguously what or where the "things" within the atom were; it was no longer possible to define antecedent causes, since the subatomic world could only be described in terms of probabilities. Electrons had to be accepted as both waves *and* particles at the same time. And perhaps most shocking of all to the world of classical science was the suggestion that quantum physics could no longer assume objective reality apart from the human experiencing of it; in a sense, what this meant was the realisation that how the scientist interprets the state of the atom at the beginning of the experiment or observation affects the final results. In short, there is no such thing as an independent observer who can watch nature without influencing it.

Realisations such as these shook physics up in the 1920s and 1930s. Heisenberg, discoverer of the Uncertainty Principle[32] described the lengthy and soul-searching conversations between himself and fellow physicists, remarking that "we fully realised how difficult it would be to convince even leading physicists that they must abandon all attempts to construct perceptual models of atomic processes".[33] So indeterminate was atomic structure that the human mind could not model it. One leading physicist who, at the time, found the concept of indeterminacy difficult to accept was Einstein, who refused, for a while at least, to accept that "God was playing dice with the universe".

This component of the paradigm shift is seen by writers such as Fritjof Capra and Hazel Henderson as significant precisely because it emphasises indeterminacy, because it blurs the subject-object distinction and because, in some ways, it is not reductionist but holistic. Notions of cause no longer run upwards from the lowest levels, as one theoretical physicist described:

According to the new view, the complete description of nature at the atomic level was given by probability functions that referred, not to underlying space-time realities, but rather to the macroscopic objects of sense experience. The theoretical structure did not extend down and anchor itself on fundamental microscopic space-time realities. Instead it turned back and anchored itself in the concrete sense realities that form the basis of social life . . . . This pragmatic description is to be contrasted with descriptions that attempt to peer "behind the scenes" and tell us what is "really happening".[34]

Reductionism, determinism, and the subject-object distinction are all distinctive features of classical science, and they are all features that have led to criticism of science. For that reason, the challenges that quantum physics poses to conventional ways of thinking about nature might indeed be a way forward, a way of beginning to think about a "new science", a point to which I will return in the next chapter.

A second suggested component of the paradigm shift is an increasing tendency to see nature in terms of transformability and interconnectedness. For Fritjof Capra, there is evidence of this in recent ideas of the capacity for self-organisation shown by organisms as well as by some chemical systems.[35] That is, the dynamics of an entire system can produce emergent levels of organisation that could not be predicted from a knowledge of the component parts (as reductionism would assume). Capra takes up the suggestion that evolution might be better understood in terms of the dynamics of self-organising systems;[36] that is, rather than the classical Darwinist perspectives of evolution, which emphasise chance events and their natural selection, Capra refers to the idea that evolution

represents an unfolding of order and complexity that can be seen as a kind of learning process, involving autonomy and freedom of choice.... Evolution is an ongoing and open adventure that continually creates its own purpose in a process whose detailed outcome is inherently unpredictable .... Its characteristics include the progressive increase of complexity, coordination, and interdependence; the integration of individuals into multi-levelled systems; and the continual refinement of certain functions and patterns of behaviour.[37]

Hazel Henderson sees similar evidence for a changing perspective in the ideas of formative causation put forward by Rupert Sheldrake. These ideas, too, address the transformability of nature, though Sheldrake's ideas are the subject of considerable controversy. The basic idea of formative causation is that biological form may be influenced across space and time by the development of similar forms; thus, for example, the form of a tadpole may be influenced across space and time by the form of all other tadpoles past and present of the same species.[38] Not surprisingly, the reaction of the scientific community to such ideas of amorphous influences was to heap scorn.

Hazel Henderson, however, finds the idea of formative causation greatly exciting because, among other things, it allows for the possibility that learning may be influenced across space and time. She refers to Sheldrake's ideas as:

research which can be interpreted to imply that species as a whole can learn from the isolated innovation of any small group. Imagine the new potentialities if learning is proved to be contagious! We would have a new scientific basis for believing in ourselves and in our collective power to pull back from the disastrous brink.[39]

Whatever one thinks of Sheldrake's hypothesis (and I for one remain sceptical—although to be fair, the hypothesis could be, but has not been, properly tested),[40] Henderson's refinement is overly optimistic once again. Even if formative causation were shown to exist in fact, Sheldrake's description is of a somewhat blind force that has the potential to influence but need not necessarily do so. More to the point, the fact of its existence need not imply that we could consciously direct it, still less in any particular direction. Outrageous though some have called the idea, Sheldrake does only suggest that formative causation might possibly explain the rapid cultural transmission of some learned traits. The question of which traits and under what circumstances is left open.

Whether or not such ideas are right, what both Henderson and Capra are arguing for is a scientific framework based on concepts such as the interdependence and interconnectedness of phenomena and events within nature, which they counterpose to the fragmented, deterministic world view that has characterised science hitherto. These ideas, I shall argue, are important to the kind of science towards which feminism might move. What I would take issue with, however, is the implication that the existence of such ideas is evidence of a paradigm shift. Granted, these "alternative" kinds of ideas are around, and are commonly opposed to reductionist science.[41] But does their existence necessarily imply a "paradigm shift" in the manner intended? Capra refers to paradigm shifts in the sense in which Kuhn used the term to describe revolutions occurring in science.[42] To be part of a paradigm shift, in the Kuhnian sense,[43] we should have to be witnessing changes in the way that most people view nature; it is only when people begin to be convinced of the value of new ways of thinking that the "revolution" can be said to have occurred. But exciting though the new ideas are, it is doubtful that they have a wide enough following for a paradigm shift to be discerned. Alternative ideas have existed before, as I have noted, yet did not necessarily result in major ideological shifts. The existence of such ideas does not mean their dominance.

A third significant component of the changes to which Henderson and Capra allude is the move away from the emphasis on competition as the motor of evolutionary history. Darwinism has laid great stress on competition between organisms, and there is no doubt that evidence for competition between organisms or species exists. Nonetheless, as a number of writers have pointed out, this is not the only—and perhaps not necessarily the primary—mechanism of evolutionary change.[44] For the first half of this century, it has been pointed out, the science of ecology viewed interspecific competition as one mechanism among many, and it was not until the 1950s and 1960s that ideas began to change, and ideas of competition and scarcity came increasingly to the fore. Michael Gross and Mary Beth Averill have called this stress on competition an instance of a "patriarchal myth" in biology, on the grounds that they perceive it largely as a myth for which there is little evidence, and as a myth which reinforces patriarchal images of nature as there for exploitation.[45] They discuss the concept of "competition" as it is used in the ecological literature, and point out how frequently the concept is confounded by biologists and lay people alike with actual combat. To illustrate this point, they cite a popular article on ecology, written in 1980, which describes the spread of grasses by likening it to:

... guerilla warfare. At its leading edge, a large (system of runners) extensively interconnected, presents an array of advanced raiders, each provisioned by an elaborate logistic network occupying already conquered terrain. The tactical advantage of this competitive strategy depends upon . . . the supply lines.[46]

What graphic detail of military tactics! As Gross and Averill point out, however, much of the evidence for actual competition between organisms is rather ambiguous,[47] and frequently overstated. They refer instead to the possibility that nature operates, contrary to the image of nature red in tooth and claw, along more cooperative lines as suggested by, for example, Peter Kropotkin. This possibility is, they suggest, central to the way in which a feminist view of evolution and ecology might view nature. There is, as Kropotkin quite rightly noted, a great deal of evidence to indicate that "mutual aid" is widespread among animals; it might, moreover, be a creative force in evolution: Gross and Averill ask:

when we turned the concept of scarcity upside down we found plenitude and opportunity as the condition for innovation. Why not see nature as bounteous, rather than parsimonious, and admit that opportunity and cooperation are more likely to abet novelty, innovation and creation than are struggle and competition? Evolution in this perspective can be seen not as a constant struggle for occupation and control of territory but as a successive opening of opportunities, each new mode of biological organization providing a new opportunity for still more diverse forms of life—new sources of food, new habitats, new means of dispersal.[48]

They also suggest that a feminist theory of evolution will need to look carefully at the concept of scarcity in nature which, they argue, has been the only, if somewhat ineffective, brake on unbridled exploitation. The concept of scarcity produces an ethic of conservation for future use which is "essentially selfish and pragmatic—fully in tune with the spirit of capital accumulation" precisely because it seeks to conserve only for further exploitation, and not because of any finer appreciation of nature. A feminist viewpoint would, they suggest, mean:

appreciating it for its own sake rather than for what can be wrenched from it: it means opening ourselves to experiencing it, learning from it, and concerning ourselves with *maintaining its integrity*. From that will follow conserving values such as minimal use of non-renewable resources, minimal tampering with the environment, and careful attention to the myriad interactions that result from any invasive act.[49]

Each of these authors has stressed that a feminist approach to ecology would emphasise concepts such as cooperation and interdependence, and would see humanity as embedded in, rather than dominating, nature. All of these ideas could well become part of a more "feminist science", and I shall draw upon them again in the final chapter. But the focus upon the ideas of Henderson and Capra was not only to do with the alternative vision of nature that they expound; it was also to do with the suggestion that we are currently witnessing a profound shift in values arising in part from the conjunction of feminism and ecology movements.

What remains unexplained is why such a shift of values should happen now: what historically specific conditions made it possible in the 1970s and 1980s but denied it in earlier generations? As I have indicated earlier, the holistic ideas about the earth and nature stressed by these writers have historical antecedents. Similarly, there have been earlier waves of feminism, periods in which women were actively struggling against their oppression. What is unique about the present time in the views expressed by Henderson and Capra is the conjunction of the two: ecology and a holistic framework have become, they suggest, specifically feminist issues.[50]

While I remain unconvinced that there is a profound shift of values of the kind envisaged, the suggestion that developing a "holistic" framework *is* a feminist issue is an important one. It is clear that the mechanistic, reductionist approach to nature that hitherto has generally characterised science is leading towards a very partial understanding which in turn facilitates our society's continued exploitation of both the environment and people. It is also clear that, if we want to reverse that system of exploitation, we will have to think about nature and science in different ways. Rita Arditti summed up the need for a more liberatory science thus:

Today, in science we know "more and more" about "less and less". Science as an instrument of wealth and power has become obsessed with the discovery of facts and the development of technologies. The emphasis on the analytic method as the only way of knowing has led to a mechanistic view of nature and human beings . . . . The task that seems of primary importance—for women and men—is to convert science from what it is today, a social institution with a conservative function and a defensive stand, into a liberating and healthy activity. Science needs a soul which would show respect and love for its subjects of study and would stress harmony and communication with the rest of the universe.[51]

Whether or not one agrees with the suggestion that feminism is already bringing about change, that "science needs a soul which would show respect and love" is something which few feminists would dispute. It is that soul which should permeate feminist science, a theme to which I will now turn.

8 Towards a Feminist Science

Much of this book has been concerned with the various ways in which feminists have been critical of the assumptions, structure and practice of existing science. A problem with criticism alone, however, is that it leaves something of a vacuum: if we do not like existing science, what is it that we are trying to put in its place? In this chapter I want to address some of the issues that have been raised by feminist writers about the concerns of a "feminist science". To some extent raising these issues is utopian, in the sense that none of these authors on whose work I draw would suggest that it is possible to remake science very much in the absence of other social change. It is not, strictly speaking, a feminist science that is being addressed, but the question of how science might look in a more "feminist" and egalitarian society, a society in which notions of gender did not imply notions of hierarchy.[1] I shall continue to refer to "feminist science" throughout this chapter as a kind of shorthand, but it should be borne in mind that no such thing is possible within our present society.

A similar sort of question is often addressed within the radical science movement as a whole, for whom the question is: can we achieve a more socialist science?[2] This would, it is generally agreed, be a science geared more to human need than to corporate greed; it would be a science that is accountable to society, rather than elitist and mystifying. It would certainly not be a science that serves a giant military-industrial complex in the exploitation of nature, but would attempt to cooperate with nature.[3]

These very general principles are, of course, ones with which most feminists would agree; in addition they would add that a new progressive science should be one that did not perpetuate in any way the subordination and oppression of women. That

143

is, it would not be a more *feminist* kind of science if, while it purported to help the community in a more socialist way, it did nothing to challenge women's oppression within that community. Women's oppression has tended to remain after socialist revolutions.

In this chapter I want to do a bit more than simply assert that a "feminist science" has to be less mystifying, more cooperative, or whatever. Some feminist writers have begun to address the specifically feminist questions that a more progressive science must address, and here I want to pull some of these more recent ideas together in the following, overlapping, ways. First, I will consider questions of the methods and process of science; how, if at all, might these be changed in a more feminist way?

This includes the question of whether or not science—at least as we now know it—is in some way inherently patriarchal; is, for example, its pursuit of objectivity essentially the pursuit of a "masculine" quality? And if it is, how should feminists evaluate it? Second, I want briefly to consider the question of the subject-matter of science. What sorts of questions might a more feminist science address? Would it consider, as present science tends to do, that *any* question can be asked, for the sake of the pursuit of knowledge? Or might we consider that some areas should be proscribed?[4] Inevitably, this raises further questions about the reorganisation of society, since some questions might be ones that feminists would abhor in a society which devalues women, while they might be questions that would be perfectly acceptable in a society which did not. For example, research into reproductive engineering raises problems for feminists at present, since it is currently being done in a society in which biological reproduction is one of the few rights that women *do* have. Reproductive engineering in a more feminist society *might*, however, bring benefits to women, as Shulamith Firestone recognised.[5] Finally, I will consider how we might organise science as an activity so that it no longer serves to mystify and is more open and accessible to everyone. Although I have tried to break down these various topics into these overlapping categories for the purposes of discussion, it will be clear that in practice they are closely interrelated: the written word is, unfortunately, linear.

1. METHOD AND PROCESS

In this section I want to consider three areas. These are (a) What counts as scientific knowledge? Is it knowledge gained only by the empirical methods of science, or would a "feminist science" change the boundaries of what are legitimate methods? (b) Science and the sexual division of labour: how does it relate to that division, and is that relationship problematic for feminism? If so, how might it be changed? (c) Subjectivity and objectivity; is science inherently masculine /objective? And if so, how does this characterisation affect women?

The first of these considerations—what counts as scientific knowledge—begs an important question. In considering that we might envisage a science "not only more sympathetic to women, but more sympathetic to all those values (often described as humanistic) which are at variance" with science as it is now, Evelyn Fox Keller asks: "What would it mean for science to change its self-conception and ideological commitments and still be considered science?"[6] She points out that science is certainly not as monolithic as its stereotype assumes, but operates in a number of different ways. As I noted in previous chapters, while the mechanistic and reductionistic framework has been dominant, there have also been other strands, beliefs in vitalism, interaction, transformability and so forth. What is poorly understood, Keller correctly points out, is how these different frameworks balance against each other at different times; different frameworks may become dominant as a result of a complex interplay of factors both internal (e.g. in terms of observations that that framework can or cannot explain) and external (e.g. prevailing ideology; vested interests).

In one sense then, science does not so much have to change its commitments, as change the balance between them; commitments to the kind of relationship with nature that feminists have envisaged are already there in the history of science—even if this is hard to see in the face of current scientific orthodoxy. But the question still remains; what does it *mean* for science to change . . . and still be considered science? The answer to that question can hardly be guessed at; in each generation, people will consider the boundaries of "science" to be somewhat different from that of previous generations. How, for instance, might physicists of the mid-nineteenth century, trained in the assumptions of a Newtonian universe, have answered the question? Yet soon after, physics changed dramatically in ways that could not easily have been predicted, and in ways that made it—at least some parts of physics—quite unlike the "science" that had predominated hitherto.

Science conducted in a truly egalitarian society would no doubt be different from that with which we are familiar. It would, presumably, have a different relationship to industry in a society unconcerned with corporate profit and the escalation of the arms race; different social priorities would require that science addressed different questions. I assume, however, that we would still call it "science" in the sense that it would still be about the discovery of the ways in which the natural world works.[7] We can, of course, only guess at how it would differ. In what follows, I will consider some of these "guesses"—though they are guesses informed by a conception of what a more feminist (or socialist) society might be like, as well as by feminist critiques of the problems of existing science.

As science is organised now, scientific knowledge comes largely from empirical observation and experiment. Scientific method is, as I noted earlier, most commonly one of methodological reductionism; that is, it proceeds by a process of isolating variables for experimental manipulation, while holding all other known variables constant or randomised. This allows science to proceed by logical sequential steps, in theory at least, testing hypothesis after hypothesis. That, at any rate, is what scientists tend to say they are doing, although their practice sometimes fall short of the logical ideal.

Methodological reductionism does, nevertheless, have implications that we might consider. In Chapter Four I noted that methodological reductionism goes hand in hand with reductionism as explanation, simply because it *does* work by isolating variables, thus forcing us to think about nature at least partly in terms of those isolated variables. Any interactions then become something that we might think about secondarily (and, indeed, this is one of the problems with interactionism, as I noted in Chapter Five, since it maintains the separation of variables). If, then, we are to move away from reductionism, we will need to consider the very methods that are used and which count as "science".

In our present society, those methods that are counted as scientific are generally held to produce knowledge that is more highly valued than other knowledge, that is thought of as somehow "more true". Associated with this is the belief that scientific methods themselves are to be more highly valued. Moreover, as Sally Gearhart has noted, it is not only knowledge for oneself that is critical to the scientific enterprise, but also knowledge that can be proven to others:

"To prove", in fact, seems to replace "to know" in Western science, thus altering the task of *discovery* to one of *justification,* and thus revealing as well a self-serving component of the epistemology. "How do I know?" or "What do I know" has become "How/what can I prove to others?" for in the service of objectivity only others can replicate and assess. The vast and proliferating desire of scientists to show knowledge to others obscures whatever noble motive—curiosity, the love of learning—might have inspired them early in the annals of science or in their personal history . . . The self-aggrandizement inherent in the drive of science to "prove" seems a far cry from even the traditionally highly touted function of science: to discover the laws of nature.[8]

To take an example from the area of women's health: if a group of women working collectively in a self-help health group discovered something about the way that their bodies worked (by, say, sharing experiences or by self-examination), then this would not be held to be scientific. That judgement would be partly on the grounds that the methods were not "scientific" and partly because the knowledge cannot be proven to others, since it would be held to be idiosyncratic, subjective knowledge. If, on the other hand, a sample of women were used as subjects (or rather, objects) in an experiment done by someone else, then this would be more likely to be classed as scientific.[9] At least in the present organisation of society, the latter method usually involves the experiment being done by a white middle-class male expert, and may well be done without the knowledge or consent of the "subjects". Precisely because of this, feminists have tended to be wary of knowledge gained by scientific method, often preferring to gain knowledge by other means, including forms of consciousness-raising, or self-examination.

On the basis of the experiences of feminists working within our present society, it seems likely that they would tend to favour a broader approach to science, one that does not assume that only certain methods and certain questions have validity. While, as Evelyn Fox Keller has noted, such a broad perspective has existed in the history of science, there remains a dominant belief in the superiority of particular methods and ways of investigation. Among other things, allowing a broader perspective to enter science might more readily allow that knowledge gained from other sources—from say, introspection—has validity, and that this is not necessarily inferior to knowledge gained by "objective" science—a point to which I will return in the discussion of objectivity a little later.

On the other hand, not all means of acquiring knowledge need to equally valued, and any future society would have to find some means of evaluating them. Indeed, some methods that are presently used and accepted as scientific raise ethical questions that a more caring and feminist society might eschew. Consider, for example, the use of clinical trials, by means of which new drugs or treatments are evaluated. The standard procedure is to give one half of the subject group the drug to be tested, and the other half a sugar pill (placebo). If "psychological" factors are to be ruled out, neither the patients nor the administering doctors should know which is which. However, this raises ethical problems, since one half of the group is deliberately being deprived of a drug which *might* be beneficial; moreover, the patients do not know what is happening—and may even not have been told about the trial at all. In the case of people with severe illness, many critics would say that this was unethical.

Similar criticism has been levied against the clinical trials used when the contraceptive pill was first launched. It was tested in this way on a group of poor Mexican and Puerto Rican women, with the inevitable result that some of the placebo group became pregnant.[10] Abortion, however, was not freely available.

A feminist society might consider such methods of testing unacceptable, both because of the way in which they deprive one group of a drug that might be helpful and because they do not always operate with the full knowledge of the "subjects".

Indeed, a feminist society might be more circumspect than our present society about the introduction of new drugs altogether; at present the introduction of new drugs has more to do with the profit margins of the pharmaceutical companies than with the direct alleviation of human suffering, and for this the industry is frequently criticised.[11] A more humane society could well place less emphasis on large-scale drug manufacture of this kind, and more on research into the prevention of disease.

On the other hand, some methods may be considered unacceptable because they are done badly, even within the currently accepted methods of science. Earlier chapters considered a variety of examples of biological determinism, some of which were founded upon science that was done badly even in its own terms. Much of the literature reporting experiments on the supposed biological bases to homosexuality are of this category; the experiments are "bad science" in that, for example, they use inappropriate control groups, poor statistics and very small sample sizes.[12] Now it is, perhaps, unlikely that my utopian feminist society would consider such research either relevant or interesting, founded as it is on assumptions about the abnormality of homosexuality. But conversely, that society should endeavour to ensure that poor methodology is not used to excuse unquestioned assumptions, as it so often is in research into topics such as human sexuality.

Another area of concern about the methods used by science might be the use made of animals. In Chapter Six I raised the question of how a feminist science might view nature, including the animals that are at present used largely without question in scientific experiments. Most feminists would advocate a view of nature that emphasised harmony and cooperation with other living things, rather than a science that was concerned with taking them apart. (I noted in Chapter Six how the cause of anti-vivisection has at times been seen as congruent with that of feminism). The view of animals that operates most commonly within science has been summarised by Cora Diamond in the following way: "Within certain limits, experimental animals may be regarded as delicate instruments, or an analogous to them, and are to be used efficiently and cared for properly, but no more than that is demanded". She counterposes this to an alternative which, at present, is more likely to be found outside laboratories: "Within certain limits, animals may be regarded as sources of moral claims. These claims arise from their capacity for an independent life, or perhaps from their sentience, but in either case, the moral position of animals is seen as having analogies with that of human beings".[13] That is, Diamond argues, the controversy is presently based on the question of whether there is, or is not, a moral issue: science operates as though moral questions do not apply to animals, or are somehow lesser.[14] Thus, the use of animals might be excused on the grounds that it would be immoral *not* to use them if there is a likelihood of some putative benefit to humanity; animals' moral claims are in this sense weighed against those of humans and are found to be of lower worth.

A more feminist science would assume, I would suggest, that the question of the use of animals is *a priori* a moral issue. It would recognise that, in the history of science, women have become associated with nature and with animals, and that this association has been important to the oppression of both women and animals. If that association is to be overcome, feminist science has to avoid methods that continue such forms of oppression in other spheres—which, at least to some contemporary feminist authors, must include the ways in which animals are presently exploited in laboratories (and elsewhere). A feminist science, then, would have to look for more cooperative, and generally non-invasive, ways of understanding nature.

The suggestion that a feminist science does not exploit animals in laboratories raises two obvious problems. First, it might be argued that it is only through the use of animals in experiments that we can learn anything about how animal bodies, including our own, function; in that sense, animal experimentation can be thought of as the basis for much medical knowledge. Second, it might be argued that we would be unable to develop new chemicals (say) because we would be unable to do any safety testing without the use of animals.

To some extent it is of course true that we can learn about the functioning of animal bodies from doing experiments with them. The question that arises, however, from ethical concerns is whether that acquisition of knowledge can be morally justified. Certainly, if, as suggested above, a feminist science would assume that the use of animals is a moral issue, then some uses of animals that are currently accepted would no longer be acceptable. Learning about function from, say, tissues taken from a dead animal might be more acceptable than learning about it from tissues from a live animal—in which case some experiments using live animals as "preparations" might be less permissible.[15] Similarly, the extensive use of live animals in undergraduate teaching might not be so acceptable.

This might, of course, seem like unjustifiable interference in the activities of other people (to wit, scientists). But it is worth remembering that it only seems that way *because* we make the moral distinctions between animals and humans to which Cora Diamond referred. And because of that distinction it is considered quite justified if, in the name of science, you do gruesome things to a sentient mammal, but it is never considered justified to do similar things to another human being, whatever their level of sentience or feeling. Moreover, the "unjustifiable interference" claim is often made on behalf of the use of animals in industrial research, where the rationale is not entirely to do with finding out about function. A feminist society would not tolerate the use of living animals in experiments which tested that bodily function when it is grossly disturbed by, say, cosmetics or nerve gas.[16]

The second argument concerns the use of animals in safety testing. Now, if we were to envisage the kind of society towards which we would strive, we might consider it important to organise industry in such a way that risks of exposure to hazards were almost non-existent, but we would probably have to acknowledge that *some* risks were likely to remain. If so, then we would wish to know as much as possible about the dangers of any particular hazard. But then the problem arises: *how* do we carry out safety tests? At present, the criteria used rely heavily on measures of toxicity obtained from animal tests and, until suitably efficient alternatives are available, only animal experiments are likely to fulfil the criteria.[17] So, if our development of a more humane science is to proceed we would need, first, to develop adequate (and this certainly means better methods and higher standards than are presently used) methods of safety testing without using living animals.

I began this section by posing a question about the boundaries of scientific knowledge and the methods used to attain it. From the discussion so far—which has largely dealt with aspects of scientific methodology—the conclusion would seem to be that the boundaries of what constitutes science and its methods might well change. Moreover, this might happen within a framework that did not necessarily assume that *only* certain methods yielded the "truth" about the world. At least part of the reason why present scientific methods are held to be better than others—to give greater truth—is that, as Evelyn Fox Keller suggests, they have become historically associated with masculinity. Other ways of knowing have become synonymous with the feminine—and accordingly are held to be less true. She notes that:

The genderization of science—as an enterprise, as an intellectual domain, as a world view—simultaneously reflects and perpetuates associations made in an earlier, prescientific era. If true, then an adherence to an objectivist epistemology, in which truth is measured by its distance from the subjective, has to be re-examined when it emerges that, by this definition, truth itself has become genderized.[18]

A feminist science would have to examine carefully the concept of "truth" and how it is presently assumed to relate principally to "objective" ways of knowing the world. Feminists would have to reject the assumption to which Keller refers, that something is often held to be more true in our society if a man has said it; they would also have to question the assumption that "objective" truth is necessarily superior. Understanding can come from many sources.

At present, of course, it is likely that scientific "truths" are uttered by men, since science remains a male-dominated preserve. It is sometimes assumed that a more feminist science would emerge if we had more women working in science. Now there are several problems with this assumption: first, having more women would not change science unless we also assume that they innately possess some quality which would make science better. In practice, women scientists are socialised in much the same way as men, and are likely to operate in largely similar ways. Second, and relatedly, just having more women is unlikely to change science unless those women are committed to feminist ideals in some way. A more feminist science might emerge if we had more feminists in science. Third, the assumption is actually untrue, at least as it is usually made. There *are* plenty of women in science: they are, however, located in lower-ranking jobs which, though necessary to the smooth operation of the scientific enterprise, do not carry as much prestige and status as the jobs in which men predominate. Women are to be found as research assistants, laboratory cleaners, secretaries, and technicians, while the more prestigious and well-paid research and administrative jobs are more often held by men.[19] This division of labour, of course, mirrors that in the larger society; science is no exception.

That women are largely excluded from the more prestigious parts of science has provoked many explanations. For some, women are scarce because they lack inherently the most suitable attributes, such as spatial ability. For others, the problem is simply one of discrimination. For yet others, women are excluded because of the prevailing masculinist ideology of science. An alternative approach to the question of why there are so few women is to start from the Left critiques of the process of science to which I referred in Chapter One. Although such analyses differ in many ways regarding the relationship between science and society, they usually start from the recognition that science is a crucial part of material production within capitalism and can, because of that, be analysed in terms of its class character. However, as feminists have often pointed out, such Marxist analyses are usually gender-blind[20] and thus fail specifically to address the question of why *women* are excluded from, as well as being subordinated by, science.

A feminist analysis of science as it is now conducted would have to do more than focus exclusively on processes of production, since that omits consideration of women's subordination in relation to processes of reproduction. Hilary Rose has suggested that this focus had led to a "one-sided materialism", on the grounds that:

this prioritisation of the production process is to ignore that other materialist necessity of history—reproduction. The preoccupation with production as a social process, with a corresponding social division of labour, and the neglect of reproduction as a corresponding social process with a corresponding social division of labour, perpetuates a one-sided materialism.[21]

That "other materialist necessity of history" includes, of course, far more than just biological reproduction, and involves a great deal of what Hilary Rose calls "caring labour"—the maintenance and care of people within the household, much of which is dismissed as just housework. This caring labour is women's province; in turn, the sexually segregated labour market assumes that women will remain principally in that province. Either they are in low-paid, low-status jobs because it is assumed that their jobs are secondary to those of their husbands, or if they enter the higher-status professions, it is similarly assumed that they will prioritise their domestic caring labour and will do two jobs.

Science is, as Hilary Rose notes, a production system in miniature, faithfully reflecting the larger labour market. In this sense, it is not surprising that we find women in the lower-paid jobs. Not only does this reflect the gender-segregation of the larger market,[22] but these jobs are also partly servicing jobs. Most women, notes Hilary Rose, in "science and engineering are relegated to those tasks which most markedly reflect their primary task as wife-mother". Women, then, unlike men, are involved both in the production of things, within the public world of production, *and* the production of people, in the private world of reproduction.

Nancy Hartsock lays similar stress on the sexual division of labour, and argues that this structures the ways in which women and men perceive the world; in turn, these perceptions have structured the history of capitalist science. She draws on the feminist writers who have emphasised the importance of childrearing practices, which remain at present firmly in the hands of women. The consequences of this practice for young boys, it has been suggested, are that a sharp sense of separation and opposition are fostered as the child grows away from his (female) parent. For girls, by contrast, gender similarity leads to identification and a sense of connection. Hartsock summarises these arguments thus: "Put another way girls, because of female parenting, are less differentiated from others than boys, more continuous with, and related to the external object world. They are differently oriented to their inner object world as well".[23]

The experience of separation, coupled with identification with the abstract world of production, shapes the construction of the male self, Hartsock suggests, and it does so in ways that have implications for science which, if nothing else, is dominated by men. She argues that:

Masculinity must be attained by means of opposition to the concrete world of daily life, by escaping from contact with the female world of the household into the masculine world of public life. This experience of two worlds, one valuable, if abstract and deeply unattainable, the other useless and demeaning, if concrete and necessary, lies at the heart of a series of dualisms—abstract/concrete, mind/body, culture/nature, ideal/real, stasis/change. And these dualisms are overlaid by gender: only the first of each pair is associated with the male.[24]

What we need then, according to Hartsock, is a social organisation (and a science) based on women's as well as men's activities, both in production and reproduction. In the short term, both Hilary Rose and Nancy Hartsock concur in advocating a feminist theory that takes caring labour into account—and more importantly, women's experiences of that caring labour.

Women's experiences in present-day society *are* grounded in caring labour: but what should we conclude from this about the possibility of a "feminist science"? The first conclusion is clearly that such a science should take caring labour into account, not least in the way that work is structured within science. It is not, however, clear what is meant by the idea of taking "caring labour" into account. In terms of the way in which science is organised, this would mean gender equality in responsibility for, and execution of, such caring labour: workplaces would have to be reorganised with, for example, the provision of adequate creche facilities.

On the other hand, this would not be enough. If Hartsock is right about the origins of the series of dualisms that she describes—that they originate in the "abstract masculinity" inculcated by existing patterns of childcare—then "taking caring labour into account" will not be enough to change the deeply rooted dualisms that pervade science. To change those we would need to change deeply entrenched perceptions of the world: and, in turn, we would have to change the patterns of childrearing that have been suggested as the source of those perceptions.

Women's experiences of caring labour have also been related to another dualism, that of subjectivity versus objectivity. A polarisation between subject and object can be seen as a particularly male perception, resulting from the separation of the male child from his mother.[25] As a result, subjectivity and objectivity have become seen in this perception as essentially separable states. Subjectivity is irrational, and closely associated with the female and her role in caring labour; while objectivity has become rational, scientific and quintessentially male. Feminists have often called this opposition into question, as Rita Arditti, writing about feminism and science, observed:

> Women, generally more in touch with their feelings, often raise uncomfortable questions about "detached, scientific objectivity". The prevalent mode in science today presents serious problems for people who have human concerns, as many women have. "Objectivity" applied to people often leads to objectifying them, or perceiving only their object aspects.[26]

Arditti, like other feminist writers, stresses that a more humane, more feminist science, must not be based on allegiance to an unattainable objectivity, but must acknowledge subjectivity and intuition.[27] These are a crucial part of the sharing of women's experiences that is central to feminism. Hilary Rose notes, for example, that:

> Unlike the alienated abstract knowledge of science, feminist methodology seeks to bring together subjective and objective ways of knowing the world. It begins and constantly returns to the subjective shared experience of oppression... within feminist theoretical production, experience, the living, participating "I" is seen as a dimension which must be included in an adequate analysis.[28]

For her, that subjective shared experience is intimately connected to women's caring labour.

It is important to emphasise that Rose is advocating a bringing together of subjectivity and objectivity, and not a rejection of the latter. There is a danger that in referring to "masculine objectivity", feminists' arguments are taken to imply a belief in objectivity as essentially male, a trait to which men are biologically predisposed. Most feminists writing about objectivity do in fact use it, quite correctly, to describe a characteristic that men in our society are stereotypically supposed to have in greater quantity than women. In that sense, objectivity becomes masculine by association.

The association of objectivity with masculinity has sometimes led feminists to reject objectivity, and to glorify subjectivity in opposition to it. While it *is* necessary to revalue the subjective as that which patriarchy has consistently devalued, we do ourselves a disservice if we remove ourselves from "objectivity" and rationality: we then simply leave the terrain of rational thought, including science, to men, thus perpetuating the system which excluded us in the first place.

The problem of objectivity for feminists is also raised by the radical critiques of science which emphasises science as a social product. At one extreme, as I noted in Chapter One, the material reality of the world fades into insignificance, and science is portrayed as virtually nothing but social relations. Now social relations in science at present are indubitably patriarchal and capitalist—science reinforces the social divisions of the larger society. But to see science solely, or even largely, in those terms constitutes what Evelyn Fox Keller has emphasised as a political threat:

The intellectual danger resides in viewing science as pure social product; science then dissolves into ideology and objectivity loses all intrinsic meaning. In the resulting cultural relativism, any emancipatory function of modern science is negated, and the arbitration of truth recedes into the political domain. Against this background, the temptation arises for feminists to abandon their claim for representation in scientific culture and, in its place, to invite a return to purely "female" subjectivity, leaving rationality and objectivity in the male domain, dismissed as products of a purely male consciousness.[29]

Moreover, such "cultural relativism" would mean that, as Elizabeth Fee suggests:

no one form of the production of knowledge could claim truth status over any other. The story of Genesis would then have as much claim to validity as the theory of evolution; the decision between sexist and feminist interpretations of social arrangements would, in the absence of any mutually agreed upon criteria of validity, be quite simply a matter of political power. It seems overly optimistic to suppose that a completely free marketplace of competing ideas and theories would result in the desired goal of a more human and more liberating knowledge.[30]

Both these authors stress that "objectivity" is not something that feminists should avoid. Indeed, there is a danger that the flight from masculine objectivity is powered by a degree of cultural relativism that, as Elizabeth Fee notes, might be antithetical to feminist interests. She goes on to argue that, not only has objectivity become masculine, but it can be a screen for political passivity. This suggestion is based on the observation that many scientists insist on the objectivity of the pure science that they do, and thus use the concept to create a distance between their science and the political and economic considerations that underlie it. That is, objectivity is used as a defence and a means of isolation from the uses to which the knowledge is put: the scientists thus see themselves as merely describing nature, while it is the politicians who are responsible for the less objective uses of that knowledge. She argues that:

> scientists who retreat behind the screen of pure science are passively abandoning their social responsibility; those who choose to become actively involved risk being seen as no longer "objective". Here, the notion of "objectivity" becomes merely a code word for the political passivity of those scientists who have tacitly agreed to accept a privileged social position and freedom in inquiry within the laboratory in return for their silence in not questioning the social uses of science or the power relations that determine its direction.[31]

There is no doubt that feminists writing thus about a feminist science will be denied validity by the accusation that they are insufficiently objective, or unscholarly; indeed the present writer has been told that she cannot be objective "on certain issues" because of her avowed feminism! In short, admitting to political interests makes the arguments less objective, and thus less valid—on top of the fact that the arguments are *a priori* less objective if uttered by a woman.

Moreover, for many scientists, failing to hide behind the screen of silence raises the spectre of "interference" in their work. If the fact that science is political were more generally accepted, then scientific work would have to be much more publicly accountable. Some work presently done might then become less acceptable. The cry of "interference!" raised when the issue of public accountability is brought up[32] is of course nonsense, since science already is political, and in that sense, science is already "interfered" with. Scientists are not at present free to pursue any line of enquiry in any way that they wish: public opinion and, to a much greater extent, sources of available funding, impose constraints upon what can be done. A woman wishing to do research relevant to feminist interests, for example, is quite likely to find it difficult to obtain funding, institutional support, laboratory space, or whatever. Yet a scientist doing military research of dubious benefit to humankind, is quite likely to obtain ample funding and facilities from defence budgets.[33]

The complaint that scientists should have individual freedom to pursue whatever line of enquiry they choose is, then, naive, since they already do operate under political and economic constraints. A second point is that such a complaint works on the liberal assumption of the priority of the individual over society, an assumption that I discussed at greater length in Chapters Four and Five. The claim that individuals should be free to pursue knowledge and that they should not be subject to social constraints implies that society as a whole has secondary status in relation to the production of knowledge. This implication is not likely to be acceptable in the development of a more feminist science, for which science should be accountable to society and thus subject to social validation or constraint in overt rather than covert ways. In the next section I will look at some of the ways in which this kind of constraint might have implications for the subject-matter of a feminist science.

2. THE SUBJECT-MATTER OF SCIENCE

It would obviously be impossible to go through the entire subject-matter of science in relation to feminist thought, and here I want only to sketch a few areas. These will be drawn from biology—in part because I am a biologist, and so can think about the problems of biology most easily. In part, too, biology is particularly relevant to feminism precisely because it is so often used as an ideological weapon against women's interests. My intention here is to highlight some of the approaches or questions that a more feminist science might take.

In discussing the subject-matter of science, I am not suggesting that such content can simply be changed to remove sexism, in the absence of the broader changes discussed in other sections. It is quite possible to ask "nicer" questions, or to improve the methodology. The science that results will be better, in the sense that it will be less obviously informed by sexist prejudices; but the patriarchal structure of science itself will not be challenged. Here, my main concern is to sketch some ways in which content might be altered if the science were being done in a more feminist, egalitarian society; this may well mean more than just asking nicer questions. On the other hand, we might also ask the question whether or not content can be changed *at all* within present society, given the extent of feminist critique: this is a theme to which I return at the end of the chapter.

I ended the last section with the theme of social constraints on scientific activity. A feminist science would, as I have already noted, have to reject the prevailing notion that scientists are free, asocial agents, with no *a priori* moral responsibility to society. What this means is that it would accept that what scientists do is very much part of society and therefore subject to social constraints. As we have seen, this is actually how science presently operates, even if individual scientists may choose to pretend otherwise. Such a recognition carries with it, of course, the implication that there will be some fields of enquiry that a feminist society would *not* consider appropriate or desirable or which it might emphasise less than our present society does. It might not consider research that for example, focusses on the differences between women and men to be as important as research that emphasises their commonality. If a feminist science emphasises a cooperative view of the human/nature relationship then it would also not consider research important or valuable that might result in renewed environmental exploitation. And some research it might even proscribe if it was seen to be against the interests of humanity, such as much military research.[34]

The first point to emphasise, then, is that a feminist science does imply social constraints upon what science does. The difference between that and the social constraints that presently operate is that those which occur in an egalitarian and humane society would be very different from those that applied in a hierarchical and competitive one. One field of research that is currently obtaining considerable funding might present problems for feminist science: this is research into reproductive engineering. During the 1970s and 1980s, ethical questions have been discussed concerning techniques such as *in vitro* fertilisation ("test-tube babies"), questions which began to fade as the techniques were improved to the point at which a baby was actually born. At the time of writing, the ethical considerations have been much to the fore again in the wake of debate about the ethics of surrogate motherhood. Discussion has centred on issues of rights and choice, asking questions such as: do women have the right to *in vitro* fertilisation if they so choose? This kind of discussion, however, raises problems for feminists, as Jalna Hanmer has pointed out:

Discussion based on "rights" and "choice" assumes a society without differential distribution of power and authority, or at least without serious differentials. But "rights" and "choice" gradually fade as coercion increases... In other words, do you have a "choice" if there are no viable options? In reality we live in a world dominated by men and the interests of men; every aspect of women's reproduction is controlled in a very collective way in the interests of their continuing power domination over women... One frequently met pattern is for the experimenter to also assume the position of the ethicist who defines the terms of the debate and offers the solution to the problem. Ordinary women, including the experimented upon, are relegated to the back wings of the stage, unseen and silenced.[35]

That is, as long as such research is being conducted in a society that so devalues women, it is unlikely to offer women real choices. In this sense, even if the technology promises fertility to some, it can be said to be likely to work against women's interests as a group. It might even, as this quotation implies, lead to coercion for some: women might, for instance, be coerced (as they are in India now) into aborting female foetuses against their will, or they might be coerced into surrogate motherhood. The latter is one reason why many feminists have opposed the idea of surrogacy, since poor women may well be forced into surrogate motherhood.

Given the context of women's powerlessness, feminists are generally very wary and worried by the "advances" in reproductive technology. But what would our view of such research be in the context of a feminist science operating in a society which did not devalue women? One possibility is that feminist science would consider such research to have importance, in order to make it possible for women to be absolved from the responsibility and problems of biological reproduction. This is the kind of scenario suggested by Shulamith Firestone, according to which children would no longer be produced principally by women, but would be produced technologically.[36] In the context of women's current subordination, this suggestion has been criticised, since it offers what has been called a "technological fix" for our oppression. Moreover, some feminists feel that biological mothering *is* one area that is, currently, unique to women and in that sense gives them some power which technology might remove. But these effects follow from living in patriarchal society; it is at least possible that technology operating in an egalitarian society might be valued very differently.

Another possibility, of course, is that a feminist society need not consider reproductive engineering to be particularly important because it would emphasise the production of children as a social, rather than individual, event. Reproductive engineering as it presently exists is geared to the notion of individual rights and choices (although these are shaped in turn by social considerations, including the powerlessness of women), and the differential allocation of rights; thus, black or Asian women or lesbians are less likely to be given access to reproductive technology. If a feminist society existed, we might ask ourselves whether or not the rights of individual women to reproduce would be of paramount importance. Among other things, a society which accorded women their true worth might not give rise to so much pressure for women to see themselves as having failed if they do not produce children. In such a society, the role of reproductive technology might be to give real choices to women, choices in which women have some control, rather than to maintain power over individual women's capacity to reproduce.

Another area in which research questions might be asked in a different way is the biology of gender. Presumably, a more feminist society would not place high value on the differences between women and men and so research into gender differences might be of relatively less interest. On the other hand, a more progressive approach to human development—whether of gender or not—should reject the additive model, outlined in Chapter Five, and might attempt to move toward an understanding of development in terms of its complexity and dynamics, emphasising the multiplicity of factors involved. A feminist research approach might be more critical of giving any single factor priority, a scepticism which should also apply to studies done of other species. Why assume—as so much of the sex differences literature does—that hormones are fairly fundamental, when we know so little about individual differences in social experience—in human or other animals? If hormones or other factors are seen as part of a dynamic and possibly constantly changing process, even something as apparently "internal" as hormones might be subject to change over time—a possibility that reductionist science does not readily permit. The task of science is then shifted from a search for effects of single causes to a search for the rules, or laws, by which processes and structures are transformed throughout an organism's life.

Asking questions about the natural world in a more feminist way would have many ramifications; it would, in the end, change the questions themselves. Questions might be asked, for instance, about how cooperative and integral the environment is, rather than the more commonplace emphasis on competition. Questions might be asked about the continua of nature, rather than the opposition of various dualities. One question that would change in a feminist society is that concerning the universality of patriarchy. As I have noted earlier in the book, this question has invited various answers, including biological determinist ones. Other apparently universal human traits have often received similarly biologistic explanations. But the "feminist society" of which I write so optimistically is a post-patriarchal one, by definition. Thus, patriarchy would no longer be a universal, either culturally or historically, and so questions about its universality would no longer be possible. Feminist historians might still wish to explain it historically, but its non-universality would at least make it less prone to biological reductionism.

It could be an entertaining armchair exercise to speculate on what forms scientific knowledge might take in a different kind of society; I have here only sketched in one or two ways in which the content of science might change in a feminist utopia. I have considered reproductive technology in particular because it is one area of current concern to feminists; how the content of the other areas of science might change is, of course, largely a guessing game—informed perhaps by feminist critiques of existing science, but a guessing game nonetheless. In the last analysis, we simply cannot tell how the content of science would look if done in a totally different kind of society. There are, though, some changes that might more easily be envisaged, even in our present society, and I will return to these in the final section.

3. THE ACCESSIBILITY OF SCIENCE

Because knowledge in some ways confers power, a feminist science would also have to operate in such a way that knowledge was open and accessible; only if this were so, could such a science be fully accountable to the society of which it is part. At present women are largely excluded from scientific knowledge. In part, this is because of discriminatory practices that deny them entry to appropriate professions.[37] In part, it is because of the overwhelmingly male characteristics of science. In part, too, it is because women are more likely to be seen as subjects of study than as participants in a process of gaining knowledge. In medicine, for example, this means that the (usually) male doctor will know far more about the bodily states of the woman patient than she is usually allowed to know.[38]

In health care, access to knowledge means both that a

woman needing health care could find out what is happening to her, and also that she could participate in the decisions made rather than having them made for her. It would also mean that she could use that information to choose between the available options (which could include various "alternative" forms of medicine, as well as orthodox "scientific" medicine). At present, such choices are constrained by factors such as access to information, status, and cost. Moreover, women, or other presently oppressed groups, need not be relegated to the status of "subjects" of scientific experiment or clinical trial. Rather, the "living, participating 'I'", with all its subjectivity might be given credibility.[39] How far that ideal is from present practice in which the "doctor knows best" and the woman's life and experiences are disregarded!

Because women are at present largely excluded from science and medicine, the access of women to scientific knowledge remains limited. Where there has been dissemination of information, it has largely been in direct relation to health care, to enable women to be rather better informed about such issues as contraceptive use, abortion, pregnancy, and so on. In other areas of biology, however, the information available within feminist literature often becomes oversimplified and distorted, helping to create new feminist myths. For instance, there is a myth in the feminist literature that all foetuses are female to begin with, and then the presence of androgenic hormones makes the erstwhile female into a male.[40] This is perhaps a comforting thought to feminists, and it certainly reverses the biological bits of the sexist myth of Adam and Eve! It is not, however, accurate, even within the logic of sexist science and so does little to help us to understand the biology of gender.[41]

If a science is to be accessible to all, we have to consider whether or not we would wish it to remain a specialist, expert, activity. Given feminist emphasis on the sharing of experience and knowledge, it is unlikely to remain an "expert" activity in a more feminist society, but might well become an activity in which a variety of people can take part. At present, there are rather few attempts to democratise science and to include other people in its decision-making processes, and none of these address specifically feminist questions.[42]

Making science publicly accountable should mean that far

more people (and notably women in relation to feminist questions) have a say in the direction that science takes. That would mean that it should more directly serve the interests of the community than it does now. This might be taken to mean that it would be a science concerned more with the solution of problems facing the community than with any abstract and esoteric attempts to understand nature. Making science accountable need not, however, necessarily mean that it *only* addresses questions of direct utility: "pure" science, addressing questions of perhaps no immediate use, *might* have a somewhat lower priority than that directed towards the solution of immediate problems, and it would of course have to be justified if that science were more publicly accountable. But "pure" science (if such a division between forms of science is ever that absolute) need not be dismissed just because of its less obvious applicability: apart from the many ways in which "pure" science has made discoveries that have turned out to be of benefit to humanity, there is another side to it, too. One mathematician, cited by J. D. Bernal, commented on the apparent uselessness of his work, saying: "This subject has no practical use; that is to say, it cannot be used for promoting directly the destruction of human life or for accentuating the present inequalities in the distribution of wealth".[43] At least within the context of present science, that seems a highly laudable reason for doing it.

4. ACHIEVING THE IMPOSSIBLE?

So far I have written about what a feminist science might be like, if we were to achieve some kind of post-patriarchal society. In doing so, I have tried to pull together various strands of ideas from the feminist literature about the kinds of goals that we might want to achieve. But it is all, of course, mere speculation since we are very far from achieving these goals. Perhaps a more immediately relevant question is: what, if anything, can we do now? As I noted at the beginning of the book, one response to the problems of science is simply to withdraw from it, or to label it as irreducibly "masculine". On the other hand, there is the possibility of making at least some challenges to the assumptions underwriting modern science now.

Among some scientists, there are attempts to move away from hierarchies in practice, and from reductionism as a mode of interpretation, though such attempts have not so far had an overtly feminist direction. And in a sense they could not have, since there are so few feminists working in science itself, who could act to change the assumptions of that science "from the inside". Even if the numbers of feminists in science were greater, of course, they would not have an easy time of it; as I noted earlier, accusations of political bias and bringing ideology into science abound. Nonetheless, that there *are* some attempts to think beyond the constraints of orthodox science does suggest that there is a possibility of change, of challenge to that orthodoxy, which might in turn provide some sort of starting point for a feminist input.

In writing about women and science, Evelyn Fox Keller has referred to the historical opposition between the organismic, holistic view of nature and the mechanistic one that is now dominant, implying that there is currently a resurgence of interest in holistic views. Unlike the interpretation put upon this resurgence by writers such as Capra or Henderson, who see in it evidence for massive ideological shifts, Evelyn Fox Keller is more circumspect, concluding: "Biology finds itself at a philosophical crossroad; we cannot yet say which route it will take".[44] To some extent, this conclusion is one with which I would agree; in a broad sense, we obviously cannot predict the future ideological directions of science. Yet that need not imply passivity: if human beings can shape their own history then there is a sense in which grappling with the problems of science, ideological or otherwise, might itself contribute to new directions. It is in that spirit that the various attempts I shall outline are operating.

First, scientific practice might be changed into at least less hierarchical forms. There have been occasional attempts to democratise scientific practice;[45] what is important about these is that such attempts do indicate that it *is* possible to make the work process within laboratories more egalitarian, even if the world outside is not. From the feminist perspective, such attempts to make the process more democratic in its day-today operation will fail if they do not adequately address the specific position of women in the process; it would not be enough merely to "democratise" relations between research workers themselves and leave untouched relations between them and the various other people that make the research possible. There is, of course, one sense in which any attempts thus to democratise workplaces *has* to fail from a feminist perspective, and that is that the entire enterprise rests on the labour of women behind the scenes, in the form of domestic labour. Unless the men involved were taking full responsibility for such work outside the lab, "democratisation" is at best a sham. Still, any attempt to remove hierarchies should be welcomed, even if it is only a partial answer.

Apart from changing hierarchical structures in individual laboratories, another way of altering practice is to place scientific expertise in the hands of the community. This is the principle behind the "science shops" that can be found in the Netherlands, to which members of the community may go for scientific information or expertise. A similar type of thing is found in work hazard groups in the U.K. (including one Women and Work Hazard Group), which generally form a link between trade-union organisations and scientists from the locality.[46] Within the Women's Liberation Movement, the nearest equivalent is the various women's health groups which provide some access to medical and health information.[47]

Scientific practice might also be challenged in another sense, through existing political channels. While it is not easy to increase the number of women in a position to influence national science policy (still less to increase the number of feminists!), feminists might consider ways of challenging their government's policies relating to science. At the time of writing, both the British and American governments are espousing a science policy overwhelmingly geared towards military-industrial interests: indeed, in both cases, defence expenditure currently exceeds 50 per cent of national research and development budgets.[48] Feminists do attempt to influence at least some aspects of that policy and its consequences by means varying from peaceful demonstration to more illicit actions, although at present a feminist influence upon the drawing up of science policy is non-existent. Science advisors to governments are almost invariably male.

Apart from changing scientific practice, there is also the possibility of changing the ideas that dominate scientific thinking. There may be many of these, of course, that I do not know about, and there are certainly many strands within biology of opposition to mechanism/reductionism. I will mention two. The first is the attempt to move away from reductionism and to think about "non-reductionist" approaches to biology, in which the organism, or other biological unit, is seen in terms of a dialectical relationship with its environment.[49] As I noted in Chapter Five, this kind of approach allows for greater complexity and flexibility, as well as the possibility that the "biology" may itself be changed as a function of that unit's environmental and historical context. When the unit is individuals, including individual humans, then the idea that the associated biology may itself be a product of its history and context is an important one with which to counteract the prevalent view that we are as we are because it is all fixed into our genes. Various tentative attempts to pursue a more progressive biology in this way have been made in different fields of biology, though it has yet to develop a characteristically feminist stance.

Another development of note is the attempt to de-emphasise competition as a catch-all excuse for social ills, by emphasising the extent and history of the concept of cooperation in nature.[50] As I noted in Chapter Seven, the notion of competition in evolutionary theory has often been used to buttress ideas of competition within capitalism, a tendency which has increased during the 1980s; yet there is also a thread of alternative ideas which stress cooperation and harmony, and it is these to which we need to draw attention. By doing so we can begin to counter the claims—often made by the Right—that feminism and socialism are delusions that cannot hope to overcome humankind's baser instincts. Attempting to understand the conditions in which humans are cooperative rather than exploitative and competitive seems an urgent task to undertake. Cooperation is more likely to be a basis for peace.

These attempts to change biological ideas are perhaps small beginnings, but they are steps in a different direction, which feminism might well heed. They are not, inevitably, without problems—an obvious one being the extent to which attempts to develop more progressive ideas will in practice change the orthodox views. Two other problems are worth noting; first, such attempts as there have been have, perhaps not surprisingly, come from within science. Precisely because of the hegemony of science, people outside it are often powerless to influence its progress. Second, there are serious limitations on ideas that have so far been produced simply because of who produces them and those people's social context. If the task is to think differently about the role of biology in the development of "human nature", then too little attention has yet been paid to human differences; biological constraints are experienced very differently if you are living in the affluent West rather than in famine-torn Ethiopia. In an article entitled "Challenging Imperial Feminism", Valerie Amos and Pratibha Parmar challenge some of the assumptions made by Western peace campaigners, including ecofeminists, by pointing out that "Internationally, while Black and Third World women are fighting daily battles for survival, for food, land and water, western white women's cries of anguish for concern about preserving the standards of life for their children and preserving the planet for future generations sound hollow. Whose standards of life are they fighting to preserve?"[51] Any attempt to "rethink" biology, to move towards more progressive ideas about the role and significance of human biology, has to take those differences in biological experience and needs into account. That, perhaps, should be the next step for the conjunction between feminism and biology with which I began this book.

In this chapter I have tried to bring together newly emerging ideas about feminism and science, particularly from the feminist literature; I have also tried to indicate their limitations. Those who have criticised science from a socialist perspective will inevitably recognise that many of the ideas raised here as "feminist" apply to broad socialist perspectives too. But a socialist perspective on its own is not likely to be enough if it is gender-blind, any more than it would be if it were blind to any other human differences, and I have tried here to focus on specifically feminist considerations. Science needs, suggests Rita Arditti, "a soul which would show respect and love for its subjects of study and would stress harmony and communication with the rest of the universe. When science fulfills its potential and becomes a tool for human liberation, we will not have to worry about women 'fitting' into it because we will probably be at the forefront of that 'new' science".[52] If science is to be changed, then it has to be done in ways that take account of gender and other differences, and that does mean that feminists have to engage actively in making that change.

Perhaps this discussion of creating a feminist science seems hopelessly utopian. Perhaps. But feminism *is,* above all else, about wanting and working for change, change towards a better society in which women of all kinds are not devalued, or oppressed in any way. Working for change has to include changing science, which not only perpetuates our oppression at present, but threatens also to destroy humanity and all the other species with whom we share this earth. If wanting to avert that danger is hopelessly utopian, then I know that there are millions of other utopian idealists around who are not content to accept annihilation from "rational" science and who are struggling to achieve change. My idealistic dream is of a better world.

Notes

INTRODUCTION

1. The Brighton Women and Science Group collectively edited *Alice Through the Microscope: the Power of Science over Women's Lives*, Virago, London, 1980.
2. See e.g. Olive Banks, *Faces of Feminism*, Martin Robertson, Oxford, 1981.
3. The "bra-burning" images of women's liberation, so beloved of the newspapers, probably stem from the demonstrations against the false standards of beauty and women implied by beauty contests. In 1968, a demonstration against the Miss America contest involved dumping garments such as bras and girdles into a rubbish bin. See Anna Coote and Beatrix Campbell, *Sweet Freedom: the Struggle for Women's Liberation*, Picador, London, pp. 10-12. And "Miss World", in *The Body Politic: Women's Liberation in Britain 1969-1972*, Stage 1, London, pp. 249-60, 1972.
4. The seven demands are outlined, for example in *No Turning Back: Writings from the Women's Liberation Movement 1975-1980*, Feminist Anthology Collective (ed.) The Women's Press, London, 1981, p. 4.
5. In its extreme form, this view considers that gender is wholly socially constructed. For further discussion, see Chapters 3 and 5, and also see Janet Sayers, *Biological Politics: Feminist and Antifeminist Perspectives*, Tavistock, London, 1982, pp. 107-24.
6. See, for example, Laurel Holliday, *The Violent Sex: Male Psychobiology and the Evolution of Consciousness*, Bluestocking Books, Guerneville, California, 1978.
7. See, e.g. Sayers, *op. cit.* pp. 187-92.
8. Since 1977 there has been a specific strand in British feminism called Revolutionary/Radical feminism.
9. Judith Stacey, "The New Conservative Feminism", *Feminist Studies* 9, 559-83, 1983.

CHAPTER 1

1. The concept of "patriarchy" has been used in various ways in the feminist literature, ranging from patriarchy defined as male domination over women (e.g. Kate Millett, *Sexual Politics*, Doubleday, New York, 1969) to patriarchy defined in terms of power relations within the family (e.g. B. Ehrenreich and D. English, *For Her Own Good: 150 Years of the Experts Advice to Women*, Pluto Press, London, 1979). For

discussions of the different meanings of the term and their uses, see Veronica Beechey, "On Patriarchy", *Feminist Review*, 3, 66-82, 1979; and Sheila Rowbotham, "The trouble with 'patriarchy' " and Sally Alexander and Barbara Taylor, "In defence of 'patriarchy' ", both in *No Turning Back op. cit.* In this book I have generally referred to capitalist patriarchy, to mean that form of male power over women existing within contemporary capitalism.
2. The notion of a "feminist science" is discussed at length in Chapter 8. I also address there the relationship between ideas of a feminist science and ideas of a "socialist science".
3. See, e.g., Ehrenreich and English, *op. cit.*
4. For an examination of the intellectual roots of feminism and their relationship to contemporary ideas within current women's liberation, see Banks, *op. cit.*
5. The ideas of self-help in women's health are dealt with in Angela Phillips and Jill Rakusen, *Our Bodies, Ourselves*, Penguin, London, 1979 (published in the U.S.A. by the Boston Women's Health Collective). For a historical account of the women's health movement in Britain, see Lesley Doyal, "Women, health and the sexual division of labor; a case study of the women's health movement in Britain", *International Journal of Health Services*, 13, 373-87, 1983.
6. This belief is based on the assumption that women, in general, are more likely than men to possess certain qualities that might be considered "good", such as nurturance, the capacity for affiliation, and for caring for others. This assumption may well be true, and these capacities are indeed encouraged within feminism. But to say that these are *inherent* qualities of women is another matter.
7. Ian Gilmour, *Inside Right: Conservatism, Policies and the People*, Quartet Books, London, 1978, p. 153.
8. See, e.g., Zillah R. Eisenstein, "The Sexual Politics of the New Right: Understanding the 'crisis of liberalism' for the 1980s", *Signs*, 7, 567-88, 1982 and Sheila Ruth, "A feminist analysis of the New Right", *Women's Studies International Forum*, 6, 345-51, 1983. Also see Lynda Birke, Hilary Rose and Steven Rose. "The New Right and the Nature of Human Nature", unpublished MS.
9. See Hilary Rose and Steven Rose, "Moving Right Out of Welfare— and the Way Back", *Critical Social Policy*, 2, 7-18, 1982. Although right-wing rhetoric is often anti-feminist, it is less overtly so in Britain than in the U.S.A. where the New Right is associated with the Moral Majority's attacks on feminism. See Lynne Segal, "The Heat in the Kitchen", in *The Politics of Thatcherism*, Stuart Hall and Martin Jacques (eds.), Lawrence and Wishart, London, 1983.
10. Shulamith Firestone, *The Dialectic of Sex*, Bantam Books, New York, 1971. The idea that reproductive differences underlie the creation of different spheres historically was also proposed by Engels in *The Origin of the Family, Private Property and the State*, International Publishers, New York, 1972, (first published 1884).

11. See, for instance, Jalna Hanmer and Pat Allen, "Reproductive Engineering; the Final Solution?", in Brighton Women and Science Group, *op. cit.*
12. See the Manushi Collective, "A New Form of Female Infanticide", in *Reclaim the Earth*, Leonie Caldecott and Stephanie Leland (eds.), The Women's Press, London, 1983, pp. 179-81, and Viola Roggencamp, "Abortion of a Special Kind: Male Sex Selection in India", in *Test-tube Women: What Future for Motherhood?*, Rita Arditti, Renate Duelli Klein and Shelley Minden (eds.), Pandora, London, 1984, pp. 266-77.
13. This is the line taken, for example, by Hans Eysenck, whose book, *Race, Intelligence and Education*, (London, Temple Smith, 1981) has been condemned as racist: see, e.g. Steven Rose, "Scientific racism and ideology: the IQ racket from Galton to Jensen", in *The Political Economy of Science*, H. Rose and S. Rose (eds.), Macmillan, London, 1976.
14. See Brighton Women and Science Group, *op. cit.*, 1980, pp. 13-19.
15. E.g. R. Young, "Science *is* social relations", *Radical Science Journal*, 5, 65-131, 1977.
16. For further discussion of this antithesis, see Hilary Rose and Steven Rose, "The Metaphor Goes Into Orbit. Science is not all social relations", *Science Bulletin*, 22, 12-18, 1979; Hilary Rose and Steven Rose, "Radical Science and its Enemies", *The Socialist Register*, 1979, pp. 317-35; and Donald MacKenzie, "Notes on the Science and Social Relations Debate", *Capital and Class*, 14, 47-60. Some of the issues raised by this antithesis will be referred to again in Chapter 8.
17. See, for example, Carolyn Merchant, *The Death of Nature: Women, Ecology and the Scientific Revolution*, Wildwood, London, 1982; and Penelope Brown and Ludmilla Jordanova, "Oppressive Dichotomies: The Nature/culture debate", in *Women in Society: Interdisciplinary Essays*, Cambridge Women's Studies Group (eds.) Virago, London, 1981. These authors point out that the nature/culture dichotomy and its association with gender occurs in recent Western science. There is much more argument about the extent to which these associations are universal cross-culturally. See, e.g., Carol MacCormack, "Nature, culture and gender: a critique", in *Nature, Culture and Gender*, C. MacCormack and M. Strathern (eds.) Cambridge University Press, Cambridge, 1980. That the status of women is not in fact uniform cross-culturally is discussed by Penelope Brown. See "Universals and Particulars in the Position of women", in *Women in Society, op. cit.*
18. This was the Aristotelean idea of a "Great Chain of Being". See E. O. Lovejoy, *The Great Chain of Being: A Study of the History of an Idea*, Harper and Row, New York, 1936. For a discussion of the association of this with gender see Lynda Birke, "Cleaving the Mind: Speculations on Conceptual Dichotomies", in *Against Biological Determinism*, The Dialectics of Biology Group, Allison and Busby, London, 1982.
19. Karen Paige, "Women learn to sing the menstrual blues", *Psychology Today*, September 1973, pp. 41-6.

20. That is, women of different cultures or social classes are likely to experience biological events differently, according to the cultural meaning given to those events. For further discussion of this see Hilary Standing, "Sickness is a Woman's Business: Reflections on the Attribution of Illness", Brighton Women and Science Group, *op. cit.* One specific example is afforded by the wide cultural variation in the experience of menstruation; see, for instance, O. Janiger, R. Riffenberg, and R. Karsh, "Cross-cultural study of premenstrual symptoms", *Psychosomatics*, 13, 226-35, 1972.
21. See Ehrenreich and English, *op. cit.*, and V. L. Bullough and M. Voght, "Women, Menstruation and Nineteenth Century Medicine", *Bulletin of the History of Medicine*, 47, 66-82, 1973.

CHAPTER 2

1. For future discussion of the debates about mothering see Nancy Chodorow, *The Reproduction of Mothering*, University of California Press, Berkeley, 1978; and Dorothy Dinnerstein, *The Mermaid and the Minotaur*, Harper and Row, New York, 1976. Also see Janet Sayers, "Feminism and Mothering: A Kleinian Perspective", *Women's Studies International Forum*, 7, 237-41, 1984.
2. See, e.g. Susan Moller Okin, *Women in Western Political Thought*, Virago, London, 1980, pp. 73-99; and Lynda Lange, "Woman is not a rational animal: On Aristotle's Biology of Reproduction", in *Discovering Reality: Feminist Perspectives on Epistemology, Metaphysics Methodology and Philosophy in Science*, S. Harding and M. R. Hintikka (eds.), Reidel, London, 1983; and M. C. Horowitz, "Aristotle and Woman", *Journal of the History of Biology*, 9, 183-213, 1976.
3. See, e.g., Fraser Harrison, *The Dark Angel: Aspects of Victorian Sexuality*, Fontana, London, 1977.
4. Bea Campbell, "Sexuality and Submission", in *Conditions of Illusion: Papers from the Women's Movement*, Feminist Books, Leeds, 1974.
5. The idea of "thwarting" does assume something like a "drive" requiring to be expressed. The notion of "drive" has a long history, but has come in for much criticism in recent years, not least because it assumes an internally driven state in the absence of environmental stimuli. Organisms do not, however, usually do things in the absence of external stimuli, and theories of motivation—human or animal—have had to be revised to take greater account of both external and internal events. See, for example, Robert Hinde, *Biological Bases of Human Social Behaviour*, McGraw-Hill, New York, 1974, and F. Toates and L. I. A. Birke, "Motivation: A new perspective on some old Ideas", in *Perspectives in Ethology V*, P. Bateson and P. H. Klopfer (eds.), Plenum, New York, 1982.

6. See, for example, J. H. Gagnon and William Simon, *Sexual Conduct: The Social Sources of Human Sexuality*, Hutchinson, London, 1973.
7. It might, of course, be argued that, while the forms of its expression may be culturally learnt, the underlying urge remains as a biological imperative. But I would suggest that this is not the way that people actually experience their sexuality: most people, if they feel an "urge" at all, experience it as an urge to do something specific, like having sex with a lover, or masturbating.
8. Interest in following psychoanalytic theory from a feminist perspective has been particularly prevalent among French feminists. See, for example, Luce Irigaray, "Women's Exile: Interview with Luce Irigaray", *Ideology and Consciousness*, 1, 1978. Also see Jacqueline Rose, "Femininity and its discontents", *Feminist Review*, 14, 5-21, 1983.
9. Wilhelm Reich, *The Invasion of Compulsory Sex-Morality*, Penguin, Harmondsworth, 1975, pp. 160-1.
10. The extent to which the prediction would hold would vary with species anyway. Female mammals are said to have a high investment in their offspring, by virtue of having to carry them to term within the female body. The difference in putative investment between males and females might be less, however, for non-viviparous animals, particularly those which lay hundreds of eggs. See Robert Trivers, "Parental Investment and Sexual Selection", in *Sexual Selection and the Descent of Man*, B. Campbell (ed.), Aldine, Chicago, 1972.
11. S, Freud, 1931, "Female Sexuality". *Standard Edition of the Complete Psychological Works of Sigmund Freud*, Volume 21.
12. Anne Koedt, "The Myth of the Vaginal Orgasm", in *Radical Feminism*, Anne Koedt, Ellen Levine and Anita Rapone (eds.), Quadrangle, New York, 1973. Beatrix Campbell has pointed out, however, that the challenge did not arise *de novo* with the present women's movement, but has a longer history. See Beatrix Campbell, "A Feminist Sexual Politics: Now you see it, now you don't", *Feminist Review*, 5, 1-18, 1980.
13. See for example the responses to Shere Hite's questionnaire on women's sexuality. Shere Hite, *The Hite Report*, Cassell, Australia, 1976.
14. See, for example, Jeffrey Weeks, *Sex, Politics and Society, The Regulation of Sexuality since 1800*, Longman, London, 1981. Especially pp. 19-56.
15. This was also a belief maintained by the feminists of the late nineteenth century, who were campaigning for women's rights on the basis of a belief in the inherent purity and greater goodness of women. See, for example, Judith R. Walkowitz, "Male Vice and Female Virtue: Feminism and the politics of prostitution in Nineteenth Century Britain", in *Desire: The Politics of Sexuality*, Ann Snitow, Christine Stansell and Sharon Thompson (eds.), Virago, London, 1983. Also, Lucy Bland, " 'Guardians of the Race' or 'Vampires upon the nation's

health"?: Female sexuality and its regulation in early twentieth century Britain", in *The Changing Experience of Women*, Elizabeth Whitelegg et al. (eds.), Martin Robertson, Oxford, 1982.
16. Harrison, *op. cit.*, pp. 217-57.
17. Alexandra Kollontai, *Selected Writings*, Allison and Busby, London, 1977, p. 264.
18. See Edwin M. Schur, *The Politics of Deviance: Stigma Contests and the Uses of Power*, Prentice Hall, New Jersey, 1980, pp. 111-13. Schur points out that such research commonly makes the assumption that women can be divided into "normal" and "deviant" (i.e. prostitutes), the difference lying in their respective backgrounds. Although such research no longer assumes a biological causation, biological theories of prostitution can still be found. See, for example, David Barash, *Sociobiology: The Whisperings Within*, Souvenir Press, London, 1980, p. 78. Prostitution, for Barash, is biological in both humming-birds and women.
19. I. H. Jones, and D. Frei, "Male exhibitionism—a biological hypothesis", *British Journal of Medical Psychology*, 52, 63-70, 1979. (My emphasis).
20. Roger Scruton, "The Case Against Feminism", *The Observer*, 22 May 1983, p. 27.
21. Barash, *op. cit.*, p. 55. Sociobiologists such as Barash are fond of using emotive terms such as rape, adultery, even prostitution, to describe the behaviour of animals or even plants. Such terms imply that the animal cases are very similar to those in human society. In the case of rape, Barash describes male mallards who dispense with the usual courtship and attempt to copulate with a female, "despite her obvious and vigorous protest" (p. 54). We cannot, of course, know whether or not the female was "willing", and it is only Barash's wishful thinking that says otherwise. Moreover, such biological "instances" further confound the issue by assuming that it has to do with sex. Rape in human society has more to do with male power over women, as feminists have often argued. (e.g. Susan Brownmiller, *Against Our Will: Men, Women and Rape*, Simon and Schuster, New York, 1975).
22. See the discussion by Diana E. H. Russell and Laura Lederer, "Questions We Get Asked Most Often", in *Take Back the Night: Women on Pornography*, L. Lederer (ed.), Bantam, London, 1980, pp. 9-15. For a discussion of differences and similarities between this "liberal" view, the conservative moral view, and feminist interpretations of pornography see M. Maureen Killoran, "Sticks and stones can break my bones and images can hurt me: feminism and the pornography debate", *International Journal of Women's Studies*, 6, 443-56, 1983.
23. And even the violence itself can become assimilated to the assumption of men's innate sex drive: The Women's Report Collective reported the case of one doctor who claimed that he would *prescribe* for men images of women being tortured on the grounds that they produced a sexual catharsis, a "masturbatory response". See the Women's Report

Collective, "Pornography", in *No Turning Back, op. cit.*

24. That a great many of the gay community also maintain those stereotypes does not of course necessarily mean that these have a biological basis.

25. John Money and Anke Ehrhardt, *Man and Woman, Boy and Girl*, Johns Hopkins University Press, Baltimore, 1972, p. 146.

26. Similar assumptions pervade animal research that purports to concern itself with homosexuality. One researcher, for example, writes about "homosexual" (male) rats that behave in a "feminine" fashion: the male rats that mounted them were, apparently considered quite normal and not homosexual! See Gunter Dorner, *Hormones and Brain Differentiation*, Elsevier, Amsterdam, 1976. For a critique of such research see Lynda I. A. Birke, "Is homosexuality hormonally determined?", *Journal of Homosexuality*, 6, 1982, 35-49.

27. M. Foucault, *The History of Sexuality Vol. 1*, Allen Lane, London, 1979. For a detailed history of changing attitudes to different forms of sexual expression see V. L. Bullough, *Sexual Variance in Society and History*, University of Chicago, Chicago, 1976.

28. See Foucault, *op. cit.,* Also see Mary McIntosh, "The Homosexual Role", *Social Problems*, 16, 182-92, 1968.

29. Jeffrey Weeks has argued that the categorisation has continued and has, paradoxically, helped to undermine the very existence of the category "homosexual" through its continuation in gay liberation. "Homosexuals" are themselves now divided up into various other categories. See Weeks, *op. cit.*, p. 287.

30. See Sheila Rowbotham and Jeffrey Weeks, *Socialism and the New Life: The Personal and Sexual Politics of Edward Carpenter and Havelock Ellis*, Pluto, London, 1977. Ellis also argued against the view that activity/passivity was always characteristic of gay male relationships: see p. 160. On the other hand, he accepted the stereotype for lesbianism!

31. For further discussion see Lynda Birke, "From sin to sickness; biological theories of lesbianism", in *Biological Woman—The Convenient Myth,* Ruth Hubbard, Mary Sue Henifin and Barbara Fried (eds.), Schenkman, Boston, 1982.

32. *Ibid.*

33. Adrienne Rich, "Compulsory Heterosexuality and Lesbian Existence", in Snitow, Stansell and Thompson, *op. cit.* (note 15).

34. See Jo Campling, *Images of Ourselves: Women with Disabilities Talking*, Routledge & Kegan Paul, London, 1981.

35. See Bell Hooks, *Ain't I a Woman: Black Women and Feminism*, Pluto, London, 1981, pp. 15-50. Rennie Simpson, "The Afro-American Female: The Historical Context of the Construction of Sexual Identity", in Snitow, Stansell and Thompson, *op. cit.*, also describes black women's experiences of sexual abuse.

36. Hooks, *op. cit.,* p. 65.

37. *Ibid*, p. 59.

38. Luisah Teish, "A Quiet Subversion", in Lederer, *op. cit.*
39. Cited in Ehrenreich and English, *op. cit.*, p. 58.
40. E. H. Clarke, *Sex in Education, or, A Fair Chance for Girls*, J. R. Osgood, Boston, 1873, pp. 156-7.
41. *Ibid.*, p. 133.
42. Cited in Ehrenreich and English, *op. cit.*, p. 103.
43. D. M. Broverman, E. W. Klaiber, Y. Kobayashi, and W. Vogel, "Roles of activation and inhibition in sex differences in cognitive abilities", *Psychology Review*, 75, 23-50, 1968. For a critical comment see Mary Brown Parlee, "Comments on 'Roles of activation and inhibition in cognitive abilities', by D. M. Broverman, E. L. Klaiber, Y. Kobayashi and W. Vogel", *Psychology Review*, 79, 180-4, 1972.
44. Corrinne Hutt, *Males and Females,* Penguin, Harmondsworth, 1972, p. 97.
45. See E. E. Maccoby and C. N. Jacklin, *The Psychology of Sex Differences*, Stanford University Press California, 1975.
46. See the discussion in Sayers *Biological Politics; op. cit.*, pp. 97-104. Also, Susan Leigh Star, "The Politics of Right and Left: Sex Differences in Hemispheric Brain Asymmetry", in *Women Look at Biology Looking at Women*, R. Hubbard, M S. Henifin, and B. Fried (eds.), Schenkman, Boston, 1979.
47. Sayers, 1982, *op. cit.*, p. 101.
48. Ehrenreich and English, *op. cit.*, p. 141. Some feminists argued for domestic science as a means of getting some *science* education into the girls' schools, but much of the propaganda did revolve around the assumption that the home was woman's natural sphere.
49. E. O. Wilson, "Human decency is animal", *New York Times Magazine*, 12 October, 1975, 35-50.
50. Barash, *op. cit.,* p. 188.
51. Nancy Tanner and Adrienne Zihlman, "Women in Evolution: Part I: Innovation and Selection in Human origins", *Signs*, 1, 585-608, 1976.
52. For further discussion of feminist objections to the Man-the-Hunter view, see Ruth Bleier, *Science and Gender: A Critique of Biology and its Theories on Women,* Pergamon, Oxford, 1984, pp. 115-38.
53. D. Barash, *Sociobiology and Behaviour*, Elsevier, New York, 1977, p. 301. Ruth Bleier quotes this piece, and comments on the language (e.g. of relegation versus satisfaction) noting that, "(Barash) then proceeds to base them *both* in biology as though they *were* equivalent. It is like claiming that repeatedly jailed offenders have an innate attachment to their cells" (Bleier, *op. cit.*, p. 21). Barash also supposes that men universally find job-satisfaction, an assumption that would not appeal to many men working long hours in dirty, noisy factories.
54. The special risks to women, or to the foetus, are largely ignored when lethal limits are calculated for any chemical or other hazard. Lethal limits are calculated on the basis of the body size of the average (male) worker.
55. Jeanne M. Stellman and Mary Sue Henifin, "No Fertile Woman Need Apply: Employment Discrimination and Reproductive Hazards in the

Workplace", in *Biological Woman: The Convenient Myth,* R. Hubbard *et al.* (eds.), *op. cit.*

56. Val Binney, "Domestic Violence: battered women in Britain in the 1970's", in Cambridge Women's Studies Group, *op. cit.*
57. Erin Pizzey and Jeff Shapiro, *Prone to Violence,* Hamlyn, Middlesex, 1982. Many feminists have been outraged by the book, for various reasons. See, e.g., Liz Kelly, "Who Needs Enemies with Friends like Erin Pizzey?", in *Sweeping Statements: Writings from the Women's Liberation Movement 1981-83,* H. Kanter, S. Lefanu, S. Shah and C. Spedding (eds.), The Women's Press, London, 1984.
58. The biology here is rather dubious, since the principal hormone of this type in humans is cortisol, not cortisone. The latter is the principle hormone in rats: one wonders if this slip is significant.
59. Pizzey and Shapiro, *op. cit.,* p. 181.

CHAPTER 3

1. Steven Goldberg, *The Inevitability of Patriarchy,* Temple Smith, London, 1974.
2. R. Verrall, "Sociobiology: the instincts in our genes", *Spearhead,* March 1979.
3. See The Women and Fascism Study Group, *Breeders for Race and Nation: Women and Fascism in Britain Today,* Undated pamphlet.
4. Verrall, *op. cit.* (sic). There are many genes on the sex (and other) chromosomes—not the other way around.
5. Scruton, *op. cit.*
6. J. Campbell, "Happy to be Prisoners of Gender", *The Standard,* 7 December 1983.
7. This is discussed by, for example, Michèle Barrett in *Women's Oppression Today: Problems in Marxist Feminist Analysis,* Verso, London, 1980, pp. 84-113.
8. G. Wilson, "The Sociobiology of Sex Differences", *Bulletin of the British Psychological Society,* 32, 350-3, 1979.
9. *Ibid.,* p. 353.
10. E. O. Wilson, *Sociobiology: The New Synthesis,* Belknap, Cambridge, Mass., 1975.
11. There have been many critiques of sociobiology. Feminist critiques include: Deirdre Janson-Smith, "Sociobiology—So What?", in Brighton Women and Science Group, *op. cit.,* chapters in Sayers, 1982, and Bleier, *op. cit.*
12. E. O. Wilson, *On Human Nature,* Bantam, New York, 1979, pp. 137-9.
13. Holliday, *op. cit.,* p. 121.
14. I am certainly not denying by this that women need women-only space. Unless radical social change occurs they will always need that. It is, nonetheless, true that some women's response to the belief in the

universality of male dominance is to withdraw completely into feminist space. At a personal level this may be very necessary, but it does nothing to challenge or change the larger society.
15. See Stacey, *op. cit.*
16. See, e.g. Eisenstein, *op. cit.*
17. Stacey, *op. cit.* Stacey refers to a number of Elshtain's essays in her analysis, but particularly the book *Public Man, Private Woman: Women in Social and Political Thought*, Princeton University Press, 1981. Also see J. B. Elshtain, "Symmetry and Soporifics: A critique of feminist accounts of gender development", in *Capitalism and Infancy*, B. Richards (ed.), Free Association Books, London, 1984.
18. Janet Radcliffe Richards, *The Sceptical Feminist*, Pelican, Harmondsworth, 1982, p. 85. (Emphasis in original).
19. *Ibid.*, p. 64.
20. For a critique of such assumptions see, e.g., Bleier, *op. cit.*, pp. 80-114; Lynda Birke, "Murderous Molecules: Hormones and Female Aggression", in *The Aggressive Female*, D. Benton and P. Brain (eds.), Eden Press, Montreal, 1985: BSSRS Sociobiology Group, "Animal behaviour to human nature: ethological concepts of dominance", in *More than the Parts: Biology and Politics*, Lynda Birke and Jonathan Silvertown (eds.) Pluto, London, 1984.
21. That Richards implies a fixed, biologically based, concept of human nature is also suggested by her phrase "men whose nature inclines them to rape". As I noted in the previous chapter, this kind of phrase assumes some sort of internally driven urge, located within the individual, and it specifically denies that rape has anything to do with male power over women.
22. This is the legacy of the post-Althusserian emphasis on ideology and cultural representation, which has culminated in discourse theory. For a discussion of feminism and discourse theory see Barrett, *op. cit.*, pp. 84-113. Of course part of the critique of biological determinism rests on the assumption that such determinism contributes to women's oppression through ideology in the first instance. That is, the biological theories operate through their representations of women. That leaves us, however, in the position of assuming that women's biology is related to concepts of gender only in terms of the associated ideology.
23. This is sometimes dealt with through the assertion that ideology is material. However, as Michèle Barrett points out, this explains little, particularly in relation to the material reality of human struggles. (Barrett, *op. cit.*, p. 95).
24. *Ibid.*, p. 73.
25. These ideas are discussed at length in Sayers, 1982, pp. 107-25.
26. See Lynda Birke and Sandy Best, "The Tyrannical Womb: Menstruation and Menopause", in Brighton Women and Science Group, *op. cit.*, and "Changing Minds: Women, Biology and the Menstrual Cycle", in *Biological Woman—The convenient Myth, op. cit.* Also see Paula Weideger *Female Cycles*, The Women's Press, London, 1979.

27. E.g. O. Janiger, R. Riffenberg, and R. Karsh, *op. cit.*
28. Menstrual pain is sometimes correlated with high levels of a particular hormone in the uterus, prostaglandin F2 α and is accordingly treated medically by drugs which lower prostaglandin levels.
29. Sayers, 1982, *op. cit.*, p. 121.
30. E.g. Katharina Dalton, *Once A Month*, Harvester Press, Brighton and Hunter House, Pomona, California.
31. Sayers, 1982, *op. cit.*, p. 123.
32. Bleier, *op. cit.*, p. 143.
33. See, e.g., J. Scott and L. Tilly, "Women's work and the family in Nineteenth Century Europe", in Whitelegg *et al.*, *op. cit.*
34. Bleier, *op. cit.*, p. 146. For discussion of the problems arising from assuming universals, see also Penelope Brown, "Universals and Particulars in the Position of Women", in Cambridge Women's Studies Group, *op. cit.*
35. Bleier, *op. cit.*, p. 157. She also notes Mary O'Brien's suggestion that it is not the *biological* fact of reproduction that has been significant in human evolution, but the *consciousness* of it. Women, argues O'Brien, experience their role in reproduction, whereas men only have abstract knowledge of theirs. See Mary O'Brien, *The Politics of Reproduction*, Routledge & Kegan Paul, London, 1981.
36. Joan Smith, "Sociobiology and Feminism: The Very Strange Courtship of Competing Paradigms, *Philosophical Forum*, 13, 281-308, 1982. Also, "Feminist Analysis of Gender: A Mystique", in *Woman's Nature: Rationalizations of Inequality*, Marian Lowe and Ruth Hubbard (eds.), Pergamon, Oxford, 1983.
37. Smith argues, for instance, that universal assumptions are implied by—among others—Nancy Chodorow *op. cit.*; Zillah Eisenstein in *The Radical Future of Liberal Feminism*, Longman, New York, 1981, and Heidi Hartmann in "The Family as the Locus of Gender, Class and Political Struggles: The example of Housework", *Signs* 6, 373, 1981.
38. Smith, 1983, *op. cit.*, p. 97.
39. Lionel Tiger, "Male dominance? Yes, alas. A Sexist plot? No", *New York Times Magazine*, October 1970.
40. O'Brien, *op. cit.*, p. 21.
41. *Ibid.*, pp. 21-2. Whether or not Technology confers any "freedom to choose" for women is of course dependent upon gender relations and power structures. At present, "choice" is constrained by women's relative lack of power.
42. Money and Ehrhardt, *op. cit.*

CHAPTER 4

1. The idea that scientific method was liberatory and progressive was central to the ideas of people like Francis Bacon, writing at the outset of the scientific revolution. It was similarly a theme supported by radical left-wing scientists of earlier decades of this century, who felt

that it was the constraints imposed by capitalism that prevented science from flowering to its full potential. J. D. Bernal, for instance, believed that science itself would contribute to the removal of those constraints, thus paving the way for a more liberatory and progressive science. See e.g., J. D. Bernal, *The Social Function of Science,* MIT press, Cambridge, Mass., 1939 (2nd paperback printing, 1973). Gary Werskey outlines some of the attitudes towards science and its liberatory potential held by Bernal and his radical associates during the inter-war years in *The Visible College,* Allen Lane, London, 1978.
2. See also Hilary Rose and Steven Rose, "On Oppositions to Reductionism", in *Against Biological Determinism,* The Dialectics of Biology Group, Allison and Busby, London, 1982.
3. For further discussion of different types of causal explanation in biology, see Steven Rose, "Biological Reductionism: its roots and social functions", in Birke and Silvertown, *op.cit.,* also see S. Rose, L. J. Kamin and R. C. Lewontin, *Not In our Genes: Biology, Ideology and Human Nature,* Penguin, Harmondsworth, 1984. pp. 265-90.
4. E. O. Wilson, *Sociobiology, op. cit.,* and J. Monod, *Chance and Necessity,* Fontana, London, 1974.
5. See, e.g., Paul Weiss, "The Living System: Determinism Stratified", in *Beyond Reductionism: New Perspectives in the Life Sciences,* A. Koestler and J. R. Smythies (eds.), Hutchinson, London, 1968.
6. This point about the ontological priority that reductionism assumes for phenomena at lower levels (that is, the priority of individual over society, of molecule over cell etc.) is discussed at greater length by Steven Rose in "Biological Reductionism" *op. cit.* (note 3).
7. W. T. Astbury, in his Harvey Lecture of 1950. Cited by J. A. Fuerst in "The Role of Reductionism in the development of molecular biology: peripheral or central?" *Social Studies of Science,* 12, 241-78, 1982.
8. The "central dogma" was originally proposed by Weismann at the end of the nineteenth century, prior to the discovery of DNA, and referred to information flow from the cell nucleus to the phenotype.
9. DNA is the molecule of which chromosomes are (partly) made. "Genes" are parts of chromosomes, and hence consist largely of DNA. The central dogma assumes that DNA directs the transfer of its encoded information to a similar molecule, RNA, which in turn uses this information to direct the construction of proteins in the cell.
10. See, e.g., N. D. Cook, "The case for reverse translation", *Journal of Theoretical Biology,* 64, 113-35, 1977.
11. See Evelyn Fox Keller, *A Feeling for the Organism: The Life and Work of Barbara McClintock,* W. H. Freeman, New York, 1983.
12. Barbara McClintock, "Chromosome organisation and genic expression", *Cold Spring Harbor Symposium for Quantitative Biology,* Cold Spring Harbor, New York, 1951, p. 34.
13. Evelyn Fox Keller, "Women, science and Popular Mythology", in *Machina Ex Dea: Feminist Perspectives on Technology,* J. Rothschild (ed.), Pergamon, Oxford, 1983, pp. 142-3.
14. E.g. Richard Dawkins, *The Selfish Gene,* Oxford University Press, Oxford, 1976.

15. E.g. S. Rose, "From Causations to Translations: A dialectical solution to a reductionist enigma", in *Towards A Liberatory Biology*, The Dialectics of Biology Group, Allison and Busby, London, 1982.
16. P. Weiss, "The living system: Determinism Stratified", in Koestler and Smythies, *op. cit.*, p. 10.
17. C. A. Barraclough and R. A. Gorski, "Studies on mating behaviour in the androgen-sterilised rat and their relation to the hypothalamic regulation of sexual behavior in the female rat", *Journal of Endocrinology* 25, 175-82, 1962.
18. See Dalton, *op. cit.*
19. Dr. Dalton was the expert witness for these court cases and argued her progesterone theory. It has provoked feminist concern on the grounds that PMT could become an excuse for overt discrimination.
20. Georgio Bignami, "Disease Models and Reductionist Thinking in the Biomedical Sciences," in: *Against Biological Determinism*, The Dialectics of Biology Group, *op. cit.*
21. *Ibid.*, pp. 98-9.
22. E.g. G. Dorner, *op. cit.*
23. See L. I. A. Birke, "Is homosexuality hormonally determined?" *op. cit.*
24. For discussion of some of the attempts, see Birke, *ibid.*
25. For example, see Holliday, *op. cit.*, pp. 122-5
26. And, of course, there is considerable variability between cultures in what constitutes appropriate behaviour for the two sexes, so that—cross-culturally at least—this component of gender cannot be said to correlate with biological sex.
27. The "sex hormones" usually means particular kinds of steroid hormone affecting the reproductive system. There are three kinds: androgens, oestrogens and progestins. What differentiates the sexes is the relative quantities of each type produced; thus, androgens are secreted in greater quantities by males, and oestrogens and progestins by females.
28. For examples of the various steps in this circular logic see the examples given in Birke, "Is homosexuality hormonally determined?" *op. cit.*
29. It has, furthermore, been argued that the tendency to dichotomise the world, to see it in terms of mutually exclusive opposites, is a particularly masculine trait, one which develops from a male's sense of "otherness". See Nancy Hartsock "The feminist standpoint: developing the ground for a specifically feminist historical materialism", in: Harding and Hintikka, *op. cit.*, pp. 296-8.
30. V. H. Mark and F. R. Ervin, *Violence and the Brain*, Harper and Row, New York, 1971. For a critique of such surgery, see Sean Murphy, "Neuroscience: the cutting edge of biology?" in Birke and Silvertown, *op. cit.* and Stephan Chorover, *From Genesis to Genocide*, M. I. T. Press, Cambridge, Mass., 1979.
31. The charge of "unscientific" has, of course, also been levied by those opposed to reductionism, albeit on different grounds. It has been, for example, one of the points of criticism of those opposed to ideas of human sociobiology, which have been referred to as "just-so" stories.

See, e.g., Steven Rose, Leon Kamin and R. Lewontin, *op. cit.*
32. See, e.g., Werner Heisenberg's autobiography, *Physics and Beyond: Memories of a Life in Science,* George Allen and Unwin, London, 1971. See especially Chapter 10, "Quantum Mechanics and Kantian Philosophy", pp. 117-24.
33. For an alternative framework to reductionism within which to understand the development of biological form, see the structuralist approach discussed by Gerry Webster and Brian Goodwin, "History and Structure in Biology", in *Towards a Liberatory Biology,* Dialectics of Biology Group (ed.), *op. cit.*
34. See, e.g., Paul Weiss, "The Living System: Determinism Stratified", and Ludwig van Bertallanffy, "Chance or law?" in Koestler and Smythies, *op. cit.* Also see Arthur Koestler, *The Ghost in the Machine,* Pan Books, London, 1970.
35. J. A. Raymond and J. Wilson, "Feminism—healing the Patriarchal Dis-ease", in Caldecott and Leland, *op. cit.,* p. 63. The emphasis in holistic health movements on the individual's own responsibility for her health does, of course, assume that the individual is free to make choices for herself—which not all women are. This point is made with respect to poor black women by Wilmette Brown in "Roots: Black Ghetto Ecology" also in Caldecott and Leland; see especially pp. 80-3.
36. See Allan Muir, "Holism and Reductionism are Compatible", in *Against Biological Determinism,* Dialectics of Biology Group, *op. cit.*
37. Koestler, *op. cit.*
38. For a useful review to that date, see L. Plapinger and B. S. McEwan, "Gonadal steroid-brain interactions in sexual differentiation", in *Biological Determinants of Sexual Behaviour,* J. B. Hutchison (ed.) John Wiley, Chichester, 1978.
39. It used to be stated that what was needed to make a male was androgen, while females developed in the absence of androgens. This was a story which some feminist writers have espoused—not least because it rather reverses the story of Adam and Eve! There is something comforting in the idea that the "basic form" is female. It is, sadly for comforting thoughts, not nearly so simple, and many hormones are capable of influencing sexual differentiation.
40. Specifically, mother rats differentiate between their male and female offspring, spending more time licking male pups! See C. L. Moore and G. A. Morelli, "Mother rats interact differently with male and female offspring", *Journal of Comparative Physiological Psychology,* 93, 677-84, 1979; G. Richmond and B. D. Sachs, "Maternal discrimination of pup sex in rats", *Developmental Psychobiology,* 17, 87-9, 1984. Maternal discrimination appears to contribute to later behavioural differentiation, as some of our own (unpublished) observations of rat behaviour have indicated, as have subsequent experiments by Moore. See C. L. Moore, "Maternal contributions to the development of masculine sexual behavior in laboratory rats", *Developmental Psychobiology,* 17, 347-56, 1984.
41. C. L. Moore, "Maternal behavior of rats is affected by hormonal

condition of pups", *Journal of Comparative Physiological Psychology,* 96, 123-9, 1982.

CHAPTER 5

1. *The Sun,* 30 August, 1979.
2. An opposition which is used to good political effect. The right-wing *Daily Mail* used this device, for example, to publicise the views of the inheritance of I.Q. put forward by Hans Eysenck, phrased, inevitably, in such a way that only a fool would disagree. See "Equality Stops Here Now" by Jane McLoughlin, *Daily Mail,* 21 May 1977.
3. See, for instance, Hugh Fairweather, "Sex differences in cognition", *Cognition,* 4, 231-80, 1976. Perhaps the most telling evidence comes from cross-cultural comparisons, which suggest that sex differences only appear in societies which are highly stratified with respect to sex. See J. W. Berry and R. C. Annis, "Ecology, culture and psychological differentiation", *International Journal of Psychology,* 9, 173-93, 1974.
4. K. Dyer, "Genetic Determination of spatial ability: conjectures and Refutations". Unpublished paper presented at seminar at the Open University, 1982.
5. The view that at birth, the infant is a *tabula rasa,* a blank slate on to which sense experiences impinge (attributed to Locke) implies for instance that reason, the rational interpretation of our sensory experiences, cannot be innate.
6. Alison Jagger, *Feminist Politics and Human Nature,* Harvester, Brighton, 1983, p. 29.
7. *Ibid.,* p. 41.
8. I. Gilmour, *op. cit.,* p. 153.
9. See, e.g., K. R. Popper and J. C. Eccles, *The Self and Its Brain: An Argument for Interactionism,* Springer International, London, 1977 — though, as Popper and Eccles point out, the idea of interaction between mind and brain is traceable throughout Western thought, back at least to ancient Greece.
10. This argument is recognisably a "neo-Lamarckian" one. Given the derision with which many biologists view Lamarck's ideas, it is perhaps not surprising that the argument is uncommon. Nevertheless there is evidence to support it, and there is much that neo-Darwinism cannot explain. For further discussion of these points, see Mae-Wan Ho and Peter Saunders, "Adaptation and Natural Selection: Mechanism and Teleology", in *Towards a Liberatory Biology*, The Dialectics of Biology Group, *op. cit.*
11. Barbara Lloyd, "Social responsibility and research on sex differences", in B. Lloyd and J. Archer (eds.) *Exploring Sex Differences,* Academic Press, London, 1976. p. 13.
12. D. McGuiness, "Sex differences in the organization of perception and cognition, in *Lloyd and Archer, op. cit.* For a discusssion of other

problems that arise from viewing interaction in this way see A. R. Buss, *A Dialectical Psychology*, Irvington, New York, 1979, pp. 161-8.

13. C. Taylor, "Mind-body identity, a side issue?" in *The Mind/Brain Identity Theory*, C. V. Borst (ed.), Macmillan, London, 1970, p. 234.

14. Jagger, *op. cit.* By stressing the dependency of human infants, I do not wish to imply that infants lack agency, the ability to act upon their world. Theorists who stress the significance of present care-giving arrangements in the development of gender asymmetry have been criticised for implying that children are passive recipients of cultural conditioning. See Jean Bethke Elshtain, "Symmetry and soporifics: a critique of feminist accounts of gender development", in *Capitalism and infancy: essays on psychoanalysis and politics*, Free Association Books, London, 1984.

15. J. Archer, "Biological explanations of psychological sex differences", in Lloyd and Archer, *op. cit.* p. 252.

16. Janet Radcliffe Richards, *The Sceptical Feminist, op. cit.* Also see Chapter 3.

17. A word derived from the Greek roots *andro* and *gynae* — meaning, respectively, male and female. Given the etymology of the word, it should be pronounced andro-gyny — not, as is frequently the case, like and*r*ogeny. Androgens are a class of hormones, sometimes (erroneously) called the "male" hormones.

18. See for example the discussion by Dorothy Z. Ullian, "The development of conceptions of masculinity and femininity", in Lloyd and Archer, *op. cit.*

19. See June Singer, *Androgyny: Towards a New Theory of Sexuality*, Routledge and Kegan Paul, London, 1977, especially pp. 224-48.

20. See Janet Sayers, "Psychological Sex Differences" in Brighton Women and Science Group, *Alice Through the Microscope, op. cit.*

21. S. Bem, "The measurement of psychological androgyny", *Journal of Consulting and Clinical Psychology* 42, 155-62, 1974.

22. This is particularly evident in Plato's *Symposium*, in which Plato discusses the existence of androgynous, or intersex, people as an explanation of the existence of homosexuality.

23. See Singer, *op. cit.* Also Stanislas Klossowski de Rola, *Alchemy: The Secret Art*, Thames and Hudson, London, 1973.

24. The Feminists, "The Feminists: A Political Organisation to Annihilate Sex Roles", in Koedt, Levine and Rapone (eds.), *op. cit.*, p. 368.

25. "Androgyny" is found particularly in liberal feminist theory (see Jagger, *op. cit.*) but is also found in discussions of transsexualism, which often centre upon the idea that people are essentially androgynous, in the context of defending transsexualism. See, e.g., Carol Riddell, *Divided Sisterhood*, (pamphlet) News from Nowhere, Liverpool, undated.

26. Particularly in Jungian psychoanalysis, which stressed the coexistence in the subconscious of the masculine *animus* and the *feminine anima*. See, e.g., J. Jacobi, *The Psychology of C. G. Jung*, Routledge and Kegan Paul, London, 1942.

27. And yet rats are relevant, at least in the sense that extrapolations are frequently made from them in the service of biological determinism! Part of our strategy against such arguments should, it seems to me, be to undermine the validity of the statements made about animals, as well as to point out their inapplicability to humans.
28. E.g., R. M. Rose, P. Bourne, and R. Poe, "Androgen response to stress", *Psychosomatic Medicine*, 31, 418-36, 1969; K. Pirke, "Psychosexual stimulation and plasma testosterone in men", *Archives of Sexual Behaviour* 3, 577-84, 1974; and M. McClintock, "Menstrual synchrony and suppression", *Nature* (London), 229, 244-5, 1971.
29. For example, C. A. Pfeiffer, "Sexual differences of the hypophysis and their determination by the gonads", *American Journal of Anatomy*, 58, 195-225, 1936.
30. For example, I. L. Ward, "Parental stress feminises and demasculinises the behavior of males", *Science*, 175, 80-2, 1972. I. L. Ward, and J. Weisz, "Maternal stress alters plasma testosterone in fetal males", *Science*, 207, 428-9, 1980.
31. F. Vom Saal and F. H. Bronson, "Sexual characteristics of adult female mice are correlated with their blood testosterone levels during prenatal development", *Science*, 208, 597-9, 1980.
32. For example L. G. Clemens and B. A. Gladue, "Feminine sexual behavior in rats enhanced by prenatal inhibition of androgen aromatization", *Hormones and Behavior*, 11, 190-201, 1978; J. L. Dunlap, A. A. Gerall and L. D. McLean, "Enhancement of female receptivity in neonatally castrated males by prepubertal ovarian transplants", *Physiology and Behavior*, 10, 1087-94, 1973. J. Stewart and D. Cygan, "Ovarian hormones act early in development to feminize adult open-field behavior in the rat", *Hormones and Behavior*, 14, 20-32, 1980.
33. For example, C. L. Moore, "Maternal contributions to the development of masculine sexual behavior in laboratory rats", *Developmental Psychobiology*, 17, 347-56, 1984; and L. I. A. Birke and D. Sadler, "Maternal behaviour of rats and effects of neonatal progestins given to the pups", *Developmental Psychobiology*, 1985 (in press).
34. For example, T. Richardson and N. Mattarella, "Hormonal substances in human milk, cows' milk and dairy products", *Journal of Food Protection*, 40, 57-63, 1977: and C. Holzhuasen, S. Murphy and L. I. A. Birke, "Neonatal exposure to a progestin via milk alters subsequent LH cyclicity in the female rat", *Journal of Endocrinology*, 100, 149-54, 1984.
35. J. C. Smith and G. D. Sales, "Ultrasonic behavior and mother-infant interactions in rodents", in *Maternal Influences and Early Behavior*, R. W. Bell and W. P. Smotherman (eds.), MTP Press Ltd., Lancaster, 1980.
36. M. A. Hofer, H. Shair and P. Singh, "Evidence that maternal ventral skin substances promote suckling in infant rats", *Physiology and Behavior* 17, 131-6, 1976.
37. H. Moltz and S. J. Kilpatrick, "Pheromonal control of maternal

behavior", in Bell and Smotherman, *op. cit.*, 1980.
38. For example, E. Hard and K. Larsson, "Dependence of adult mating behavior in male rats on the presence of littermates in infancy", *Brain, Behavior and Evolution*, 1, 405-19, 1968.
39. C. H. Waddington, *The Strategy of the Genes*, Allen and Unwin, London, 1957.
40. Certainly, large areas of the perineal region are differentially sensitive to hormonal stimulation in female rats. See D. Pfaff, C. Lewis, C. Diakow and M. Keiner, "Neurophysiological analysis of mating behavior as hormone-sensitive reflexes", *Progress in Physiological Psychology*, 5, 253-98, 1973.
41. For example, F. M. Schultz and J. D. Wilson, "Virilization of the Wolffian duct in the rat fetus by various androgens", *Endocrinology*, 94, 979-86, 1974.
42. For further discussion of the relationship between interactionist views and the ideas of constraints, see P. P. G. Bateson, "Rules and reciprocity in behavioural development", in *Growing Points in Ethology*, P. P. G. Bateson and R. A. Hinde (eds.), Cambridge University Press, Cambridge, 1976.
43. The major theories derive from psychoanalysis, social learning theory and cognitive developmental theory. For a review see S. J. Kessler and W. McKenna, *Gender: An Ethnomethodological Approach*, John Wiley, New York, 1978, especially pp. 81-101.
44. I realise that this may be contentious in the context of transsexualism, since it implies that the sense of gender identity held by a woman who is biologically a woman will be different from that of a male-to-female transsexual.

CHAPTER 6

1. See Carolyn Merchant, *The Death of Nature: Women, Ecology and the Scientific Revolution*, Wildwood House, London, 1982.
2. See various articles in C. MacCormack and M. Strathern (eds.), *Nature, Culture and Gender*, *op. cit.*
3. Luther Standing Bear, quoted in J. E. Brown, *The North American Indians* (The Photographs of W. S. Curtis), Aperture, New York, 1972, p. 86.
4. C. P. MacCormack, "Nature, Culture and Gender: A Critique", in MacCormack and Strathern, *op. cit.*, p. 9.
5. Merchant, *op. cit.*, pp. 1-41.
6. L. J. Jordanova, "Natural facts: a historical perspective on science and sexuality", in MacCormack and Strathern, *op. cit.*, and P. Brown and L. J. Jordanova "Oppressive Dichotomies: the nature/culture debate", in *Women in Society*, The Cambridge Women's Studies Group, *op. cit.*
7. Jordanova, "Natural Facts", p. 65.
8. E. O. Lovejoy, *The Great Chain of Being*, *op. cit.*

9. That is, the structure of the universe as set out by the Greek astronomer, Ptolemy, a system which had the earth at its centre. This was finally superseded by the Copernican sun-centred system during the sixteenth and seventeenth centuries. The Ptolemaic system was favoured by the church precisely because it did put the earth at the centre, though it fitted uneasily into the Great Chain; after all, if the earth was important enough to be Man's home, why was it put by God *underneath* us? See discussion in Lovejoy, *op. cit.*, pp. 101-16.
10. *Ibid.* pp. 183-241. As new species were discovered, they were slotted into the chain.
11. See essays in R. Needham (ed.), *Right and Left: Essays on Dual Symbolic Classifications*, University of Chicago Press, Chicago, 1973.
12. Unattributed. Cited in G. Jones, *Social Darwinism and English Thought: The Interaction between Biological and Social Theory*, Harvester, Brighton, 1980, p. 102.
13. C. Lloyd Morgan, *The Springs of Conduct*, Routledge & Kegan Paul, p. 241. Cited in G. Jones, *op. cit.*
14. Frederick Olmstead, cited in Hooks, *op. cit.*, p. 39.
15. It is still common practice, for example, for biologists to refer to "higher" mammals and so forth. Rank order is implied very strongly, too, in the attempts to refute Darwinism by advocating creationism (i.e. the story of Genesis). Modern creationists argue that God created all living things and that humans are distinct from other species, that they are special. Interestingly, the creationists assert that it is evolutionary theory, not ideas of rank orders, that has helped to perpetuate racism and other immorality and evil. As Philip Kitcher notes in his account of creationist ideas, this argument is surely a "desperately unwise choice of weapons", given the history of Christianity in rationalising all kind of immoral action. See P. Kitcher, *Abusing Science: The Case Against Creationism*, Open University Press, Milton Keynes, 1983, p. 197.
16. This kind of view of creation is evident, for instance, in the Gnostic writings and much alchemical work. See, for instance, Singer, *Androgyny, op. cit.* pp. 125-35.
17. Merchant, *op. cit.*, pp. 1-41.
18. *Ibid.*, pp. 19-41.
19. *Ibid.*, pp. 42-68.
20. Cited in Merchant, *ibid.*, pp. 111-17.
21. Jordanova, *op. cit.*, p. 66.
22. *Ibid.*, pp. 66-7.
23. Merchant, *op. cit.* p. 127.
24. *Ibid.*, pp. 127-48. Ironically, those accused of being witches were often accused of doing just what the emerging mechanistic world view eventually came to do—that is, harnessing the forces of nature to their own ends. The witch-hunts were, in one sense, about the control of women, whose sexuality was feared and condemned by the patriarchal Christian church, although there is argument about the extent to which the witch-hunts represented actual and direct forms of woman-

hating, or whether women were hunted as ideological deviants from Christianity. There is also controversy, in feminist writing at least, over the numbers of women involved: just how acute a form of social control over women was it? See Christina Larner, *Enemies of God: The Witch Hunt in Scotland*, Chatto and Windus, London, 1981. For comments on the ideas put forward by Larner, see Lynnette Mitchell, "Enemies of God or victims of patriarchy?", *Trouble and Strife*, 2, 18-20, Spring 1984.

25. This notion is attributed particularly to Renè Descartes, who viewed the functions of animal bodies in general as operating according to mechanism. What made humans different from other animals was the possession of a soul or mind. This philosophy has had two significant effects. First, it contributed to the development of mind-body dualism which has ever since pervaded Western thought, and second, it contributed to the idea that animals did not suffer or feel pain, an idea subsequently used in defence of rather cruel physiological experimentation during the eighteenth century.

26. The empirical school of philosophy is generally said to have been founded with the ideas of John Locke (1642-1704), particularly in *An Essay Concerning Human Understanding*, although empiricist ideas can be traced back to classical times. For a brief history of empiricist ideas (from a Marxist perspective), see G. Novak, *Empiricism and its Evolution*, Pathfinder Press, New York, 1971.

27. The question of subjectivity v. objectivity is a theme to which I return in connection with feminist science in Chapter 8.

28. See, e.g., Merchant, *op. cit.,* pp. 172-90. The sexual metaphor was, however, more complex than that, at least according to some interpretations. Evelyn Fox Keller, for example, wrote of the "dialectical, even hermaphroditic" nature of the "marriage between Mind and Nature" in Bacon's writing. Science, in Keller's interpretation of Bacon, becomes both virile masculinity, probing nature's secrets, but also femininely receptive to nature. See Evelyn Fox Keller, "Baconian science: a Hermaphroditic Birth", *The Philosophical Forum*, 11, 299-308, 1980.

29. Merchant, *op. cit.*, p. 190. While Bacon employed the sexual penetration metaphor quite extensively, he also saw science as a force for harmony, since otherwise unresolved tensions between people might, through science, become deflected on to nature, leading in time to the end of human disunity. See J. Haberer, *Politics and the Community of Science,* Van Nostrand Rheinhold, New York, 1969, p. 42.

30. Merchant, *op. cit.,* p. 190.

31. See the collection edited by MacCormack and Strathern, *op. cit.*, and *Sexual Meanings: the Cultural Construction of Gender and Sexuality*, S. B. Ortner and H. Whitehead (eds.), Cambridge University Press, Cambridge, 1981.

32. That is, some of the values culturally associated with science, such as objectivity, or single-mindedness, are also stereotypically masculine qualities. In this sense, science can be thought of as "masculine".

33. See Ruth Wallsgrove, "The Masculine Face of Science", in Brighton Women and Science Group, *op. cit.*, and Karen Messing, "The Scientific Mystique: Can a White Lab Coat Guarantee Purity in the Search for Knowledge about the Nature of Women?" in *Woman's Nature: Rationalizations of Inequality*, Marian Lowe and Ruth Hubbard, *op. cit.* Both authors point out that women face greater problems in science than "just" those of masculine values.
34. Two legendary occupations of Medieval alchemists were the search for a means of transmuting base metals into gold, and a search for the "elixir of life" that would prolong human life indefinitely. In the light of modern views of nature, such pursuits seem quaint, if not downright deluded. However, they typify the alchemical concern with the *transformability* and perfectibility of nature. The alchemists' role was considered to be that of providing the conditions in which such transformation to greater and greater perfection could take place. See Klossowski de Rola, *Alchemy: The Secret Art, op. cit.*
35. Janus was a god of classical mythology, having two heads facing in opposite directions. (Hence, January, the month that faces both the old and the new year).
36. In 1976 a cloud of deadly poisonous dioxin escaped from a chemical works near Seveso, Italy, killing and injuring numbers of people. Similarly, in 1984, large clouds of a cyanate gas escaped from a chemical works, near Bhopal, India, killing some 2000 people.
37. For examples of predictions see Paul R. Ehrlich, *The Population Bomb*, Pan, London, 1971. For more sophisticated predictions, using computer-simulated forecasts, see D. H. Meadows, D. L. Meadows, J. Randers and W. W. Behrens, *The Limits to Growth*, Earth Island, London, 1972. The assumptions made in the "Limits to Growth" arguments have more recently been criticised, however. See, for example, H. S. D. Cole, C. Freeman, M. Jahoda and K. L. R. Pavitt, (eds.) *Thinking About the Future: A Critique of 'The Limits to Growth' "*, Chatto and Windus, for Sussex University Press, London, 1974.
38. Andrè Gorz, *Ecology as Politics*, Pluto, London, 1980, p. 3.
39. Susan Griffin, foreword to Caldecott and Leland *op. cit.*, p. 1.
40. Ynestra King, "The Eco-feminist Imperative", in Caldecott and Leland, *op. cit.*, p. 11.
41. Anita Anand, "Saving trees, saving lives: Third World Women and the Issue of Survival", in Caldecott and Leland, *op. cit.*, p. 182.
42. See note 26.
43. Madame De Grignan, cited in Brian Easlea, *Science and Sexual Oppression: Patriarchy's Confrontation with Woman and Nature*, Weidenfeld and Nicholson, London, 1981, p. 71.
44. See, e.g., G. R. Taylor, *The Science of Life*, Panther, London, 1976, pp. 206-08; and W. Coleman, *Biology in the Nineteenth Century: Problems of Form, Function and Transformation,* Cambridge University Press, Cambridge, 1977, pp. 118-59.
45. See, e.g., A. Brown, *Who Cares for Animals?* Heinemann, London, 1974, (in conjunction with the RSPCA), pp. 1-35.

46. Cited in Brown, *ibid.*, p. 9.
47. Many feminists of this era saw their campaigns as being campaigns for the moral elevation of society, linking them, for instance, to issues such as temperance. See Olive Banks, *Faces of Feminism, op. cit.*, especially pp. 63-84.
48. *Ibid.*, pp. 81-2.
49. Carol Adams, "The Oedible Complex: Feminism and Vegetarianism" in *The Lesbian Reader*, G. Covina and L. Galana (eds.), Amazon Press, Oakland, California, 1975, pp. 149-50.
50. Norma Benney, "All of One Flesh: The rights of Animals", in Caldecott and Leland, *op. cit.*, p. 151.
51. This is one solution to male violence offered, for example, by Laurel Holliday in *The Violent Sex, op. cit.*
52. I have argued this point elsewhere. See Lynda Birke, " 'They're worse than animals': animals in biological research", in *More Than the Parts: Biology and Politics*, Birke and Silvertown, *op. cit.*, pp. 219-35.
53. This is often written about in the guise of women's (innate) spirituality. One letter-writer to the feminist magazine *Trouble and Strife* wrote, for instance, of how women were "harnessing a deep source of spiritual power . . . This is a power, and an 'hystery' that men do not and never can possess. Seldom recognised, it is a secret strength that has carried women through worse times than these. It is the fundamental life energy which all women share." See Jill Chadwin, "Religion as a basis for politics", in *Trouble and Strife*, 2, 1984, pp. 3-5.
54. From Rosalie Bertell, "A Micronesian Woman", in Caldecott and Leland, *op. cit.*, p. 111.
55. See Laura Conti, *"Visto da Seveso: l'evento straordinario e l'ordinario amministrazione"*, Feltrinelli, Milano, 1977. Also see essay review of Conti's book by Gianna Pomata, "Seveso: safety in numbers?" *Radical Science Journal*, 9, 69-81.
56. Women's Working Group, Seveso, "Seveso is Everywhere", in Caldecott and Leland, *op. cit.* p. 39.
57. S. de Beauvoir, *The Second Sex*, Penguin, Harmondsworth, 1972, pp. 95-6.
58. Mary Daly, *Gyn/Ecology: The Metaethics of Radical Feminism*, The Women's Press, London, 1978.
59. Ruth Wallsgrove, "The Masculine Face of Science", in Brighton Women and Science Group, *op. cit.*, p. 232.

CHAPTER 7

1. E.g., Hazel Henderson, "The Warp and the Weft: The Coming Synthesis of Eco-Philosophy and Eco-feminism", in Caldecott and Leland, *op. cit.*, and Fritjof Capra, *The Turning Point: Science, Society and the Rising Culture*, Wildwood, London, 1982.
2. Henderson and Capra refer to this as a paradigm shift, much in the same way that T. S. Kuhn describes scientific revolutions. See T. S. Kuhn, *The Structure of Scientific Revolutions*, University of Chicago

Press, Chicago, 1970. Whether such "revolutions" occur as precipitously as is generally implied is open to controversy however. For further discussion of the ideas of revolutions in science see John Krige, *Science, Revolution and Discontinuity*, Harvester, Brighton, 1980. For discussion of the controversy concerning Kuhn's ideas of scientific revolutions, see I. Lakatos and A. Musgrave (eds.) *Criticism and the Growth of Knowledge*, Cambridge University Press, Cambridge, 1970.

3. Merchant, *op. cit.*, pp. 226-7.
4. D. Kubrin, "Newton's Inside Out!: Magic, Class Struggle and the Rise of Mechanism in the West", in *The Analytic Spirit: Essays in the History of Science*, H. Woolf (ed.), Cornell University Press, Ithaca and London, 1981. For a broader discussion of dissident ideas during this period see C. Hill, *The World Turned Upside Down: Radical Ideas During the English Revolution*, Maurice Temple Smith, London, 1972.
5. Kubrin, *op. cit.*, Merchant, *op. cit.*, pp. 111-17.
6. Kubrin, *op. cit.*, p. 105.
7. *Ibid.*, p. 114.
8. Merchant, *op. cit.*, pp. 99-126.
9. *Ibid.*, pp. 114-5. The context of Merchant's discussion at this point is the naturalism of the Italian Renaissance philosophers, such as Bruno, Telesio and Campanella. The ideas of transformation are, she points out, essentially dialectical (i.e. a form of dialectical idealism, rather than dialectical materialism: also see Kubrin, *op. cit.*).
10. See Stephen Jay Gould's discussion of the current state of Darwinian theory in *New Scientist* 17, May 1984, p. 28. In this he discusses some of the reasons why opposition to the theory of evolution continues to be strong (e.g. in the form of creationism). Racist ideology was similarly both supported and refuted by evolutionary theory. See Nancy Stepan, *The Idea of Race in Science: Great Britain 1800-1960*, Macmillan, London, 1982. Stepan notes how the rise of racialist ideas in science at the beginning of the nineteenth century was accompanied by a return to ideas of a Great Chain of Being with which to buttress such ideas. Darwinism implied the homogeneity and commonality of humankind, although this too was brought into the service of racism in the form of social Darwinism.
11. See, e.g., Greta Jones, *op. cit.* Also see W. Coleman, *Biology in the Nineteenth Century*, *op. cit.*, and Jonathan Silvertown, "Ecology, interspecific competition and the struggle for existence", in *More than the Parts* Birke and Silvertown *op. cit.*
12. Quoted in Silvertown, *ibid.*, p. 185.
13. See note 11. Most of the criticism of the period was directed against the racism of eugenics and social Darwinism. A few authors did, however, address the issue of sexism in the writing of social Darwinists such as Herbert Spencer. See, for instance, Antoinette Brown Blackwell, "Sex and Evolution", in *The Feminist Papers*, A. S. Rossi (ed.), Bantam,

New York, 1974, pp. 356-77, and D. G. Ritchie, *Darwinism and Politics,* Swan Sonnenschein, London, 1889, pp. 77-92.
14. Ritchie, *op. cit.*, pp. 44-5. The idea that competitive capitalism would eventually evolve into a more socialist organisation based on cooperation is an idea which is sometimes, if rather simplistically, attributed to Marx. For a discussion of the relationship between Darwin's ideas of biological evolution and Marx's views of social change, see Valentino Gerratana, "Marx and Darwin", in *Marx: Sociology, Social Change, Capitalism,* D. McQuarie (ed.), Quartet Books, London, 1978.
15. Peter Kropotkin, *Mutual Aid,* 1902 (republished by University Press, New York, 1972), quoted by M. Gross and M. B. Averill, "Evolution and patriarchal myths of scarcity and competition", in Harding and Hintikka, *op. cit.*, p. 88.
16. Merchant, *op. cit.*, p. 294.
17. Or what sort of change she might envisage. That it might be a narrowly defined change is suggested by her description. We might not all agree, for instance, that *reform* of capitalism is what we should seek, nor that capitalism exploits only *working* people (children? the elderly?). And do we necessarily want to equalise male and female work options—do women *or* men want to work in the dangerous and polluted industries that men are traditionally assigned to?
18. Learning to deal with the notion that the atomic universe is essentially *un*predictable put physicists through a considerable reappraisal of their assumptions. For an interesting account of how that transition was experienced, see the autobiography of Werner Heisenberg (discoverer of the Uncertainty Principle by which the unpredictability of electrons is described), *Physics and Beyond, op. cit.* Quantum physics inevitably describes the world through highly sophisticated mathematics which are beyond most people's abilities! For a very readable, non-mathematical account of the essential ideas of modern physics, see G. Zukav, *The Dancing Wu-Li Masters: An Overview of the New Physics,* Fontana, London, 1980. The title referes to the parallels drawn between ideas in physics and ideas deriving from Chinese Taoism.
19. Lin Simonon, "Personal, Political and Planetary Play", in Caldecott and Leland, *op. cit.,* p. 198.
20. Henderson, *op. cit.,* p. 206.
21. *Ibid.*, p. 206.
22. *Ibid.*, p. 211.
23. Capra, *op. cit.*, p. 11.
24. *Ibid.*, p. 11.
25. *Ibid.*, p. 466.
26. This passivity in the face of ideological change does imply a different view of change from that employed by earlier opponents of mechanism. The opponents of mechanism writing during the Renaissance and early scientific revolution utilised a dynamic and

interactive (dialectical) concept of change in nature. The role of the human observer then became that of facilitating nature's changes rather than merely observing them. While both Henderson and Capra refer to the need (cf. in twentieth century quantum physics) to reappraise our view of the role of human observer, their descriptions of associated cultural change remain essentially passive. No reason is given for human activity in one sphere (human involvement in the observation of nature) and not in another (the proposed revolution in cultural mores).

27. That feminism and the Left in general are *not* winning over the populace is evident in the rise of the new anti-feminist Right, in Europe and the U.S.A. What Henderson and Capra's optimism fails to deal with is the element of co-optation of feminism. That is, the way in which some feminist demands have been co-opted by the establishment and even taken on board by some of the Right Wing. See, e.g. Zillah R. Eisenstein, "The Sexual Politics of the New Right: Understanding the 'Crisis of liberalism' for the 1980s", *op. cit.*, and Judith Stacey, "The New Conservative Feminism", *op. cit.*, for discussions of attitudes of the "New Right" towards feminism. Also see Andrea Dworkin, *Right Wing Women*, The Women's Press, London, 1983. Dworkin sees the beliefs of anti-feminist women as a strategy for survival in the face of a woman-hating patriarchy.

28. Some feminists involved in the WLM appear, however, to believe in the power of ideological change, withdrawing from political engagement into what has been dubbed "cultural feminism", rooted in beliefs in the essential superiority of women. On the other hand, the seven demands of the Women's Liberation Movement concern women's *rights*, which might be achieved by political struggles. These are not likely to be given to us on a plate.

29. Henderson, *op. cit.*, p. 211.

30. For consideration of the various problems for women involved in new reproductive technology, see *Test-Tube Women*, Arditti, Klein and Minden *op. cit.*

31. Capra, *op. cit.*, p. 64.

32. See note 18.

33. Heisenberg, *op. cit.*, p. 76.

34. H. P. Stapp, cited in Zukav, *op. cit.*, p. 64 (see note 18).

35. The notion of self-organisation in certain chemical systems has been put forward by Ilya Prigogine; see G. Nicholis and I. Prigogine, *Self-Organisation in Non-equilibrium Systems,* John Wiley, Chichester, 1977.

36. Capra is not unique in this suggestion, but I deal with it here in the context of discussing his work. The suggestion is very similar to the ideas about evolution and organismic development proposed by Gerry Webster and Brian Goodwin, *op. cit.*

37. Capra, *op. cit.*, pp. 312-3.

38. R. Sheldrake, *A New Science of Life*, Paladin, London, 1983. A measure of the reaction of the establishment to these ideas is provided

by the verdict of the prestigious scientific journal *Nature*, which commented acidly: "Infuriating ... the best candidate for burning there has been for many years".
39. Henderson, *op. cit.*, p. 205.
40. That is, to date no adequate test of the hypothesis has yet been devised. It is, however, a testable hypothesis in principle, if a suitably unambiguous method of testing it could be devised.
41. See, e.g., The Dialectics of Biology Group, *Against Biological Determinism* and *Towards a Liberatory Biology'*, both *op. cit.*
42. Kuhn, *op. cit.*
43. That is, Kuhn viewed paradigm shifts as being fairly revolutionary and happening quite quickly, representing a discontinuity in perception. That scientific revolutions may not have been such rapid affairs is suggested, however, by John Krige (*op. cit.*). Whatever the speed, the suggestion is that the paradigm shift is already occurring: it is this which I would dispute.
44. See, e.g., Gross and Averill, *op. cit.* and Silvertown, *op. cit.*
45. Gross and Averill *op. cit.* They note that "A feminist task is to reconsider patriarchal images: to understand them as reflections of a male mentality; to consider whether they even answer any questions feminists wish to ask; and to remake the image of nature in metaphors conformable to women's reality." (p. 27)
46. *Ibid.*, p. 86. Cited from Robert Cook in *Natural History*, 89, 1980, 91.
47. *Ibid.*, pp. 76-80.
48. *Ibid.*, p. 85.
49. *Ibid.*, pp. 85-6. Emphasis in original. Some of the ideas about cooperation in nature were also discussed by Lynda Birke, "Outgrowing Selfish Genes", *New Socialist*, 16, 40-2, 1984.
50. A related question is, of course, why it is only now that feminism has emerged as a strong social movement; why not (say) in the 1950s? Sandra Harding has noted that "During the last decade of feminist inquiry, a new 'object' for scientific scrutiny has emerged into visibility: the sex/gender system"—although she does emphasise that this new visibility "calls for a revolution in epistemology" since existing epistemologies fail to tell us anything about why the sex/gender system should become so visible and so salient at the present time. See Sandra Harding. "Why has the sex/gender system, become visible only now?" in Harding and Hintikka, *op. cit.*
51. Rita Arditti, "Feminism and Science", in *Science and Liberation*, R. Arditti, P. Brennan and S. Cavrak (eds.), South End Press, Boston, 1980, pp. 366-7.

CHAPTER 8

1. I am not suggesting that gender would necessarily disappear altogether, rather that "gender" would come to mean something quite

different, and would not be evaluated in a hierarchical way. Some feminist theorists have assumed that what we are working towards is a genderless society (or one in which gender differences are minimal); others have continued to emphasise the differentness of women and men. Maggie McFadden, in a recent review of differences in perspective between feminists, refers to this as a difference between "minimisers" and "maximisers" (McFadden, "Anatomy of Difference: Toward a Classification of Feminist Theory", *Women's Studies International Forum*, 7, 495-504, 1984). I suppose that my view falls somewhere in between, since I neither believe that gender differences would disappear, not do I believe in the female superiority which McFadden attributes to at least some maximisers. My vision of science might also be called "humanist", and it is certainly true that there are dissenters from the mechanistic view among both women and men. This book, however, makes reference to feminist literature, and I have retained the "feminist science" appellation.

2. Talk of a "socialist science" sometimes raises the spectre of social interference in science (as though science is somehow divorced from the rest of society). In this context, critics often refer pejoratively to Soviet science and the work of T. D. Lysenko. Lysenkoism failed for many reasons; its failure need not however, mean that the creation of socialist science is impossible. For discussion of the Lysenko affair and its political context in Soviet agriculture, see Dominique Lecourt, *Proletarian Science: The Case of Lysenko*, New Left Books, London, 1977. Also see the chapter on Lysenko by Richard Lewontin and Richard Levins in *The Radicalisation of Science*, H. Rose and S. Rose (eds.), Macmillan, London, 1976.

3. Though some Marxist accounts do continue to emphasise a domination of nature. For a discussion of this emphasis see W. Leiss, *The Domination of Nature*, Braziller, New York, 1972.

4. To say that some areas might be proscribed begs the question of how. Presumably we would not prefer to legislate directly, but might adopt a system similar to the present one. That is, areas of research are facilitated or otherwise basically by two methods: peer group approval, and funding. The two overlap but are not quite synonymous. On the other hand, a future society might wish to police directions of science in some more organised way. The most important point is, however, that some areas are already proscribed, either by being starved of funding or by social pressure from within the scientific community.

5. Firestone, *op. cit.*

6. Evelyn Fox Keller, "Women, Science and Popular Mythology", in Rothschild, *op. cit.*, p. 139.

7. It will be evident that throughout this book I have used the term "science" to refer to the "natural sciences" and I have not used it to cover the social sciences as well. This is the common usage of the word "science", although Renate Duelli-Klein and Shelley Minden have objected to such "elitist" usage: see R. Duelli-Klein and S. Minden,

"Feminists in Science Speak up: *Alice through the Microscope*—the latest in a series of books on women and science", *Women's Studies International Quarterly,* 4, 241-52, 1981, p. 241.
8. Sally M. Gearhart, "An End to Technology: A Modest Proposal", in Rothschild, *op. cit.*, pp. 174-5.
9. While this statement is generally true, it might be argued that medicine does not really constitute a science. Medicine is often not scientific, and often operates by informed guesses. Nonetheless, medical research normally proceeds by means of the scientific method in the form, for example, of "double-blind" trials in which one group of people receives a drug while the other receives a sugar pill. It is double blind in the sense that the administering doctor does not know which is which either: only the researcher keeps records of the groups.
10. The contraceptive pill was launched in part because of Western fears of overpopulation in Third-World countries such as Puerto Rico, and newer forms of hormonal contraceptive are still tested largely in the Third World. For a critical review of the history leading up to acceptance and testing of the Pill, see Vivien Walsh, "Contraception: The Growth of a Technology", in Brighton Women and Science Group, *op. cit.* Also see Lesley Doyal, *The Political Economy of Health* (with Imogen Pennell), Pluto, London, 1979, p. 283. For a similar consideration of the hormone injection, Depo Provera, see Jill Rakusen, "Depo-Provera: the extent of the problem. A Case Study in the Politics of Birth Control", in *Women, Health and Reproduction,* H. Roberts (ed.), Routledge & Kegan Paul, London, 1981.
11. Particularly in relation to the operations of multinational pharmaceutical companies in the Third World. See, for instance, The Haslemere Group, *Who Needs the Drug Companies?* Haslemere Group, War on Want and Third World First (pamphlet) 1976. Also see Doyal, 1979 *op. cit.* pp. 266-73, and Lesley Rogers, "Pharmacology: Why Drug Prescription is on the Increase", in Birke and Silvertown, *op. cit.* For a broader discussion of the political context of Western scientific medicine, see Len Doyal and Lesley Doyal, "Western scientific medicine: a philosophical and political prognosis", in Birke and Silvertown, *op. cit.*
12. See, for example, my discussion of such research and its problems in L. I. A. Birke, "Is homosexuality hormonally determined?", *op. cit.* And Lynda Birke, "From sin to sickness: hormonal theories of lesbianism", in *Biological Woman—The Convenient Myth,* Hubbard, Henifin and Fried *op. cit.*
13. Cora Diamond, "Experimenting on animals: a problem in ethics", in *Animals in Research,* D. Sperlinger (ed.), Wiley, Chichester, 1981.
14. That is not to say that some individual scientists do not behave differently—just that the prevailing *ethos* of science is to operate in this way.
15. Some experiments might conceivably be permissible—*if* they are of proven benefit to human or animal well-being and the animal is suitably anaesthetised. This is a particularly contentious issue, and it is

not easy to predict how any future society might deal with the moral claims of animals. What would be less likely to be permitted is the use of animals for, e.g., testing drugs to treat a disease for which there is already an effective treatment. By saying that the issue is contentious, I am not suggesting that I would necessarily condone such experiments; simply that *it is conceivable* that a conflict of interests (or moral claims) might arise.

16. The majority of animals used in the name of scientific research are used by industry testing a wide variety of drugs, chemicals, etc.
17. The criteria are, however, themselves based on animal tests. The most common measure is the LD_{50} test according to which the substance is measured according to a criterion of lethality. LD_{50} means the lethal dose at which 50 per cent of the animals die. The remainder, of course, having suffered agony from the sub-lethal effects of the substance are killed anyway after the end of the test. Not surprisingly, the use of the LD_{50} test has been often criticised; but until it is abandoned, there is not likely to be any serious effort to find other criteria. In Britain there are several organisations concerned with the development of alternatives, such as the Fund for the Replacement of Animals in Medical Experiments (FRAME). For a discussion of alternatives to animals in research see A. N. Rowan, "Alternatives and laboratory animals", in Sperlinger, *op. cit.*
18. Evelyn Fox Keller, "Gender and Science", in Harding and Hintikka *op. cit.*, p. 198.
19. See, e.g., Libby Curran, "Science education: did she drop out or was she pushed?" in Brighton Women and Science Group *op. cit.*, for a description of ways in which the British educational system pushes women out of science at different stages. The division of labour in science is at least partly the product of this process of exclusion.
20. The fact that Marxist analyses are usually gender blind was pointed out, for example, by Heidi Hartmann in "The Unhappy Marriage of Marxism and Feminism: Towards a More Progressive Union", *Capital and Class*, Summer 1979, 8, 1-33.
21. Hilary Rose, "Making Science Feminist", in *The Changing Experience of Women*, E. Whitelegg *et al. op. cit.,* p. 361. That reproduction has been ignored is a claim made by several critics of Heidi Hartmann's analysis of Marxism and feminism in *The Unhappy Marriage of Marxism and Feminism: A Debate on Class and Patriarchy* Lydia Sargant (ed.), Pluto, London, 1981. See, for instance, Sandra Harding "What is the real material base of patriarchy and capital?", and Ann Ferguson and Nancy Folbre, "The Unhappy Marriage of Patriarchy and Capitalism". None of these specifically addresses the division of labour within science, but they discuss it more broadly.
22. Feminist analyses of gender segregation in the labour market have tended to assume that this derives from capitalist social relations, particularly in the family. However, this approach may be insufficient, not least because gender segregation certainly predated the rise of capitalism. Veronica Beechey has suggested therefore that feminism

needs to consider the problem of gender segregation in the labour market from a perspective more directly concerned with gender divisions *per se*. See Veronica Beechey, "What's so special about women's employment? A review of some recent studies of women's paid work", *Feminist Review*, 15, 23-46, 1983. It should also be stressed that women have contributed to science in the past (although these were usually upper-class, educated women), but they have been largely written out of history. The reasons for women's relative exclusion in the late twentieth century are probably very different from those operating in early epochs. Some consideration of earlier women scientists is given by Merchant in her book, *The Death of Nature, op. cit.,* pp. 253-74. Also see H. J. Mozans, *Woman in Science*, MIT Press, Cambridge, Mass., 1974, Margaret Alic, *Hypatia's Heritage: A History of Women's Achievements in Science*, The Women's Press, London, (forthcoming); and Autumn Stanley, "Women hold up two-thirds of the sky: notes for a revised history of technology", in Rothschild, *op. cit.*

23. Nancy C. M. Hartsock, "The feminist standpoint: developing the ground for a specifically feminist historical materialism", in Harding and Hintikka, *op. cit.*, p. 295.
24. *Ibid.*, p. 297.
25. See, e.g., Jane Flax, "Political philosophy and the patriarchal unconscious: a psychoanalytic perspective on epistemology and metaphysics", in Harding and Hintikka, *op. cit.*
26. Rita Arditti, "Feminism and Science", in R. Arditti, P. Brennan and S. Cavrak *op. cit.,* p. 364.
27. That is not to say that intuition is not already integral to science, simply that, at present, it is insufficiently acknowledged. As Evelyn Fox Keller notes, in her biography of Barbara McClintock, intuition is centrally important to the generation of ideas in science, as elsewhere. See Keller, *Feeling for the Organism, op. cit.*
28. Rose, 1982 *op. cit.,* p. 368 (note 21).
29. Keller, E. F. "Feminism and Science" *Signs: Journal of Women in Culture and Society* 7, 1982, p. 593.
30. Elizabeth Fee, "Women's nature and scientific objectivity", in *Woman's Nature: Rationalizations of Inequality*, Lowe and Hubbard *op. cit.*, p. 16. Sandra Harding also considers the question of cultural relativism raised, for example, by the theorists of the "Edinburgh school" of the sociology of knowledge. In discussing the relativism espoused by these theorists, Harding notes the problems for feminism, stressing that "it leaves unexamined the reasons that research directed by some 'social values' is scientifically more valuable than research directed by other 'social values'. Is research directed by feminist values (and which 'feminist values'?), anti-racist, and anti-classist values only equally scientifically fruitful to research directed by sexist, racist, and classist 'values'?", Harding, in Harding and Hintikka, *op. cit.* p. 319.
31. Fee, *op. cit.*, pp. 17-8.
32. One area where this is currently obvious is in the context of discussing

the public accountability of scientists regarding their use of animals. When animal welfare lobbyists demand greater accountability and the opening of laboratories to the public eye, scientists usually respond by implying that this would be interference, interference in work that the public would not understand or be able to evaluate.
33. In Britain currently, defence expenditure is over 50 per cent of the total research expenditure.
34. I am not suggesting that such a society would be naive enough to assume that it would never require defence. What I am suggesting is against the interests of humanity is the continued research into *new* developments, better ways of killing more people, particularly in terms of nuclear weapons or chemical and biological weapons. Or, of course, research into "improved" forms of conventional weaponry. Proscribing areas would not be unique to such a utopian science, since there are a number of controls at present on the development of genetic engineering, in the United States and Britain, which were implemented partly because of the risks to humanity involved.
35. Jalna Hanmer, "A Womb of One's Own", in Arditti, Duelli Klein and Minden, *op. cit.*, p. 441.
36. Firestone, *op. cit.*
37. See, e.g. Jonathan Cole, *Fair Science: Women in the Scientific Community*, Free Press, London, 1979. Although Cole gives evidence of discriminatory practices in science, his interpretations have been open to feminist criticism. See Hilary Rose, *op. cit.*, p. 371, note 21.
38. See, e.g., Lesley Doyal, *op. cit.*, 1979, pp. 221-8. A particularly chilling account of how women are treated, and the lack of information they are given, by the medical profession is provided by an anonymous contributor in an article "Abortion: one woman's horror story", in: H. Kanter *et al.*, *Sweeping Statements, op. cit.*
39. As I have noted, clinical trials etc. deny individual subjectivity in the pursuit of "Scientific objectivity" when drugs or new treatments are being tested. Yet, in the end, treatments *can* only be evaluated against subjective experience for each individual; some people know, for instance, that they are particularly sensitive to some kinds of drugs, while other drugs have little effect. This kind of variation cannot be determined by clinical trials. By contrast, many forms of alternative medicine, such as acupuncture or homeopathy, do attempt to allow for individual idiosyncrasies.
40. E.g., Stephanie Leland, "Feminism and ecology: theoretical connections", in Caldecott and Leland, *op. cit.*, pp. 67-8. "If the foetus is to be male the hormone androgen occurs (sic) triggering the process which alters the female into a male".
41. The genital structures which exist prior to differentiation are more female-like than male-like, but both sexes still have to differentiate further. As differentiation occurs, hormones seem to be involved in influencing the process so that it goes in one or other direction. Certainly, androgens are critical for male-like development, but there is evidence that there are hormones which affect the course of female

development too. See Chapter 5, note 32 for references relating to behavioural differentiation in animal studies. There is no reason to suppose that genital differentiation in humans differs fundamentally.

42. Though there have been some attempts. See, e.g., R. Lewontin, "Work collectives: utopian and otherwise", *Radical Science Journal*, 8, 133-7, 1979. And Uriel Kitron, Brian Schultz, Katherine Yih and John Vandermeer, "The Tomato is Red: Agriculture and Political Action", in Birke and Silvertown, *op. cit.*

43. J. D. Bernal, *op. cit.*, p. 9.

44. Evelyn Fox Keller, 1983, p. 143, note 6.

45. See note 43.

46. These are normally affiliated to the British Society for Social Responsibility in Science; such groups aim to provide information to workers and their union health and safety representatives about the particular work hazards to which they are exposed in that specific industry.

47. In Britain, there is also a Women's Health Information Centre in London which acts to collate information about a variety of health issues. Small women's health groups exist in many towns.

48. See, e.g., C. Joyce, "Science under Reagan: the first four years", *New Scientist*, 24 January, 1985, pp. 24-5. Also see Tam Dalyell, *A Science Policy for Britain*, Longman, London, 1983, for an account of a suggested approach to science policy under a future Labour government.

49. As characterised by the work of the Dialectics of Biology Group, which met in Bressanone, Italy, in 1980 and which subsequently published two books, *Against Biological Determinism* and *Towards A Liberatory Biology*, (Allison and Busby, London, 1982). Although several feminists were among the group, its concern at that time was not specifically to address feminist questions.

50. This was the theme, for example, of a conference organised by the Antonio Gramsci Institute of Parma, Italy in 1983, with the title "The Biology of Cooperation". It was one of a series around the theme "War and Peace: Understanding the Reasons for War in the Construction of Peace". Some of the issues arising from it were discussed by Lynda Birke in "Outgrowing selfish genes", *New Socialist*, 16, 40-2, 1984.

51. Valerie Amos and Pratibha Parmar, "Challenging Imperial Feminism", *Feminist Review*, 17 (Black Feminist Issue), p. 17, 1984.

52. Arditti, *op. cit.*, p. 367 (note 26).

Name Index

Acton, W., 18
Anand, Anita 119
Aquinas, Thomas 109-10
Arditti, Rita 142, 156
Aristotle 15
Averill, Mary Beth 140-1
Bacon, Francis 114-5
Banks, Olive 120
Barash, David 26, 30, 177n, 179n
Barrett, Michele 46
Beechey, Veronica 200-1n
Bentham, Jeremy 120
Bernal, J. D. 166, 182-3n
Bertell, Rosalie 123
Bignami, Georgio 68
Bleier, Ruth 49-51, 179n
British Society for Social Responsibility in Science 203n
Brovermen, D., 28
Brown, Wilmette 185n
Bruno, Giordano 113
Campanella, Thommaso 113
Campbell, Beatrix 15
Capra, Fritjof 126, 133, 134, 136-141, 167
Clarke, E. H. 27
Cobbe, Frances Power 121
Daly, Mary 124
Darwin, Charles 129-30
de Beauvoir, Simone 124
Descartes, Rene 120, 191n
Diamond, Cora 149-51

Dorner, G., 178n
Ehrhardt, Anke 21, 23
Einstein 137
Ellis, Havelock 22
Elshtain, Jean Bethke 42-3, 187n
Fee, Elizabeth 157, 158
Firestone, Shulamith 6, 144, 162
Foucault, M., 22
Freud, S., 16-17
Friedan, Betty 42
Gearhart, Sally 147
Gilmour, Ian 5, 86
Goldberg, Steven 36, 41
Gorz, Andre 117
Griffin, Susan 118
Gross, Michael 140-1
Hanmer, Jalna 161
Harding, Sandra 197n, 201n
Hartsock, Nancy 154-5
Heisenberg, Werner 137, 195n
Henderson, Hazel 126, 127, 132-41, 167
Henifin, Mary Sue 32
Holliday, Laurel 41-2
Hooks, Bell 25
Hutt, Corrinne 28
Jagger, Alison 85, 90
Jordanova, Ludmilla 113
Keller, Evelyn Fox 63, 145, 148, 152, 157, 167, 191n
King, Ynestra 118
Kitcher, Philip 190n

Name Index

Koedt, Anne 17
Koestler, Arthur 77
Kollontai, Alexandra 18-19
Kropotkin, Peter 130, 140
Kuhn, Thomas 139
Lerna, Gerder 25
Lloyd Morgan, C., 110-11
Magendie, F. 120
McGuiness, D., 88
McClintock, Barbara 63, 76
McFadden, M., 198n
Merchant, Carolyn 114-15, 127, 129, 131
Money, John 21, 23
Newton, Isaac 128
O'Brien, Mary 52-3
Paige, Karen 9
Pizzey, Erin 33-4
Raymond, Janice 76
Reich, Wilhelm 16
Rich, Adrienne 23
Richards, Janet Radcliffe 43-6, 91
Ritchie, D. G. 130
Rockefeller, J. D. 129
Rose, Hilary 153-6
Rose, Steven 64
Sayers, Janet 29, 47-8
Scruton, Roger 20, 37-8
Seveso feminist collective 123
Shapiro, Jeff 33-4
Sheldrake, Rupert 138-9
Simonon, Lin 132
Smith, Joan 51-2
Stacey, Judith x, 43
Stall, S., 27
Stille, A., 26
Stillman, Jeanne 43
Tanner, Nancy 31
Taylor, Charles 89
Tiger, Lionel 51
Waddington, C. H. 100, 102
Wallsgrove, Ruth 124
Weiss, Paul 64-65
Wilson, E. O. 30, 40-1, 60, 89
Wilson, Glenn 38-40
Wilson, Janice 76
Zihlman, Adrienne 31

Subject Index

Additive models of development 44-5, 49-55
and homosexuality 73, 83-90
and feminist science 163
Androgyny 91-3
Animal rights:
 and mechanistic science 119-20
 and nineteenth century feminism 120-1
 and feminist science 149-52

Binary classifications (dualism) 70-3, 110, 11, 155,6
Biological determinism:
 and radical feminism ix
 and feminist critiques 3-5, 41-3, 46-55
 in relation to men 10
 and paid work 27-30
 and medical interventions 34-5
 acceptance of, 36-43
 irrelevance of, to feminism 43-6

Causality:
 and reductionism in science 59, 61, 74-5
 and holism 77, 81
 reciprocal 87
 as formative causation 138-39
Central dogma, the 62

Clinical trials 148, 199n, 202n
Competition in nature:
 versus cooperation 129-30, 140-1, 160, 163, 169
 in evolution 139-40
Conservative feminism:
 and biological determinism 42-3
 and theories of gender construction x, 42-3
Cooperation in nature (see competition)
Creationism and evolution 190n

DNA:
 and the central dogma 62
 as a master molecule 63
 in relation to biological form 75-6, 95-6
Domestic labour:
 and women's biology 30-2, 50-1
 and "caring labour" 154-6
Domestic violence 33-5
Drive:
 and repression 175n
Drugs:
 and domestic violence 34-5
 and menstruation 48
 and clinical trials 148-9
Dualism (see binary classifications)
Dual systems theory 51-2

Subject Index

Ecofeminism xi, 116-25, 132-4
   and environmental concern 118, 119, 123-5
   and animal rights 119-21
   critique of, 119-22
   and contemporary physics 132-3
   and the peace movement 134
   and racism 170
Employment (also see domestic labour):
   and women's biology 26-30
   of women as scientists 28-9
Evolution:
   timescale of, 69
   and neoDarwinism 87
   as implying change 129
   and social Darwinism 129-30
   and self-organising systems 138
   and competition as driving force 139-42
"Ex juvantibus" logic 68, 75

Feminist science vii, xi, 1, 135-6, 143-71
Formative causation 138-9
Funding, as constraint on science 161, 168

Gender development 5-6
   and separation of biological from social 54-5, 83-106
   and interactionist view 88-106
   and interaction with biology 103-6
   and feminist science 163
   and transsexualism 189n
Gender divisions:
   as natural 2, 36-55
   as dichotomous category 70-3
   and gender development 104-5
Great Chain of Being 9, 109-12, 129
   and the Ptolemaic universe 109

Heterosexuality:
   as natural 21-5
   as a political institution 23-4
   and reductionism 70-3
Higher education for women 11-12, 26-7
Holism 75-82
   in medicine 76
   versus mechanism 126-9
   as a feminist issue 142
   and feminist science 167
Hormones:
   and women's moods 9
   and women's work 28-9
   and violence towards women 33-5
   and male dominance 44-5
   and homosexuality 53, 68-9
   and reductionism 65-8
   and sexual differentiation 54, 80-2, 96-9, 102-3, 163, 165
   as dichotomous 80-1
Homosexuality:
   as pathology 22-3, 149
   and gender concepts 23, 70-3
   and hormonal determinants 53, 68-9
   and reductionism 70-3
Human nature:
   and the New Right x, 5
   versus women's nature 5
   as primary 43, 86
   within liberal philosophy 84-6
   in feminist science 170

Indeterminacy, and causality 75, 132, 136-37
Individualism, and human nature 86, 159
Intellectual ability, and women's biology 2, 28
Interaction:
    and self-organisation of biological systems 78
    and gender 82, 96-9
    as alternative to additive model 86-106
    critiques of, 88-9, 146-47
    and explanation of patriarchy 91
    retention of dualism in 88, 92-3
    and biological transformation 95, 169
LD_{50} test on animals 200n
Lesbians:
    as specific kinds of people 22
    and hormonal determinants 68
Levels of analysis:
    in reductionism 57-65
    and reality in nature 64
    and holism 77-8
    and interactionism 93-4
Liberalism 84-5
    and reason 89-90

Male exhibitionism 19
Man-the-Hunter theory of evolution 30-3, 49-52
Masculine science 9-10, 114-16, 144, 153, 155
    and objectivity 157-8
Mechanistic philosophy of science 114-15, 126, 167
Menstrual cycle:
    and women's moods 9, 27
    and social construction of gender 47-8
    and premenstrual tension 67-8, 83
    and gender development 104
Mind-body dualism 87, 191n

National Front, the 37
Natural, the concept of 13-14
    gender differences as 39
Nature/culture dichotomy 9-10, 107-25
    cross-cultural comparisons 108-9
    historical specificity 109-15
    and the Great Chain of Being 110-11
    and organic philosophies 112-13
    and the rise of mechanism 114-15
    and feminism 115-25
    and animal rights 119-21
New Right, the, and human nature x, 5, 42, 131, 133, 135

Objectivity, in science 94-5, 114, 132, 136, 144, 147-8, 156-8
Organic philosophies 112-13, 127-9

Parental investment 176n
Parenting, and women's role 154-6
Patriarchy:
    and science 1
    and biological determinism 36-7
    and dual systems theory 51
    disintegration of, 133
    and subjectivity 157
    definitions of 172-3n
Prostitution 18
Public accountability in science 159, 164-6, 168

Subject Index

Pure versus applied science 166
Quantum physics:
  wave-particle duality in 94-5
  and indeterminacy of 132
  as representing ideological shift 133, 136-7, 146

Racism:
  and women's sexuality 25
  and the Great Chain of Being 110-11
  and biological constraints 170
  and evolutionary theory 194n
Radical feminism:
  and biological determinism ix-x
  and gender ix
Rape 19-20
  and pornography 21
Reason:
  and human nature 84-5, 89-90
Reductionism 56-82
  and scientific method 57-9, 99, 164, 166
  as explanation 59-65, 74
  and the aims of science 60
  in molecular biology 62-4
  versus holism 76-82, 145, 167
Relativism, in social theory 157-8, 201n
Reproduction:
  as dialectical process 52-3
  and liberalism 85, 90
  and materialism 153-4
  and women's rights or choices 162-3
Reproductive technology 6-7, 144, 161-3

Scientific method 57-9, 145-59

Scientific knowledge, as patriarchal 8
Self-organisation, and evolution 138
Sexual differentiation 80-1
  of behaviour in animals 96-106, 185n, 202-3n
Sexual division of labour (see also gender divisions)
  in science 153-4, 200-1n
Sexuality:
  and gender differences 14-15
  as innate 15-21, 24-5
  and repression of 16
  and male promiscuity 17
  and racism 25
Social construction of gender 38, 46-55, 172n
Social relations of science 7-8, 157, 167-8
Socialist science 143-4, 170, 182-3n
Sociobiology:
  and promiscuity of males 17
  and rape 20
  and the Man-the-Hunter theory 30-1
  and sex differences 38-41
  and male dominance 51
  and reductionism 63-4
Spatial ability:
  and women's work in science 28-9, 153
  and human evolution 69
  and the additive model 84

Timescales of biological explanation 66-7, 69
  and the relationship between levels 79
  and interactionism 86-7
Transformability of nature 95-105, 137
  and formative causation 138

Truth, as genderised 154

Vaginal orgasm, myth of 17-18

Women's health movement 3, 147, 173n, 185n
    versus scientific medicine 165
Women's Liberation Movement vii-x, 46, 92, 107, 134, 168, 172n, 196n
Work hazards:
    and women's reproduction 32
    in relation to safety testing 151-2
Work Hazards Group, Women and 168